D1263311

don juan
east/west

SUNY series, The Margins of Literature
Mihai I. Spariosu, Editor

don juan
east/west

on the problematics of
comparative literature

Takayuki Yokota-Murakami

STATE UNIVERSITY OF NEW YORK PRESS

Published by
State University of New York Press, Albany

© 1998 State University of New York

All rights reserved

Printed in the United States of America

No part of this book may be used or reproduced in any manner
whatsoever without written permission. No part of this book may be
stored in a retrieval system or transmitted in any form or by any
means including electronic, electrostatic, magnetic tape, mechanical,
photocopying, recording, or otherwise without the prior permission in
writing of the publisher.

For information, address State University of New York Press,
State University Plaza, Albany, NY 12246

Production by Marilyn P. Semerad
Marketing by Fran Keneston

Library of Congress Cataloging-in-Publication Data

Yokota-Murakami, Takayuki.
    Don Juan East/West : on the problematics of comparative literature
/ Takayuki Yokota-Murakami.
        p.   cm. — (SUNY series, the margins of literature)
    Includes bibliographical references and index.
    ISBN 0-7914-3665-9. — ISBN 0-7914-3666-7 (pbk.)
    1. Don Juan (Legendary character) in literature.   2. Literature,
Comparative—Themes, motives.   3. Literature, Comparative—History
and literature.   I. Title.   II. Series.
PN57.D7Y65   1998
809'.93351—dc21   97-16828
                                                                          CIP

10 9 8 7 6 5 4 3 2 1

contents

illustrations

preface

This book was first conceived when a good friend and colleague of mine, Junko Saeki, published a history of Japanese courtesans through literary representations, a theme that had always interested me greatly. As her work was rather comprehensive, I felt, although her theoretical/ideological position was quite different from mine, that I had to switch to a new topic for research. At that moment a change from a study of "amorous" women to that of licentious men appeared to me to be a natural choice.

This decision, however, eventually gave me cause for serious theoretical reconsideration. Launching on the task, I was not content, from the beginning, to write a history of only Japanese "libertines" or *iro-otoko* as such, but wanted to locate this type in relation to other debauchees belonging to different literary/cultural traditions. After all, I was a scholar who had first received training as a comparativist. The subject of my research at this stage was a comparative analysis of the "libertines" of the world.

Nonetheless, the more I worked, the more I found the whole idea suspicious. In this project, locating a candidate for comparison was naturally the first task. The choice was, however, not natural. If I selected one, emphasizing the difference, I felt, I could not justify the comparison. If I stressed similitudes, my argument turned out to be a senseless tautology.

I became, then, more interested in analyzing/deconstructing the presumptions of comparative scholarship themselves. I decided eventually to reverse the task, that is, to write about why I could *not* pursue my own project and how I should demystify the notion of an "Eastern Don Juan" (just as I should not have been deluded by the concept of a "female Don Juan" as a construction theoretically symmetrical to "male Don Juan"). That is to say, I decided that I should compare in order to un-compare. If some readers find my book somewhat self-contradictory, that exactly is my aim and I prefer to consider this contradiction as a strength of the book.

The other day, I saw in a supermarket an ad for a detergent that said, "Dare (not) to compare" with the negative "not" deftly inserted in relief. If I may risk sounding superficial, this motto very neatly represents the problematic of comparative literature to me. American advertisements are full of encouragements for comparison: Please compare and find out for yourself that our product is the better. Now, the above motto at once encourages and discourages comparison: obviously, ours is the better detergent; we want you to compare and find that out for yourself; but, as our product is superior beyond comparison, you will just waste your time and energy by comparing. Hence, the negative "not," which does not change the meaning of the two sentences: compare in order to know that you do not have to compare, or, do not compare because the comparison has already been made.

Transcivilizational comparative literature functions in a like manner. It encourages us to compare the literatures of the world. But as we move on, we realize that the same motto is also bidding us not to do so, for there is nothing really to compare. The answer is already there as we are comparing the same thing. In the chapters that follow the reader will find out how and why comparativism has worked this way.

Turning to personal matters, my project started shortly before my first child died at birth. At his funeral service, I read from *Psalms*: "They that sow in tears shall reap in joy"

(125:5), trying not to lose hope. Almost five years have passed since then. The research project is now being completed and my second child is thriving, about to stand up and walk. With a combination of remorse, sorrow, relief, joy, and hope, I thank Jin, Yū, and Gerry Yokota-Murakami for always being beside me when I was struggling with the present work.

acknowledgments

Several teachers, colleagues, and friends of mine, whose names I list below with gratitude, read my manuscript at various stages and provided a number of useful critical comments and suggestions: Earl Miner (Princeton), Hosea Hirata (Tufts), Caryl Emerson (Princeton), Theodore Goossen (York), Darko Suvin (McGill), Rolf J. Goebel (Alabama), Pamela Abee-Taulli, Stephen Clark, Paul R. Wright (Osaka), Charles Shiro Inoue (Tufts), Deryn P. Verity (Osaka), Karen L. Myers (Osaka), and Gerry Yokota-Murakami (Osaka). My sincerest gratitude is also due to some dozens of people whose names do not appear here but whose help in locating material for me, offering encouragement, giving various tips and so on, was nevertheless instrumental in bringing this book to light.

The major part of this work was done during my stay in Moscow at the A. M. Gorki Institute of World Literature, Russian Academy of Sciences (1990), at Princeton University, as an Overseas Researcher of the Japan Society for the Promotion of Sciences (1990–1992), and at the University of Illinois, Champaign-Urbana, as a Fellow of the Summer Research Laboratory on Russia and Eastern Europe, hosted by the Russian and East European Center (1993). I am grateful to these organizations for enabling me to pursue this project. The publication of this book was made possible partly by the generous support from the Suntory Foundation, Osaka, Japan, and also from the Japan Foundation.

Portions of chapter 4 appeared in *Hikaku bungaku kenkyū* (*Comparative Literature Studies* 65 [1994]). Material used in chapters 3 and 4 is largely included in my book *Sei no purotokoru* (*Protocols of Sexuality*) forthcoming from Shin'yōsha, 1997. Michigan State University Press (East Lansing, Mich.) has generously given permission to use extended quotation from *The Crisis in Comparative Literature* by René Etiemble, translated by Herbert Weisinger and Georges Joyaux, 1966. I thank the editors and the publishers concerned for their permission to reproduce the material here.

Texts in foreign languages whose English translation is not available are translated by me unless otherwise noted.

1 problematizing comparative literature

*[E]verywhere under God's sky all humans express in their
language the same and kindred emotions. . . . [T]he importance
lies in our discovery of the eternally unchanging human in all
guises.*

—Max Koch, Introduction to *Zeitschrift für
vergleichende Literaturgeschichte*

Comparative Literature as a Discourse of Identification

To analyze two or more literary phenomena that transcend national, cultural, or linguistic boundaries, the
discipline of comparative literature must depend on the legitimacy of an act of bringing two items together. What
makes this act legitimate? The ground is usually sought in
"similarity," empirical, speculative, or other. Therefore,
comparison is a kind of perception that is first realized by
ignoring a distance from a certain "common" axis. Comparative literature is, then, fundamentally a discourse of
identification: we begin comparing when we identify, not
when we differentiate, two objects.[1]

1

This presumption of "comparative" methodology becomes clearer if one thinks of the traditional form of comparative literature at its incipient stage, when it took shape in the latter half of the nineteenth century in Europe. As many have pointed out, the term *comparative literature* was a misnomer. Scholars of comparative literature in nineteenth-century Western universities hardly "compared," but were simply engaged in a literary history that crossed national borders. If the discipline of comparative literature shared something with comparative linguistics, a discipline that had a large role in formulating the concept of comparative literature, it was a general framework of the objects of research which these two disciplines equally possessed.

This framework was, of course, Europe. A common root for a set of any phenomena was guaranteed beyond doubt as long as a researcher was confined within the realm of the greater European linguistic/cultural unity, rendering it a subsequent task to establish the genealogy of related entities, and to describe variants in sundry soils. It was not necessary to give reasons for comparison, for crossing boundaries, and for bringing together the two "different" items within the monolithic and homogeneous entity of Europe, fictional though it may be. It was the tacit but unshakable presupposition of early "comparativism" that objects of inquiry were variants, stemming from the same root.

For instance, comparative linguistics had two main tasks:

1. To find out the general laws of phonetic transformation, in which case identification of objects was pregiven; in other words, we took it for granted from the start that πατηρ (pater) and "father" meant much the same thing, a recognition from which derived Grimm's law: "Classic Greek (ancient Indo-European) [p] changed to English (Germanic) [f]."

2. To reconstruct the lost root (an unknown signifier of the Indo-European for the original signified "Father"), applying these laws, a gesture in the quest

for an origin that could relate all its various manifestations in the later linguistic formation.

In the field of comparative literature during the first half of this century, when the so-called French school was dominant, the discipline also abided by a principle of identification, similar to that utilized in comparative grammar. The study of "influence" and the search for "sources," for which French comparativism has now fallen into bad repute, quite faithfully reproduced the disciplinary model of comparative linguistics, that is, the determination of the common root and the analysis of its variations in multiple but restricted milieux. The *Stoffgeschichte* (history of a theme) approach, which René Etiemble labeled as "one of the favorite subjects of the so-called French school" (*Crisis in Comparative Literature* 43), was also the application of the traditional model of comparativism in terms of a literary theme and a character within the boundaries of Western literary tradition. Thus, the field of research continued to be based on, and to contribute to, a common European destiny. When such typical literary themes as Don Juan, Hamlet, or Faust in various national traditions were discussed, the emphasis was not so much on the comparison of two markedly different objects as on the historical transformation of one specific denominator that served as the common origin of its various spatial/temporal embodiments. It was a primary identification and an undoubted continuation of the phenomenon that further motivated an investigation of a difference, humbly attached to the original, that is, in more concrete terms, a feature which has turned an original Don Juan into a classical Don Juan, a romantic Don Juan, a Byronic Don Juan, a rationalist Don Juan, and so on. That a given researcher was speaking about one and the same topic was so obvious that it would have amounted to absurdity to doubt it: despite varied nuances and overtones, what we call "Don Juan" remained "Don Juan" after all.

Naturally, such "Eurocentrism" in the methodology of earlier comparative literature largely discouraged East-West comparison, where there was no such common origin, and where a historical connection, which was a prerequisite of the French method, was scarce or nonexistent. One of the major early theoreticians of the French school, Ferdinand Brunetière, unhesitatingly dismissed the East from the scope of inquiry with the following statement: "[T]hese faraway and mysterious civilizations [of the Far East] have developed outside ours, and, having therefore few points of contact with ours, consequently offer very few possibilities of comparison" (158).

Then, sometime in the middle of this century, a new task was acknowledged, mainly on the other side of the Atlantic, of subsuming two literary phenomena without any historical contact as objects of research. Instead of genealogy, source studies, and the historical account of a theme in literature, uses of a comparative frame of two (or more) completely different phenomena that may or may not have actual connection began to insist on its legitimacy as a task for comparative literature.

The new move was made possible by a method of "criticism." By devising a form of explanation, based on some "critical" term, or a "theoretical" concept which can bridge separate phenomena, the comparativist was now authorized to make any kind of comparison. In the formulation of one of the dominant proponents of the emerging methodology, A. Owen Aldridge, "[c]omparison may be used in literary study to indicate affinity, tradition, or influence. Affinity consists in resemblances in style, structure, mood, or idea between two works which have no other connection. As an example, the Russian novel *Oblomov* may be compared to *Hamlet* because each work is a character study of indecision and procrastination" (3).[2] It is the "critical" concepts about characters, "indecisive" and "procrastinatory," not the historical relations, that now relate the two heroes to the same category. Thus, this shift in methodology, which can roughly be encapsulated as a shift from the dominance of the "French" to the "American" school,[3] can also be characterized as one from historicism to criticism.

René Etiemble's *The Crisis in Comparative Literature* vividly captured this shift in the history of comparativism, and was itself a manifesto of the new thinking, passionately defending comparison not among nations belonging to the same civilization but among historically unrelated civilizations:[4] "The other tendency [the American school] considers that even though two literatures have not had historical relations, it is legitimate to compare the literary genres which each developed for its own use" (35).

The new tendency naturally legitimatized an East/West comparative scheme, which had hitherto been taboo. If the earlier comparative literature had relied on the relatively high degree of sociocultural, linguistic, and historical homogeneity of Europe, the new principle opened up a way to incorporate any writing deemed "literature" into comparative research.[5]

We should be aware that in this newer form of comparative literature that deals with non-European literary traditions, "literature" is often presented as a given empirical reality. The question as to what constitutes literature in non-Western discourse is seldom asked. Instead, works that are considered "literary" are first cited, then compared, and finally a conclusion is given as to what it is that may be called "literary," and what these examples show as a universal feature of literariness. For instance, we have a comparison of *La Chanson de Roland* and *The Tale of Heike*, a classic study by a Japanese comparativist, Satō Teruo.[6] It compares the two works as representatives of oral literature and as "epics." Whether either belongs to the category of "literature" is not self-evident, though. Then, what makes it so ostensibly obvious as Satō presumes that it is an issue of comparative "literature"? The Japanese comparativist should have begun by defining "literature," and then convinced us of the "literariness" of *The Tale of Heike* and of the general nature of the "oral literature" which could be revealed through comparison with *La Chanson de Roland*. Satō's method was contrary to this and "tautological." He took it for granted that *The Tale of Heike* was a work of literature, from which he subsequently drew conclusions as to the nature of (oral) literature.

Conversely, Hutcheson Posnett starts his *Comparative Literature* by asking "What Is Literature?" in an effort to specify objects of the discipline. The study radically points to the diversity of the phenomena, and the infeasibility of the standard of "literariness" as something universal. However, at the end of the first chapter, he reduces all his arguments to an anticlimactically conventional definition of literature: "works which, whether verse or prose, are the handicraft of imagination rather than reflection, aim at the pleasure of the greatest possible number of the nation rather than instruction and effects, and to appeal to general rather than specialized knowledge" (18–19). Actually, though, this standard definition puts the status of *The Tale of Heike*, which is a historical narrative, in a debatable position.

Let us return to the examination of the new school of transcivilizational comparative literature. "Comparison" in this newly established method claims to encompass the poetic features of the literary discourse of the world as it is an analytical tool, based on philosophical, metatexual abstraction. What associates Pushkin's *The Stone Guest* and Da Ponte-Mozart's *Don Giovanni* is the Russian poet's familiarity with the opera and the actual use, in the drama, of motifs and characters taken from it (historical method). In contrast, what puts Tirso di Molina's Don Juan and, say, the Shining Prince (Hikaru Genji), the hero of *The Tale of Genji* of eleventh-century Japan, in the same arena is one or more features that a comparativist may project upon both characters through speculation and critical analysis, whether those features be "love," "passion," "lust," "seduction," and so on (analytical method).

This new concept of "comparison," based on critical considerations of "similarity," "analogy," and "affinity," well answered the need to expand horizons, pointing to infinite possibilities, gloriously described as "an inexhaustible reservoir" that "[p]urely comparative subjects constitute" (Remak, "Comparative Literature, Its Definition and Function" 5). Or it could have been, on the contrary, that the latter, that is, the expansion of the field, responded to the shift in approach. In any case, "expansion" now became legitimate, and theoretical. The result was the emergence of such methodological concepts as comparative stylistics, genology, typology, thematology, and so on, in systematic collaboration.

"Analogy" and the notion of abstract "types" are the theoretical tools that have enabled the Euro-American scholarly discourse to incorporate other "literary" traditions. An American comparativist asserts: "One field in which the possibilities for research are almost limitless is that kind of comparative literature study which seeks to provide pictures of world literature as shown by the investigation of *typological analogies* as distinct from cultural interactions" (Wrenn 19; emphasis added). Or, in the formulation of Friederich, a pioneer of American comparative literature, "it is often not at all important to dwell on influences that are actually demonstrable but to find evidences of a so called 'Zeitgeist' or a spirit of the time which produced, independently of each other, *similar* mentalities and hence *similar* works and styles in the most diverse countries" (40–41; emphasis added).

Claudio Guillén's formulation of the models of a comparative method may correspond to the above described history of comparative literature. In *The Challenge of Comparative Literature* he proposes three models of what he calls "supranationality." They are: (model A) the study of "phenomena and supranational assemblages that imply internationality, that is, suggest either genetic contacts or other relations between authors and processes belonging to distinct national spheres or common cultural premises"; (model B) "phenomena or processes that are genetically independent, or belong to different civilizations, [but] are collected and brought together . . . to the extent that common sociohistorical conditions are implied"; and (model C) "genetically independent phenomena [which] make up supranational entities in accordance with principles and purposes derived from the theory of literature" (70). Obviously, he evaluates the last method most highly, judging that it displays the greatest degree of "theoreticity" and "supranationality." Guillén's models, in which model A probably refers to the "French" method and models B and C to the "American," thus show a sense of evolution and hierarchy, although he is not explicit about it, nor does he completely dismiss the type of research done according to model A. We see here in collaboration the ideal of "theoreticity" and that of "supranationality" just as "criticism" was responsible for opening up the horizons at the dawn of the "American" school. The higher one climbs on the ladder of theoretical abstraction, the wider the scope one is endowed with.

Another concept that has formed part of such a constellation, and that needs some examination, is the idea of "aesthetics." In *Truth and Method* Hans-Georg Gadamer remarks, quoting Graf Yorck: "Comparison is always aesthetic, it is always concerned with the form" (206). René Etiemble, too, justifies comparativism on the ground of "aesthetic" considerations:

> [A]s soon as we enter the realm of the abstract, the concepts of a given language only rarely coincide with those of another language[.] Rather, they overlap, each being composed of parts of several foreign concepts, and the latter varying with the language in question: in German *Volk* is charged with an affective and racial meaning which does not inhere in our term *peuple*. *Völkisch* does not mean *populaire* at all, but rather adds to *rassisch*, a quasi-scientific notion which can be translated by *racial*, a romantic and leftist nuance which did not prevent it from deviating toward the monstrously normative meaning of *raciste* under the Nazi influence. Historically, German classicism has few traits in com-

mon with French classicism. *Aesthetically* [my empha-
sis], however, they do possess some characteristics in
common. How can one explain historically that all the
themes of European pre-romanticism are found . . . in
ancient China and the China of the T'ang? Yet, aesthetically, the analogies *force* themselves into consideration.
(*Crisis in Comparative Literature* 40)

We will have to return to the problematic of what I
would call the "metaphysical" elements of Etiemble's
thought in respect to the relationship between a signifier and
a signified. A special note, however, should be made now
about the "violence" with which the metaphysics of
aestheticizing is justified. Etiemble starts his discussion by
giving an example: *Volk* and *peuple*, two notions that he
strongly insists upon differentiating. A reference to Nazism
must suggest an essential discrepancy between these two
terms. Nonetheless, when Etiemble abruptly mentions
French and German classicism, which "possess some characteristics in common," the context conversely requires readers to understand that *Volk* and *peuple* are after all the same
concepts, or at least, have the same core of meaning in spite
of their differences. This is not an idea difficult to accept,
for we probably believe at the bottom of our hearts that *Volk*
translates into *peuple*.

The unexpected shift in the course of logic may demonstrate Etiemble's predominant interest in what is identical,
rather than what does not overlap. Given this new direction
of argument, he can conclude, without much reasoning, that
European and "Chinese" preromanticisms belong to one and
the same order despite all the apparent differences, just as
French and German classicisms are essentially identical literary phenomena. This twist is, finally, reinforced by the
claim to "aesthetic" terms: classicism is classicism in any
sociolinguistic formation; therefore, we are "forced" to notice
the aesthetic affinities of French and German classicisms and
European and "Chinese" preromanticisms.

Although it is unclear how the interrelation of the signs *Volk* and *peuple* helps to demonstrate that French and German classicisms are comparable, Etiemble pushes his argument even further by expanding the discussion to the transcivilizational comparison of "aesthetic" phenomena. This is a suspicious move, since he is engaged in two different kinds of activity. In a European context, he compares what is called classicism in Germany and what is so called in France, and then concludes that there is something in common in the final instance. In a transcivilizational comparison, he first decides to call some features in a Chinese work "preromantic," and then insists on the ubiquity of preromanticism, the basic feature of which, he argues, is shared by every culture "aesthetically," if not historically.

Whether or not preromantic features are to be found in Chinese literature is a theory that can be agreed upon or contested. But such considerations are dismissed by Etiemble's unchallenged formulation: "Chinese preromanticism." To put it differently, comparison is already legitimatized the moment he has started to perceive some aspects of Chinese culture as "preromanticism." When the two are compared (under the rubric of "preromanticism" in this case), they are already identified with some signification projected onto one or the other.

This is quite a different procedure from comparing French classicism and German classicism, both of which are, after all, categorized as classicism of some kind. In defiance of such problems, Etiemble violently closes the argument by writing: "aesthetically, analogies *force* themselves into consideration."[7]

Probably, a certain aesthetic "violence," revealed by this sentence, is invariably required in comparison. Now the axiom has been arrived at: even among cultures belonging to different civilizations, based on different linguistic formulae, essential aspects of culture are always identifiable and comparable if only one observes them from an "aesthetic" point of view. The complicity of aesthetics and comparison is thus achieved.

In this manner, the comparative method of the American school as endorsed by Etiemble has such an anti-historicist, "metaphysical" character. The object of the present study is to analyze the nature of "criticism," "theoreticism," "aestheticism," and "metaphysics" as concepts of comparative study, especially in the American method, taking the comparison of "Don Juan" across civilizations as an example.[8]

Problems of Transcivilizational Comparison of Don Juans

What is the nature of a comparative study of Don Juan(ism) on an "international" (or "supranational," if you will) scale? What enables a transcivilizational comparison of Don Juans? While French scholars on the whole have been intent on the variation of a character identically called "Don Juan" in the West, a scholar is now, according to the new American concept, or to Guillén's models B and C, expected to find and compare "Don Juan-*like*" figures in other, non-Western literatures.

It is the abstractness, or the theoreticity of thematology, aesthetics, and criticism that enables the concept of "Donjuanesque," which authorizes this kind of comparison. Such an attempt, however, can be a futile endeavor. In order to achieve higher "theoreticity" and abstractness, and to subsume ever larger groups of objects to be studied and compared, a researcher in turn has to resort to ever broader and therefore even vaguer terms. The more theoretical it gets and the more one subsumes, the more trite it becomes. To find a candidate for comparison of a Don Juan in radically different cultural milieux, and to discover the gist of Don Juanism, the concept of "Donjuanesque" has to be as broad and comprehensive as possible.

Let us take a look at some of the candidates for the point of comparison of Don Juans East/West that have been proposed so far. Guillén variously suggested "an inveterate woman-chaser," "an untiring and incorrigible lover," or an even plainer "seducer" (84). Etiemble (and his English translators) proposed a comparative chart of "Men who love" (xxii). Other candidates have been: (a man who embodies) inconstancy (Gendarme de Bévotte), betrayal (Jonathan Miller), insincerity, passion, desire, sensuality, lust, and ultimately, of course, masculinity, that is, Don Juan as the "man": "Don Juan is the man who before the woman is nothing but man, neither father, nor husband, nor brother, nor son" (José Ortega y Gasset, *Don Quijote, Don Juan y la Celestina: ensayos de simpatía*; qtd. in Weinstein 3–4).

It is, however, open to question whether, by retreating from a tangible Don Juan to a supposedly more abstract, inclusive notion of a "seducer," a "lover," and so on, a scholar of literature enters the realm of neutrality, comprehensiveness, and universality. Take the concept of "seduction," for example. According to *The Oxford English Dictionary*, the verb "seduce" changed its central meaning in the sixteenth century from "1. To persuade (a vassal, servant, soldier, etc.) to desert his allegiance or service" via "2. To lead (a person) astray in conduct or belief" to "3. To induce (a woman) to surrender her chastity." The date of the first example of definition 3, which the dictionary notes is "now the prevailing sense," is taken from A. Scott's poem of c. 1560. The note further remarks, under definition 3, that: "[I]n English law, the plaintiff in an action for seducing a virgin is the parent or master who is supposedly to have been deprived of her services."

Thus, "seduction" in the sense of corrupting a woman is a historical phenomenon. It must depend on a social structure, on that of the modern West, for example, where women's sexuality belongs to someone else, most likely, to men. This is why their loss has to be described as "deprivation," and why "the parent or master" can report to the court for the damage done to them. Chastity is ultimately a property to be defended not by women, but by men, the real possessors. Seduction is imaginable solely in the confines of the ideology implicit in such a gender hierarchy and with a notion of "property" actively operating in it. Let us remember that most of the adventures of Don Juan involve his confrontation and conflict with a father, a brother, or a fiancé.

In other words, seduction is a meaningful category only where "chastity" is at work; for instance, in the framework of Catholic society, where virginity is categorically encouraged, or of Puritan married lives, where constancy and loyalty are emphasized, or of Edo samurai society (1603–1868), where "feudal" morality strictly harnessed women.[9] Conversely, it could not have been meaningful, say, in the polygamous society as described by Morgan and Engels (if there was such a society), or, in Tokugawa Japanese rural communities, where an occasional sexual orgy was institutionalized, or, more evidently, in the Edo (Tokyo) urban system of masculine sexuality, where an erotic relationship largely lay within the boundary of the pleasure quarters. For can a man "seduce" a prostitute? Seduction, therefore, is a concept which functions under particular social conditions, and in conjunction with certain related denotations and connotations, historically formulated.

Not only Euro-American comparativists, but also Japanese scholars of the "American school" explore paths for evoking transcivilizational comparison. A professor in comparative and Spanish literature, Ōshima Tadashi, makes a preliminary call in his *A Study of Don Juan Types* for comparison of Western Don Juans and corresponding figures in Japanese literature such as Hikaru Genji (the hero of *The Tale of Genji*) and Yonosuke (that of *The Life of an Amorous Man*). This, to my knowledge, is the only attempt of this kind of some length up to the present day.[10] He writes in the preface:

> The theme [of Don Juan] spread from its native Spain, via Italy, France, England, Germany, to Northern and Eastern Europe, Russia, and America. One may say that Japan also has its own image of Don Juan. . . . Hikaru Genji and Yonosuke are said to be Japanese Don Juans. (5)

What is already questionable in Ōshima's proposal, though, is the way he surreptitiously and smoothly switches from a *Stoffgeschichte* (history of a theme) to a more general thematology, that is, from the actual spread of the Don Juan legend in Europe and America to the transcivilizational comparison of Donjuanesque types, as if these were one and the same approach: "Japan *also* has its own image of Don Juan." Such a tricky reasoning in the preface is justified by reference to a French comparativist, Guyard, whose comment in his supposedly classic text, *Littérature comparée*, is quoted by the Japanese scholar in the postscript:

> We have, in our culture, such Donjuanesque figures as Hikaru Genji and Yonosuke. Maybe, some Japanese should write a book *Don Juan in World Literature*, analyzing all the Donjuanesque types of the World. Marius-François Guyard states that: "And the history continues to the present day: more and more Don Juan is regarded as a symbol," and that: "It is better to study Don Juanism than Don Juan." (217)

Transcivilizational comparison is thus justified by the recognition that it is Don Juanism, not Don Juan, that has to be studied. Given this, Ōshima can safely insist that the crucial object is what it means to be "Don Juan," not individual manifestations which carry that name; it is the comparison of Donjuanesque figures, East/West, not the spread of the Don Juan theme in Euro-American literatures, that may prove to be more significant.

In a subsequent publication, *Invitation to Spanish Literature*, Ōshima himself launches on such a project: a comparison of Western Don Juans and such Japanese "equivalents" as Hikaru Genji and Yonosuke. In the preface of the book he attempts to justify the possibility of the project:

> Just like Don Quixote, Don Juan will continue to exist as an eternal philanderer. Perhaps we could say that the image of Don Juan has settled down in our soil, being confused or overlapped with representative Japa-

nese philanderers such as Hikaru Genji, Narihira, Yonosuke, and so on. However, even if we tentatively conceive Hikaru Genji and other figures as Japanese Don Juans, there is a profound difference. (14)

The proposed scheme of comparison, upon which Ōshima's entire project depends, raises several questions. First of all, it raises a question about the basic meaning of comparison itself. Ōshima begins with an ostensible and meaningful similarity of the Don Juan phenomena in the West and the East, and then concludes that they differ significantly. But if the two are completely different, the ground for comparing collapses, and if the two are almost identical, why do we bother to compare? What do we learn from it? Comparison on an international scale is always such an operation, a tightrope walk which sways between identity, elementary and essential, on the one hand, and difference, contingent and marginal, on the other. A comparativist gains nothing by reaching either end of the rope.

Of course, comparative studies are expected to negotiate these conflicting poles. They are highly evaluated when they convincingly identify and meaningfully differentiate two objects: the Shining Prince *is* basically a "Don Juan," with a distinct character that is expected to represent cultural differences. However, the primary identification must necessarily imply hierarchy: identity is essential and primary; difference, peripheral and secondary. Don Juan as an eternal masculine type is central; cultural mutations are ancillary. For all the differences Ōshima claims to be significant, within the comparative scheme Hikaru Genji is *essentially*, that is, at the most profound layer of his existence, a Don Juan, an identification that is open to question. In other words, whatever differences a comparativist may later offer, by formulating the Shining Prince as a "Japanese Don Juan," the features in common with a Western Don Juan are taken to be central in his characterization.

Now, with such a precarious presupposition, Ōshima proceeds to compare them in the eighth chapter of the above book, entitled "A Study of Don Juan, East and West." In that chapter, he resumes his discussion by reconfirming the definition of Don Juan. However, it now has a slightly different nuance.

> The Don Juan that appears in European literature is, in short, the incarnation of male instinct. Or he is a symbol of a man who arouses a swirl of lust *(aiyoku)* between a man and a woman, confronting each other.
>
> When we turn to Japanese literature, we find figures comparable to Don Juan, such as Narihira (*the* man [*otoko*]), Hikaru Genji, and Yonosuke. (225)

We are not really sure what Ōshima means by "male instinct." Is it lust? Is it an urge to chase after women? Is it desire to seduce? Neither are we sure what "*the* man" is except in the specific context of *The Tales of Ise*, of which Ariwara no Narihira is supposedly a hero, who is, however, referred to simply as "a certain man from bygone days (*mukashi otoko*)" in the tale. Ōshima, it appears, though, is trying to make a broader statement in the above quotation than that. Most likely, he is using the term *otoko* as representing *the* Man, or the essential masculinity that is transcendentally acknowledgeable in any male on earth. Under the pretext of a scientific and "neutral" but powerfully convincing term, "instinct," Ōshima strengthens a not unanimously acceptable presumption that every man has the deeply embedded urge to excite a "swirl of lust" in men and women, an urge which, however, Don Juan is believed to incarnate in a perfect manner.

Given this presumption, he makes another ultimate comparative definition of Don Juan, East/West: "The only feature shared by the Don Juans of the West and of the East is the huge number of women they have loved" (245). If it is only the number of women conquered that associates "Don Juans" of the two civilizations, if the rest of the features are not shared by them, if they are that different, are we speaking of the same character, Don Juan, or not?

This ultimate characteristic of Don Juans, as claimed by Ōshima, is all the more doubtful because the above statement of Ōshima is immediately belied, or at least downplayed, by his subsequent observation: "Male homosexuality is a special feature of the Japanese Don Juan, Yonosuke" (256). Have we not understood that Don Juan is a symbol of "male instinct," which is paraphrased as a will to inflame lust between two sexes? Have we not reconfirmed that the only common element shared by the Western Don Juan and Japanese "Don Juan" is the number of *women* they conquer?

The difference between Don Juan and the Japanese heroes that Ōshima calls attention to, namely, the absence or the presence of the homosexual passion, also belies Guillén's definition of the "archetype" of Don Juan as "an inveterate *woman*-chaser." Thus, even the supposedly most elementary definition is prone to collapse.

There are two ways for comparativists to respond to this situation. One is to retain the definition of an archetype as it is, and consider the Japanese hero as a deviation. We will be exploring the problems of this solution later. The other is to change the definition of the archetypical Don Juan to "an inveterate chaser of human beings of *both* sexes," and then consider the Western Don Juan also as a deviant subtype. Both explanations involve marginalization, yet the latter does not seem to have been attempted in any relevant comparative studies. Most accounts of Don Juan expect him to be a paragon of masculinity, challenging, confronting, and conquering the feminine world. In the Western conception, Don Juan is a heterosexual myth. This leaves out the possibility of conceiving the archetypical Don Juan as a chaser of women *and* men as a point of comparison.

In truth, however, the Edo "Don Juan," Yonosuke of *The Life of an Amorous Man*, is a bisexual, not homosexual, figure. "Exploring both homosexual and heterosexual love so intensely day and night that people nicknamed him 'The

Dreaming Guy' " (*Kōshoku ichidai otoko* 101).[11] This partially prevents Ōshima's definition of Don Juan (a conqueror of a number of women) from completely collapsing: he chases after men [boys], but he hunts women, too. In the Edo paradigm of sexuality, expertise in "both ways" of sexuality (*ryōdō*) was considered a great accomplishment for a playboy. Saikaku's *The Life of an Amorous Man*, demonstrating the hero's development toward a perfect "libertine," includes a chapter of his initiation into homosexual activity immediately after his first adventures in heterosexual affairs. While being an expert in "both ways" was considered to be an ideal, however, there was also rivalry between these two orientations. Literature abounds in the Edo period representing one camp or the other, each insisting on its superiority over the opponent. This, however, merely demonstrates the independent standing of homosexual love in feudal Japanese culture. Consequently, in the Edo sexual context, there could even be a homosexual (and purely homosexual) "Don Juan," an inveterate lover of boys, a concept that is probably inconceivable, or unacceptable, within the Western tradition.

Thus, the conclusion of Ōshima's comparative analysis contradicts his initial proposition, which defines Don Juan (as a transcivilizational literary phenomenon) as a philanderer, a chaser and conqueror of women. With the initial definition which has allowed us to set forth a comparison of Don Juans East/West undermined by the subsequent analysis of their differences, we come back to where we started, still uncertain in our search for the irrefutable ultimate core of what a Don Juan is, and what standard authorizes a transcivilizational comparison once and for all.

In such a manner, comparison according to Guillén's model C, that is, comparison on a supranational scale, is subject to infinite problematization, at least until one decides to be content with nearly pointless theoretical schemes such as "a man who loves," "a man with desire," "a man who is (especially) sexual," and so on. Admittedly, these schemes, which are apparently too general, may serve as a point for comparison. For instance, the problem that has arisen through the comparison of the Western Don Juan and the Japanese "Don Juan," of the possibility of a homosexual Don Juan, may tentatively be circumscribed by the formulation of Don Juan as "a man who loves" (provided, of course, that it be granted that homosexual passion is also an expression

Figure 1. A scene showing the first homosexual adventure of Yonosuke. Courtesy of Osaka Nakanoshima Library.

of "love"). However, even such a framework of comparison, which appears unproblematically applicable but is instead too general to be analytically meaningful, is also open to question, as we will see in subsequent chapters.

The "Metaphysics" of Comparativism

As we have seen, the move in the focus of comparative research from the study of Don Juan versions to a comparison of Don Juan-like figures conceals in itself a switch from an interest in Don Juans to an interest in Don Juanism. While a study of the evolution, variation, or ramifications of Don Juan types may be justified by the common name "Don Juan," comparison of a Western Don Juan and a non-Western Don Juan presumes some category of Don Juanness, which will be, it is now believed, represented by a variety of signifiers such as Don Juan, Casanova, playboy, libertine, *iro-otoko*, Xi Menqing,[12] and so on. In schematic terms, then, the shift from the French method to the American can be defined as a shift from the axis of the signifier to that of the signified. A scholar of the French school seeks various versions of signifieds for one signifier "Don Juan." Conversely, an American scholar attempts to make an inventory of signifiers that represent one single signified "Don Juanism."

In other words, the American discipline is based on a belief in the primacy of a signified, or, more precisely, a belief that a signified precedes a signifier. One can compare a Don Juan and a (Edo) Japanese dandy, *iro-otoko*, as "Don Juan-like" types on the condition that this concept "Don Juan," then unverbalized in Japan, is embedded in human nature, awaiting expression.

We should not take the contrast of two schools too seriously, though. This shift from the French to the American discipline was not anything resembling a sudden rupture, or an epistemological break such as Foucault describes. The French comparativists, too, appear to have been ultimately interested in signifieds. As a matter of fact, Gendarme de

Bévotte, the French scholar who achieved the most extensive survey of the ramifications of Don Juan in Europe, voiced his metaphysical conviction when he wrote: "Don Juanism had existed before having received its formula in the story of the Stone Guest. The story merely gave Don Juan his name, but not the life" (2). Don Juan is an ideal type in the Platonic sense, which exists before finding a shadowy substance and a name in the real world. François Guyard even encourages his colleagues to abandon the common name, calling for a study of Don Juanism, that is, a study of what it means to be Don Juan, rather than that of Don Juan per se. His was, then, a move that somehow departed from the traditional spirit of French comparativism:

> [I]t is better to study Don Juanism than Don Juan, and to discover, under diverse masks, such as Faust, Manfred, or Cain, the same revolt, and the same affirmation of the individual. Both the history of ideas and the history of literature profit from this. A type is not a theme: it is preferable, in the future, to trace an idea, a way of feeling, a life-style, through the heroes, different but close, than to group, under an artificial unity of one single name, such as Oedipus, or Prometheus, morals and the theories that are not related to one another. The choice of the point of observation is no less important than the observed territory. (53)

To Guyard, one idea, one sentiment, or one lifestyle is expected to constitute a concept that may be signified by "one single name." The name itself, however, is inconsequential since it is "artificial." It is the concept that unites various ideas, feelings, and lifestyles that matters.

An emphasis on the signified, or more concretely, a call for Don Juanism, was thus heard even in the context of the supposedly monocivilizational comparative approach of the French school. It appears, then, that a search for a universal concept has always been at the root of comparativism. The American camp has merely pushed such universalism to an extreme by breaking loose from the restriction of the common signifier, not only across national borders, but also civilizational ones. Under the French system, a possibility was open to trace infinite modification of the signifieds, represented by a common signifier. Without a common signifier, American scholars have had to resort to a signified of some kind.

In this search, the question as to which signifiers should be used to signify this definitive core has appeared to be contingent. American scholars believe that they seek the common signified, represented by varied signifiers, which is tentatively represented by the term "Don Juan." *Iro-otoko* signifies a "Japanese" Don Juan; Xi Menqing a "Chinese"; and (Western) "Don Juan" simply signifies the "Don Juan," from which stem all the other such-and-such "Don Juans," although they are not so called unless a comparative exegesis is attempted. Theoretically speaking, in the critical discourse of (American) comparative literature, the choice of one single denominator that can subsume all the other versions is held to be a matter of chance. In respect to a signifier, anything goes, or could go. Ostensibly, one speaks of a certain (common) "lifestyle," a (shared) "way of feeling," and so on, using the term "Don Juan" for sheer convenience's sake. Hence, the possibility of speaking of the "lifestyle" of a Western Don Juan and a Japanese "Don Juan" in one breath.

However, as American comparative literature has been an extreme form of universalism with an ambition to bridge civilizations as well as nations, it has to search not only for a single signified but for the *ultimate* concept. In other words, in order that a Western Don Juan, a Japanese "Don Juan," a Chinese "Don Juan," and so on, may point to one signified, that is, in order to make a transcivilizational comparison, it is necessary that a comparativist find a "core" of meaning, the very essence of a denotation—a basic feature, be it a lifestyle, a way of feeling, or what not, which permits most varied referents to be called by the same term. In this case, (American) comparativists strive to answer the question:

What is the one aspect (or a set of aspects) that bestows upon a certain alien entity the signifier "Don Juan"?

At stake, then, is the belief that distinguishes the contingent and the essential, the belief of a Platonic kind that presumes that one can strip off all that is irrelevant, accidental, and historical, eventually arriving at the core of the meaning, as if one can unclothe Don Juan to reveal his real self as the original Seducer (or, Lover, Playboy, or whatever you will).

The yearning for such a transcendental signified is a "metaphysical" move in the Derridean sense, insofar as a transhistorical and transspatial core concept, an Ur-signified, shared by "all the humans under God's eye," is being presupposed. For Derrida, the metaphysics of presence is the exigent, powerful, systematic, and irrepressible desire for a transcendental signified (*Of Grammatology* 49). We can argue that American comparativists follow this desire when they regard "seduction" as an Ur-concept that one can supposedly find at the root of the systems of sexuality of all cultures: *ars amatoria, courtoisie,* romantic love, Don Juanism, *iki* of Edo Japan, *fengliu* of China, and so on. Such an Ur-concept is considered ideal and universal. "[I]t is the unique experience of the signified producing itself spontaneously, from within the self, and nevertheless, as signified concept, in the element of ideality or universality" (*Of Grammatology* 20).[13]

Of course, it may be argued that comparative projects have aimed at the careful mapping of both the universal/ideal and the contingent/historical, not to mention a close analysis of the meaning of the map that results from the initial research. Some studies emphasize the importance of differentiation, while others point to the danger of overemphasizing it. A major shift, however, seems to have occurred in the cultural sciences in general between the latter half of the nineteenth century and the first half of the twentieth; one that saw what is common as theoretically more significant than what differs. The anthropologist Ralph Linton asserts that the great leap forward took place (around the turn of the century) in the science of culture when ethnographers realized that eye-catching superficial differences of cultures were less illuminating to the understanding of the culture of a human being than hidden similitudes (19).

Linton does not give a precise date for the change except for the statement that fifty years ago (from the date of the publication of 1945) ethnographic study of a modern European cultural pattern would have been considered out of place, and that scientists were still more interested in something different, and were engaged in "curio-hunting." This may indicate that the change occurred sometime early this century.

The discipline of comparative literature seems to have followed a similar trajectory. An early comparativist, Max Koch, expressed a theoretical position analogous to Linton's insistence, in the quotation that I have cited as an epigraph to this chapter: "All humans express in their language the same and kindred emotions . . . the importance lies in our discovery of the eternally unchanging human in all guises" (74). It is the search for the identical, not the curious diversities, that substantiates comparativism. A comparison that is not a "misnomer" began when an interest in the common feature, rather than differences, was evoked. This search, in turn, has been in collaboration with a search for the one conclusive meaning.

Paradoxically, the shift in emphasis from a signifier to a signified, or more precisely, from multiple signifiers to the universal, ultimate signified, entailed a significant impoverishment of the latter. The notorious *Stoffgeschichte* approach was an exploration of the infinite possibilities of the signifier "Don Juan," which could mean a naughty playboy (Tirso di Molina), a rational atheist (Molière), an eternal lover (E. T. A. Hoffmann), a romantic poet (Pushkin), and so on. Now, with the signified as the basis for the linkage, and with the loss of the signifier "Don Juan," the meaning-content is monolithically reduced to the basics of "the

Lover" of Etiemble and "the Seducer" of Guillén at best, and "*the* Man" of Ortega y Gasset at worst.

It is one of the principles of ancient logic that comparison always requires a third object (*tertium comparationis*) that functions as a point of reference. Modern philosophers such as Immanuel Kant developed this idea in various formulae (126 [B 194], passim).[14] If so, comparisons of a Western Don Juan and a non-Western "Don Juan" can only be materialized by referring to the ideal third "Mr. Man,"[15] or the definitive masculinity, that unspoken concept one finds nowhere on earth, which defies feminism and the theory of gender. To think that "seduction" is universal/eternal male instinct, having nothing to do with patriarchal ideologies, is this not already metaphysics?

To invoke anthropological terms, one may remember Clifford Geertz's warning against the temptation a student of a culture may feel to imagine a context-free bare humanity. "There is, there can be, no backstage where we can go to catch a glimpse of Mascou's actors as 'real persons' lounging about in street clothes, disengaged from their profession, displaying with artless candor their spontaneous desires and unprompted passions. They may change their roles, their styles of acting, even the dramas in which they play; but as Shakespeare himself of course remarked they are always performing" (36).

From a perspective of conventional comparative literature, Don Juan, *iro-otoko*, Xi Menqing, and so on, are all roles that a spontaneous "Seducer" acts out. Comparativists insist on having witnessed the "real person" backstage. But which language, returning to sociolinguistic terms, does this "real person" speak? Not a known language. Such cabalistic, magic gestures, as it were, as imagining a place where a real person does not speak an existent language, are the gist of the new comparativism.

The belief in a nonverbal essence, in a signified without a signifier, or a signified preceding a signifier, is not only a strategy of the metaphysics of presence but also a seduction of universalism. It is the humanist conception that certain essentials of human nature are shared by all nations, cultures, communities, linguistic groups, and, finally, individuals, and that diversities stemming from them are mere spatial, or temporal, contingencies. It is, consequently, also a belief in essentialism, a creed that all human beings possess some essential features whose true forms, however, can be observed solely in an ideal situation, just as a "real person," concealed under the clothing of all sociocultural contingencies, may be revealed "backstage," in his or her naked reality. Humanist essentialism is a doctrine that believes in the existence of such an idealistic space.

Metaphysical essentialism-universalism of this kind leads Guillén to the following statement. "[N]o matter how broad the interpretation may be, its point of departure will not have been a universal figure, but a Don Juan who is European, Spanish, even Sevillan. The possible universality will have to start from model C, from an archetype, a man who is an inveterate woman-chaser, an untiring and incorrigible lover, who is found in the most varied cultures and literatures: in Africa, India, China, Japan" (84). This is a belief in the most essential "third referent" of comparison, an archetype that is neither Sevillan Don Juan nor a Japanese Don Juan, but *the* Don Juan who speaks spontaneously its grammar of "love" divested of any linguistic or cultural robe.

It is this sense of a "primordial" origin, an idea of "archetype," which will be radically challenged in the chapters to follow. It is not so much a material existence as a Platonic essence, as it were ("Platonic," for, while Tirso di Molina's Don Juan is known to be the first of the series of legends, no one knows the most archaic type of a "Donjuanesque figure" in a material text), that will be put to question: a Don Juan that untiringly "loves" (or does not love); a Don Juan that "seduces"; a Don Juan that "chases" women; and so on.

Admittedly, such a search for a "primordial origin" is an attempt to break through Eurocentrism and should deserve credit as such. Guillén proposes to speak not of "Don Juan" but of "a Seducer, of which Don Juan is no more than the European variety" (84). However, he still has to propose some alternative as a referent of comparison in order to subsume other "Don Juans." For this purpose, Guillén adopts a "Seducer." This procedure of substitution is permitted by resorting to the theory, credible to many, that "seduction" is a universal, ideologically neutral term, applicable to any culture of the world. In this operation, the concept of the arbitrariness of signs is instrumental. The concept "Seducer" is ontologically stable; we simply choose to give it an arbitrary signifier: seducer, Don Juan, *iro-otoko*, and so forth. Such a substitution is, however, open to question, provided that "seduction" is also a culturally specific signification.

In the above passage, Guillén implies that, while "Don Juan" may not be universal, the "Seducer" is, since "seduction" is. In the next few chapters, we will examine some other "primordial" features of sexuality that enable Don Juan and other non-Western Donjuanesque characters to emerge as figures in typology, permitting comparativists to substantiate their comparison. Let us also be reminded again at this point that this gesture toward a primordial type is based on a presumption of a nonverbal concept. Within a comparative discipline, it is ostensibly a meaning-content, a signified, never uttered, that allows us to compare. A "Seducer" is supposed to be an ideal seducer; consequently, it is an essence awaiting to be materialized in varying linguistic forms (seducer, Don Juan, playboy, *iro-otoko*, and so on). This represents a bizarre move away from language, all the more bizarre because we are here to speak of "literature" as seemingly one of the factors which have facilitated American comparativism in its divorce from French comparative literature. In a chapter on "The French Hour," Guillén, making a critique of the French obsession with "influence" and its positivist conception (although he does not dismiss the French school as blatantly as Etiemble) points to the possibility of a case of "influence" that may not be "visible" but is "more significant," in other words, an influence "manifested in a more *theoretical* than *verbal* form" (57; emphasis added). At the root of American comparativism is such a queerly twisted notion of nonverbal (or, little verbalized) theory. But can a theory be nonverbalized?

The universalist argument that there is always some irreducible, general core of meanings that all languages and cultural paradigms share, constituting universal human essentials, has been generally assumed by modern critics. Let us, though, remember in passing, since we will be dwelling on this theme in the following chapters, that the idea of universal humanity is not as ancient or as long-standing a notion as it might appear. There was a lengthy debate in sixteenth-century Spain between those who held that American natives were human beings just like Europeans and those who claimed they were animals (Todorov, *Conquest of America* 151–57). The medieval Russian church seriously pondered the issue of whether women had souls, indicating its ambivalence about including women in the category of "humans." Of course, one can argue that these instances only show various, and therefore incomplete, undeveloped notions of "humanity." Yet if the concept of "humanity" itself is so variable, are not "human essences" even more so? Can "human" features be as simplistically conceived and listed as comparativists believe when, to begin with, what exactly constitutes human beings has been that unclear?

Exactly what features constitute humanity? A "soul," which used to be an absolute, unchallenged candidate for the human essence in the Judeo-Christian world, seems not so promising any more, as the examples I have just cited may show. Are we, then, to resort to "goodness," "amity," "maternal instinct," "democracy," and so on, as unquestionably universal features of humanity which everyone is expected to possess, demonstrate, or eventually achieve?

The ontotheological status of some of these "human essences" is in the process of being questioned and deconstructed. Naturally, I do not mean that these features should simply be abandoned. I am just pointing to the problematic of modern Western humanism's regarding them as *essentially* and *unquestionably* valuable. Rather, it appears to me that, as human constructs, they are all ideologically charged, and prone to change for better or for worse. For instance, "good" in a religious sense and "good" in a secular sense can be diametrically oppositional. So can "democracy" in a capitalist sense and a communist sense. In *Madness and Civilization*, Michel Foucault reveals the ideological implications of the Quakers' "friendly" attitude to "mad" men. Elizabeth Badinter in her *The Myth of Motherhood* convincingly argued that the concept of "maternal instinct" is a patriarchal myth. The allegedly "human" feature of maternity is an ideological apparatus to perpetuate sexism and the modern family with the claim to its being essentially human (or womanly).

The project of the following three chapters is another attempt to criticize some of the major candidates for such universals. They seem to have infiltrated the basis of comparative literature when the translators of Etiemble wrote:

> The ultimate core of human nature whatever we might define it to be seems finally to be occupied by the same questions of life and death and the future life, whether here on earth or elsewhere; of birth and growing up; of the challenges to the emerging person; of marriage and family; of love and ambition and joy, and of overcoming the obstacles in their path; of hate and anger and fear and sorrow, and of their consequences; of despair and hope; and all that tragic protest against the utter indifference of a universe too large, too strange, and too unconcerned for human comfort, comprehension, and control; and around these few great central themes literature wondrously weaves its manifold threads, over and over again, into new and unforeseen shapes, countless in their variety, yet single in their origins and purpose. (*Crisis* xxi)

As the translators rightly point out, in Etiemble we find an array of "human essentials": marriage, family, love, ambition, joy, hate, anger, fear, sorrow, despair, hope, and so forth. They sound all very well, but the question is whether it would, then, be wrong, or completely abnormal *not* to demonstrate any of those feelings. In fact, the major danger of such "humanism" is the marginalization of cultures that do not demonstrate these "human essentials" as deviant, degraded, and perverse. Is a culture that does not instill in its members a sense of ambition an "inhuman" society? Is a society which is not interested in hope "abnormal"? Could the Mayan society, as described by Tzvetan Todorov, be an example of such a society, where the course of one's life and events in society is completely predetermined (*Conquest* 63–67)?

Etiemble's list is a typical inventory of humanism. But it is, probably, not such human essentials that consolidate the humanist belief; it is, on the contrary, the ideology, termed humanism, that makes the inventory of those essences crystallize. My polemic is not against the "ideological bias" of humanism, but against its ostensible freedom from any ideological content, and its claim to "objectivity." In my opinion, it is not the entities that exist universally and transhistorically such as love, marriage, ambition, and other "human" traits, that allow us to embrace a creed called humanism. Instead, it is modern Western humanism that demands that we see those entities. Humanists reject such a view. For them, human essentials are universal, eternal, objective, and independent of interpretation. Given only this belief, humanists-comparativists can launch on a search for love, hope, ambition, and so on, in any culture they encounter.

In this search, a comparativist's belief lies more in the existence of a phenomenon in the physical world than in its linguistic formula. It would not be a problem if a certain culture is lacking in an expression for, say, "love." Transcivilizational comparativism, as I have repeatedly noted, is a search for human essences prior to the linguistic and cultural differences. The human feature that refers to "love" is presumed and the meaning of "love" is expected to be known to all, even when the word for it may be absent. The task of comparativism is, then, to pinpoint a certain phenomenon in a different culture, and then to find a corresponding term if there is one. Now that comparativists know or have decided that they know there is such a phenomenon in that culture, they can assume that there is probably also a name for it. It does not matter if they cannot find one. They would point to the "phenomenon," and then call it "love."

To return to the investigation of René Etiemble's position, and to show such preference for a signified to a signifier and the universalist bent of comparative literature, I here cite his remarkable proposal, recalling that of Descartes and Leibniz, that we should use Chinese ideographs as a universal working language:

> Was it really such a "bold" proposal? What did I do except take over, in a form hardly changed, an idea which Descartes expressed . . . whereafter expounding all the inconveniences of an artificial universal language, he says: Thus, all the usefulness I can see as resulting from this invention [of an universal language] is for writing: namely that he [Mr. Hardy] had a large dictionary printed with all the languages in which he would like to be understood, and assigned to each basic word common characters corresponding to the meaning and not to the syllables, as an identical character for *aimer, amare,* and *philein*: and those who would have these dictionaries and know its grammar could, by looking for all these characters one after the other, interpret in their own language those which should be written. (*Crisis* 29)

Signifieds link the signifiers of the languages of the world, being, at the same time, independent from them. Hence his plan of using "Chinese ideographs, each of which expresses a concept and which everyone can, according to his own desire, *pronounce* in his own language, as long as he knows the *meaning* of the characters" (29; emphasis original). The Chinese character, *ai* (愛), which Etiemble does not cite in the passage, but must imply, is an Ur-signifier, an original "meaning," from whence spring all the other signifiers in various ways to be "pronounced": *aimer, amare, philein*, and of course, the Chinese *ai*.[16]

Descartes's choice of the example of "*aimer, amare*, and *philein*" was probably no accident. In the Judeo-Christian tradition, "love" has always been one of the most powerful candidates for the title of the deepest human essence. What else is the reason that one begins a lesson of Latin by memorizing the inflection of "*amo*," which surely symbolizes the Western obsession with "love"?[17] As a concept of unquestionable importance in the Western tradition, "love" is easily believed to transcend cultural, national, and linguistic differences entirely.

That is to say, in the quest for the interrelationship of beliefs in primary signifieds, in universalism, and in essentialism, "love" is a representative notion, more so than the rest of the dozens of "cores of human nature" that the translators of Etiemble give. These other "cores," too, however, invite us to a humanist-comparativist project. Hence, the translators' comment:

> [A]s we learn more and more about the different ways of men, we learn as much about the universal in man. To voyage with Odysseus, to cry aloud with Oedipus, to rage with Lear, to laugh with Don Quixote, to love with Don Juan, to defy with Ahab, and despair with K is to voyage, cry aloud, rage, laugh, love, defy, and despair with particular men of particular times and particular places, but we can do so only as we can transcend the difficulties of those particulars, even at the moment of savoring them, and participate in their common humanity. This is the justification of those disciplines we call the humanities, of which comparative literature is most profoundly one. (xxii)

Thus, human nature, humanities, and humanism are combined. Together they construct the disciplines about "men," men who "cry, rage, laugh, love, defy, and despair" as a universal experience that ultimately transcends the particulars of times and places. The creeds of humanism, universalism, essentialism, a belief in prelinguistic human features, the discipline of comparative literature, or humanities in general, begin to function in a certain complicity. As a preliminary objection against what comparativists believe to be the features of "common humanity," I will investigate in the next chapter whether all of us really "love" (with Don Juan), or not.

2 the introduction of "love" into modern japan

The fact that there is no word corresponding to iki *in the West is proof that, in Western culture, the phenomenon of consciousness of* iki *has no place with any fixed meaning in the national existence.*

—*Kuki Shūzō*, The Structure of "Iki"

Love is not something that you can put chains on and throw into a lake. That's called Houdini. Love is liking someone a lot.

—*Jack Handey*, Deeper Thoughts

The New Concept of Romantic Love

Etiemble's optimistic program of discovering a universal language for love and other human essences meets a serious challenge when we look into the cultural change that took place in early modern Japan. His belief that every nation possesses a sense of "love" and an appropriate signifier to represent it does not seem to have a solid ground in light of the reorganization of sexual ideologies that Japan (and most East Asian countries) underwent.

Troubled by the obvious disparity between the love of the West and "love" in Japan, and by the absence of an appropriate signifier, the Japanese invented a word for it. This new signifier was to be adopted even in China, a culture which, from the viewpoint of Leibniz-Descartes and Etiemble, is supposed to offer the world a basis for the universal system of signs. The speculation concerning this fact, whose historical trajectory we will trace soon, leads us to view with suspicion a metaconcept of "love" that can serve as a universal point of reference, that is to say, "love" that exists beyond an immediate cultural/linguistic formula. The belief in "love" existing in a linguistic void, from which signifiers of various languages only afterwards spring forth to represent it, is not as evident as Etiemble and the Western humanists would have us believe.

When the "modern" Japanese literati started to read European literature in the early years of the Meiji period (1868–1912), among the most conspicuous features that radically challenged their traditional paradigm was the representation of heterosexual relationships.[1] For instance, the "equality" between male and female lovers or spouses described in Western literary discourse was often quite incomprehensible to Meiji intellectuals. The following episode typically demonstrates the Japanese encounter with this alien conception. A major early translator of Russian literature, Futabatei Shimei, asked his senior comrade in the literary coterie, Tsubouchi Shōyō, for advice on his translation of Turgenev's *Fathers and Sons*. The latter suggested that Futabatei correct the dialogue of the spouses in his translation because it sounded too casual, and hence, "proletarian" to him. Futabatei protested that it had to be rendered this way. Spouses in the West, he argued, were equal partners who could have an informal conversation unlike Japanese husbands and wives, whose relationship was strictly hierarchical (qtd. in Tsubouchi, *Calyx* 24).

If Shōyō was blind to the different kind of male-female relationship with which he was not familiar, Futabatei may have been somewhat naive as to the patriarchal structure of modern Western culture hidden beneath the apparent "equality" of the sexes. In spite of his naiveté, though, it was true that there really was a certain ideological/discursive formation, in European literary texts, of "equality" between man and woman, which only progressive Japanese writers who were sensitive to the tenets of Western culture could discern and introduce to the Japanese cultural scene.

This "equal" relationship was tied to the concept of "friendship." Calling one's lover a friend is a routine procedure in the literary discourse of the West, or even in everyday conversation. One of the earliest occurrences of such a usage in Western discourse is *Abelard et Héloïse* in which the former addresses the latter as friend.[2]

The principle of friendship and comradeship between lovers immediately became popular with Meiji intellectuals who were attracted to the Western style of loving. It was no coincidence that Kitamura Tōkoku, a romantic poet who advertised the new fashion of love, repeatedly addressed his fiancée in letters as his "dear friend." A friend and a (heterosexual) lover came to stand in a paradigmatic relationship with each other in the Japanese linguistic system for the first time in its history.[3]

If the premodern regime of Japanese male sexuality, which mostly encompassed prostitution, entailed condescending patronage on the part of a man and humble servitude on that of a woman, love as friendship required mutual respect. Concern for love and respect had, apparently, never been concurrently expressed in premodern Japanese texts. One's object of passion was someone whom one hoped to become intimate with, but not someone one wished to admire and respect. Only through reading European literature did a connotation of "respect" arise within the significative system of "love" of Japanese literati.

The origin of such a combination in Occidental cultures is often sought in courtly love, that is, in its idioms of adoration and lady-worship. The real nature of *courtoisie* and its heritage in the modern West have been fundamentally reexamined today. However that may be, the ideal of so-called chivalry or more broadly, the association of love with courtesy and respect, actively functioned in the discourse that Meiji intellectuals had access to. To give a few examples from works that were well known to Meiji writers, based on such a conception, Catherine of *Wuthering Heights* assures Mr. Linton that she does *not despise* him, and then paraphrases it as loving him more than anyone (ch. 23). In Jean-Jacques Rousseau's *La Nouvelle Héloïse*, the hero, addressing Julie as "ma charmante amie," writes: "You will always be respected" (Letter VIII). The theme of respect has eventually been combined with Don Juanism, too, although, naturally, in a reverse form. Théophile Gautier observed: "Don Juan is a man who has too lofty an idea of the woman not to despise women in general" (qtd. in Gendarme de Bévotte 5). If romantic lovers respect each other, Don Juan despises the women he seduces.

Such a Western concept of love quickly found its way into the writings of Japanese enlightenment thinkers. For instance, Nakamura Masanao wrote in his treatise from 1875 on motherhood that: "Equal rights [of a husband and a wife] should cause no harm if spouses love and respect each other" (301). The notion of love as respect subsequently spread to literary discourse. Futabatei's *Drifting Clouds* (1888) demonstrates an obvious reference to progressive writings of the previous decade: "[The hero Bunzō] was certain that love went hand in hand with respect and that no woman could love a man she did not respect" (*Japan's First Modern Novel* 275).

Such a concern for "respect" naturally instills a large amount of moralism into Western romantic love ideology. In modern European discourse, love is often primarily a moral issue, even when it takes the form of defiance to the codes of ethics. The conditions of morality have been integral to the very nature of love itself: one has to be virtuous to be a good lover. Such a feature is absent in the premodern

Japanese conception of passion; being in love has little or nothing to do with being personally moral. In Chikamatsu's classic puppet/Kabuki play, *The Love Suicides at Amijima*, the clerk Jihei's affection for the courtesan Koharu is measured only by its intensity. It is irrelevant to his diligence, religious piety, loyalty to his parents, a sense of charity, and other virtues, which, in fact, do not seem to be the major concerns of the author. By contrast, for the modern lover, Bunzō, in *Drifting Clouds*, the heroine Osei's affection should be directed toward him precisely because he is more honorable than his rival in love, Noboru, whom he considers to be a wicked scoundrel.

The concept of the love-relationship as friendship and moral achievement is interlaced with that of spiritual love. A physical relationship is downplayed as long as love is regarded as a kind of comradeship for achieving some lofty goal transcending material concerns. Puritan discourse, which was one of the major sources for romantic love ideology in modern Japanese literature, underscored spirituality as an aspect of heterosexual love. The dichotomy of *rei(-sei) no ai* (spiritual love) versus *nikutai no ai* (carnal desire) became a favorite motif for Western-oriented Japanese writers, especially Christians.

Furthermore, spirituality translated into "internality." It was now the internal, mental, but not the bodily, traits which should spur affection: "[Bunzō] had mistaken [the] superficial [literally, "external"] beauty [of Osei] for true ["internal"] virtue" (*Japan's First Modern Novel* 334). "Love," thus, was forced to depart from the physical arena to the metaphysical. It is here that the standard of compatibility arose. "Love" has to be based on the deep (since it concerns internality) understanding of, and sympathy with, characters and sentiments of those whom one loves: "Love requires mutual understanding [of the nature and temperament]. . . . [Osei had lost interest in Bunzō since] their personalities were in conflict" (*Japan's First Modern Novel* 334).

Such a model of the male-female relationship was in complete contradiction to the hierarchical gender structure and the hedonistic masculine sexuality of the premodern Edo upper- and middle-class society. The semifeudal (male) system of passion depended on the division between prostitutes (*yūjo*) as objects of love, and housewives (or, literally "ordinary women"; *jionna*) as domestic servants and agents of reproduction. A wife in Edo culture was seldom conceived of as an object of passion; one's own wife almost never. The general dissociation of love with nonprostitutional women is typically expressed in the following quote from Saikaku's *Five Women Who Loved Love*: "She showed coquetry (*sui*) unusual for an ordinary woman" (*Kōshoku gonin onna* 230).[4]

The same ideology is expressed in the development of *Onna daigaku* (*Women's Learnings*). In what is generally considered to be the first version of the series of Books of Conduct for women that are loosely categorized *Onna daigaku*, Kaibara Ekiken emphasizes that housewives should not make themselves appear sexually attractive. Consequently, the Confucian author suggests that they should use the humblest clothing, should not wear makeup, or show coquetry, and so on, implying that they are not objects of male passion (21). Conversely, the modern version of the Book of Conduct after the Meiji Reformation (1868) advises them to look neat and tidy so that the husbands may not lose interest in them (e.g., Doi Kōka, *Modern Women's Learning* [1874] 115). Only at this moment did housewives change from asexual servants to erotic "companions."

Till then, in the Edo system of sexuality, masculine desire was expected to be fulfilled predominantly in the pleasure quarters. The sexual ideologies developed within this system are variously encapsulated as *kōshoku, iki, sui, tsū, iro,* and so forth, entailing carnal hedonism, playfulness, aesthetic rather than moral concerns, male patronage, and other features.[5] Those ideals precluded the concepts of love as anything resembling respect, comradeship, and a quest for

an ideal that characterized the Western romantic representation of spiritual love.

Creation of the Signifier *Ren'ai*

I have briefly described some characteristics of Western romantic love which struck Meiji literati as incompatible with
the traditional Japanese principle of a male-female relationship. The latter, based on the distinction between prostitutes
(*yūjo*) and housewives (*jionna*), that is, on feudal/patriarchal
familial ideology and commercialized male-chauvinistic hedonism, was completely lacking in any of the elements of
(alleged) "equality," senses of respect, "chivalry," friendship, and so on, that constituted romantic love ideology.
Spirituality and morality were absent, too. Values encouraged in the *iki* or *kōshoku* sexual ideology of playfulness and
detachment were in contradiction to the requirements in
Western romantic passion to be intense and in earnest.

Such major differences in sexual ideology as perceived
by the Japanese literati caused a terminological difficulty.
It is reported that Futabatei Shimei, while translating one
of Turgenev's novels, could not hit upon an appropriate
rendering of "I love you," uttered by a woman. He finally
translated it into *shindemo ii wa* ("I could die for you").[6]
Ai(-suru), which we encountered earlier as a universal term
for love in the Leibniz-Descartes-Etiemble proposal, and
which is a normal Japanese translation for English "love"
(and "to love") today, up to this point had signified in Japan only the hierarchical, condescending passion of the male
patron toward a courtesan. Therefore, a woman was not permitted the use of this verb, but could only indirectly com-
municate a sense of devotion. This feature was at first
tenaciously retained even in a Western-oriented context. In
Karyū shunwa, a free translation of Bulwer Lytton's *Ernest
Maltravers*, partly incorporating material from *Alice* by the
same author, "love" between Ernest and Alice is translated
into several different Japanese words, including *ai. Ai,*

however, is always ascribed to the male, Ernest; the others, including *koi, kenren,* and so on, indicating devoted affection are carefully allocated to the female, Alice. Consider, for example, the following diametrical opposition: "The man loved (*ai*) the woman; the woman also loved (*koi*) the man (*Otoko moto onna o aishi, onna mata otoko o* kou)" (Niwa 38). The usage of *ai* as a sentiment involving mutual respect and ostensibly equal footing commenced only after the introduction of the Western concept of romantic love. Besides, other related terms such as *iki, kōshoku, nasake, iro,* and so forth, through which the ideology of sexuality in Japan had traditionally been expressed, were devoid of the sense of spiritual comradeship that appeared to permeate Western counterparts. Futabatei's choice of not translating "love" into *ai* was inevitable.

Meiji literati recognized this absence of a corresponding signifier in the native vocabulary to express the signified of Western romantic love. This caused a problem in introducing the new idea. The first, natural solution was to use the English word "love" as it was, or its closest phonetic equivalent in Japanese, *rabu.* One of the earliest of such usages appears in Suehiro Tecchō's *Plum Blossoms in the Snow* (1886): "Seeing that he was staring at your face all the time, he must have fallen in 'love' (*rābu*) with you" (123). The long vowel sign (*rābu*), which can be absent in other occurrences (*rabu*), attests to the instability of the new usage. As a matter of fact,"love" was first rendered in quite a varied fashion: "love," *rabu, rābu, raabu, rabbu,* and so on. These variations would ultimately vanish except for *rabu.* The quotation marks in the above quotation, which show that the concept was new and alien at this point, would soon be unnecessary.

That the new signified was yet to be established is testified by those usages whose meanings were reduced to traditional concepts. The following is an example from Tsubouchi Shōyō's *The Characters of Modern Students* (1885): "Did he know that Komachida was a regular customer (*rabu* [love]) of that singer [geisha]?" (321) Here "love" is used to refer to a "patron (of a prostitute)," representing the Edo system of male-oriented sexuality.[7]

The second phase was to use a Japanese (Sinified) form with a gloss (*furigana*) indicating that it was to be read in English, that is, "love." Tsubouchi's early works often took advantage of such a method: "He was carried away in so-called love" (*Characters* 6: 50; the original text is quite dexterously expressed with one gloss, *koi*, the Japanese pronunciation of the Chinese character 恋 [love], to its right, and another, *raabu*, the phonetic rendering of English "love," in parentheses below. The qualifier "so-called" shows that the use of the English term (and the concept) was still relatively new to the readers.

However, *raabu* in this example may represent a case of the empty signifier. It denotes hardly anything, having, instead, a good deal of connotations. The definition of (English) "love" was probably not clear either for the author or for the readers. The word simply conveyed the sense of fashionableness and civilization that a progressive readership associated with the Western texts. The use of empty signifiers was, during this period of relentless change and modernization, a gesture to imply something new. It was newness that was always quickly recognized even when its exact content was vague.

Finally, by the early 1890s, a consensus had been somehow formed that the Western notion of romantic love should be expressed with a new coinage, *ren'ai*. According to Yanabu Akira, one of the first writers to use *ren'ai* in the sense of Western romantic love was Iwamoto Yoshiharu. He wrote in 1890 in the review of a Japanese translation of a Balzac novel: "Japanese men love (*ren'ai-suru*) very superficially. They don't love (*ai-suru*) from deep within their soul" (*Jogaku zasshi* Dec. 1890). This usage was later popularized by contributors to such journals as *Jogaku zasshi* and *Bungakukai*, popular belletristic magazines that catered to progressive young readers. *The Dictionary of Meiji Terms* does not give the date of the first occurrence, although it mentions that *ren'ai* was generally acknowledged and was popularly used in the third decade of Meiji, citing Yamaji Aizan's "Philosophy of Love (*Ren'ai*)" from the twenty-third year of Meiji (1890). The date *The Dictionary* gives coincides with Yanabu's theory. The first example of such a usage recorded in Shōgakkan's *The Great Japanese Dictionary* is from the translation of *Self-Help* (*Saigoku risshi hen* [1870]). *The Dictionary* also comments that *ren'ai* came into circulation in the early years of Meiji, as a translation for English "love," along with *ai-ren*; *ren'ai* became the more popular of the two from around the twenty-second year of Meiji (1890).

That *ren'ai* among other choices was finally chosen and accepted as a Japanese signifier for an English (and European) signified "love," seems to have been largely a matter of coincidence. In the contour of changing signifiers, other candidates such as *ai-ren* were also used, but then discarded. It is quite unclear why this particular coinage (*ren'ai*) was preferred to other options, or why it eventually survived in the glossary of Japanese terms for sexuality. As we have seen, several traditional words appeared in early Meiji texts with a gloss indicating that they were translations for English "love." Why did they fall out of grace? One possible explanation for the advantage of *ren'ai* over *ai-ren* is the absence of homonyms. *Ai-ren* can be rendered either 哀憐 (pity-mercy) or 愛憐 (love-mercy). The latter two are long-standing classical terms, dating back to the medieval period. Both of them have a connotation of condescending, patronizing sentiment, not necessarily confined to a sexual context. They had Buddhist associations as well. These two renditions, then, might have given *ai-ren* a nuance which conflicted with the Western concept. Other words such as *kenren*—meaning strong, almost karmic attachment—probably suffered from similar traditional connotations. *Ren'ai*, conversely, had no such association from the past. It was a completely new coinage, appropriate for expressing an alien Western term. It was the radical newness and the utter differentiation of the concept that the new signifier was expected to convey.

The evolution of the sign *ren'ai* from the original English "love" (*rabu*) via Chinese characters and compounds read "love" eventually to *ren'ai*, reveals the origin of the latter as a translated coinage. *Ren'ai* was, at least originally, another name that Meiji literati gave to what was signified by the English word "love," whatever ramifications and distortions it was to receive afterwards. The fact that "love" had to be first called *rabu*, the nearest phonetic equivalent in Japanese for "love," and that it was subsequently necessary to invent a completely new signifier, strongly suggests that the signified of "love" was, at least to the eyes of Japanese literati, in no way similar to the related concepts in the Japanese vocabulary. Kitamura Tōkoku, himself one of the most influential figures in disseminating the translated coinage *ren'ai*, insisted on its total disparity from the Japanese concepts foregrounding heterosexual relationships. In articles such as "The Pessimist-Poet and the Woman," which was to prove the most influential manifesto in advertising the concept of "love" and Western romantic love ideology, and "On *Iki* with Criticism of *Kyaramakura*," Tōkoku declared that *iki* was one-sided while *ren'ai* mutual, that *iki* was a reserved attitude while *ren'ai* a total devotion, and that *iki* was sobriety while *ren'ai* was madness. If *ren'ai* was a translated coinage, the notion of "love" was also a translation in a broad sense of the word. For translation is commonly considered an act of finding a signifier in the vocabulary of the target language, whose signified is either identical, or closest, to that of the word to be translated. An act of translating, then, must be based on the conviction that a corresponding signifier with a relatively and sufficiently similar meaning content must necessarily be somehow available in other cultural/linguistic vocabularies. However, we are now dealing with a case when a new concept is imported first, and a new signifier is only subsequently created in a target language. Is this also an act of translation? The word was missing; so was the concept.

The "Meaning" of Love

The fact that Edo Japanese culture lacked the signifier /love/ (and, most likely, the signified «love»,[8] too) is in serious contradiction with the humanist principles of comparative literature. They are typically presented by Etiemble's proposal of metalanguage, namely, of giving a single symbol to a series of signifiers from multiple languages that are considered to possess the same content. 愛 (or any arbitrary symbol) can substitute for the signifiers /love/, /Liebe/, /amour/, /liubov'/, /ai/, and so forth. This would enable us to compare various forms of "love" in the cultures of the world, and to speak of it, using a transcendental symbol that supposedly represents the original signified from which spring forth all the local expressions. However, underneath such a formula is a presupposition that /love/, /Liebe/, /amour/, and so on, ultimately represent the same signified. Only on such a premise can parochial signifiers conveniently be substituted by a metalinguistic symbol that allegedly allows the scholars of different backgrounds to speak of the "same" phenomenon.

Underlying Etiemble's model is a belief in the universality of humanistic values: it is expected that a term (and, therefore, a corresponding sentiment) for such an essentially human concept as love has to be existent in any culture, possessing essentially an identical content. Then, what if the word "love" was missing in premodern Japan? The chain of synonyms that must endorse Etiemble's project would collapse. Furthermore, what if the concept of "love" was also absent? The universalist-essentialist ideology that must underwrite the project would become moot.

There are several ways to tackle such difficulties with a view to reinstating the humanist essentialism of comparative literature:

1. In spite of the terminological deficiency, the concept of romantic love was prevalent in effect in Japanese culture before Westernization. The lack of a signifier

is a mere historical contingency. If "love" is one of the most important tenets of humanism, it has to be universally existent; it cannot be missing. (This is an opinion largely held by American comparativists and Japanologists.)

2. The concept of «love» was embedded in the mind of Edo Japanese, but was dormant or suppressed. Therefore, its verbalized and institutionalized form did not materialize. (This is the idea of the Japanese humanist-philosopher Abe Jirō, whose writings I will examine in detail in chapter 5.)

3. Both the concept «love» and the expression /love/ were absent in Edo Japan since it was an inhumane, semifeudal society. If "love" is an important humanist category, a society lacking it has to be a terribly unfortunate one. (This is basically Kitamura Tōkoku's view.)

What are the problems of such arguments? The first and second views represent the kind of metaphysical thinking that I called into question in the previous chapter: the notion of a signified without a signifier, awaiting to be signified. It is, as it were, a religious belief in that it presumes the unspoken-of, unnamed ideal entity, not contaminated by the materiality of language. So arguing, a literary critic dreams of the existence of ideal essence just as an anthropologist imagines a "real" human being without any sociocultural masks on, to use Geertz's terms again. There is, however, no backstage where one can observe a signified without any sociolinguistic contingencies. A sign functions solely in social/ideological milieux.

In fact, it is highly unlikely that a notion, if it was consciously or unconsciously operating in a culture, could remain without a signifier for centuries, and suddenly, at the end of the nineteenth century, find its happy expression /love (rabu)/. If, as in the second argument, it was not in operation but was dormant, and if its embodiment in a tangible form was unavailable, we do not know where it was hiding latent, except in an idealistic backstage.

Furthermore, a theory that a concept, either in a conscious form or in a dormant state, was not represented by a native term, but was signified only by a foreign word, must be suspected for its Orientalism in the Saidian sense. For it is a typical Orientalist conception that a certain signified in (Eastern) cultures can be perfectly signified not by a signifier from the vocabulary of the native cultures, but by one in other cultures (of the West). Given this theory, related Japanese terms such as *iki, kōshoku, tsū, sui, nasake, koi,* and so on, are considered either hardly relevant to, or only partially expressive of, a real human essence, "love." It is the European vocabulary, not the inefficient, dormant language, which takes over the assignment of representation.[9]

The third argument (that Edo society was so abnormal that it lacked both the word and the concept of "love") is a cruder form of Eurocentrism, which conceives any deviation from the European standard as marginal, perverse, or barbarian. It theorizes that it would not be surprising that "feudal" backward Japanese society should necessarily have lacked a modern, progressive, and Western notion of love. Evidently, such a Euro-chauvinistic faith in modernization and Westernization is no longer tenable.

Many may yet hope that my foregoing objections can be overcome by resorting to the theory of a core meaning,[10] that is, by imagining *the* notion of love, or the ultimate «Love». In such a theory, it is the most fundamental essence of "love," which, having shed all its cultural and historical contingencies, must be shared by every human society as a basic human sentiment. «愛», «love», «*Liebe*», «*amour*», «*ai*», and so forth, are, then, considered not exactly identical signifieds, as Etiemble seems to be suggesting. Indeed, they are part of a constellation of concepts that, overlapping each other, configure around a certain core. In short, it is expected that /love/, /Liebe/, /amour/, /philia/, /liubov'/, /iki/, /nasake/, /ai/, /koi/, and so on, all express something of an ideal notion «Love», but only imperfectly. These signifiers signify merely subconcepts of the original «Love», and consequently are all equally parochial paradigms. It is only «Love» that transcends cultural and linguistic differences. Given this theory, the charge of Orientalism is presumably evaded. The absence of a signifier in some cultures is not to be wondered at any more; perhaps no single signifier of any language will ever perfectly express this ideal concept. The absence of a signified, a case observed in Edo Japan, would not be too serious, either; since an ideal concept can only be partially represented, the embodiment of its full content is merely a potential.

Even with such theorizing, however, we are still within the problematics of metaphysics: signifiers continue to be the mere shadows of Platonic Ur-signifieds. At the same time, the substance of these ideal concepts is extremely ambiguous. What exactly is «Love»? If it transcends its contingent linguistic renderings, how do we know it except by some Kantian a priori perception? Discovering what all cultures regard as the basis of "Love" is necessarily more complicated a task than determining what "love" means in a certain single culture.

Furthermore, a theory of a core inevitably leads to unwelcome political consequences. A quest for a core meaning, that is, a construction of the "essential," is by nature a marginalization of the "contingent." This centering and decentering in order to differentiate the core and the periphery of a meaning is largely an ideological decision. For instance, one area of sexuality that came to be deleted from the field of signification of "love" at some points in history in various cultures was homosexuality.[11] The shift from Greek "love" to Christian sexual "love" described by Foucault in his *The History of Sexuality* was one such point. We have also referred to the legitimate tradition of homosexual love in Edo sexual ideology in the previous chapter. This field of signification disappeared when the traditional sexual ideal of *iki* was replaced by *ren'ai* (love), which differed from *iki* in that it could not be applied to homosexual passion, at least in the Meiji period.

Selection of a "core," then, reflects ideological agenda. A conservative thinker would define universal «Love» as "an intensely passionate and tender feeling between two people of different sexes (potentially leading to reproduction)," and consider homosexual "love" a deviation. This has been the hegemonical view of the modern West. Sexological discourses, as we will see in chapter 4, played an immense role in "modernizing" and legitimating such a view. An early sexologist, Auguste Forel, declared: "[I]t is obviously absurd to apply the term 'normal' to a sexual appetite absolutely devoid of its natural object, procreation. But this is quite characteristic of the sentiments of inverts" (*Sexual Question* 242). Conversely, a gay Edo Japanese writer would define "love" as a homosexual passion, and consider heterosexual "love" as perversion. Saikaku argued, though in a playful manner, in his *The Great Mirror of Male Love*: "Why, when there is no form of amusement more elegant than male love, do people nowadays remain unaware of its subtle pleasures? . . . Truly, female love is something that all men should fear" (51-52). Today a progressive would simply formulate it as "a (hetero-/homo-)sexual passion." The choice of a formulation is not an issue of linguistics. Nor does it reflect the "real" nature of Love, universal, essential, and unchanging. It is an issue of ideology and politics.

If heterosexuality is often considered an integral part of «Love», so is "intensity." In the light of the Edo sexual ideology, however, "intensity" appears more or less contingent. The standards of loving proposed in later Edo fictions were sobriety and playfulness. A serious involvement was considered *yabo* (uncool), contrary to the ideal of *iki*. This is exactly why the poet-essayist Kitamura Tōkoku, representing Western romantic love, denounced *iki*: for him, love had to be soul-consuming. Conversely, this is probably why Chikamatsu's plays featuring lovers' double suicides have been much more favorably received in the West than later

Edo pulp fictions emphasizing detachment. And this is why Tōkoku prefers Chikamatsu, who, he insists, *occasionally* succeeded in depicting true love, by which Tōkoku means crazily acute involvements ("Upon Reading *Utanenbutsu*" 85–86).

Also relevant here is the reason that Tōkoku selects *Utanenbutsu* as one of the very few plays in which the ideal of love is expressed. It is because the heroine is *jionna* (literally, an "ordinary" woman), while in Chikamatsu's many other works heroines are prostitutes. The evaluation is based on the modern, Protestant standard that love is domestic and private, not on the Edo (masculine) sexual ideology, which maintains that "love" is prostitutional. Tōkoku writes: "Most heroines of Chikamatsu's plays dealing with domestic subjects are taken from the pleasure quarters. Plays whose setting is the *pure* environments are very few. Among them *Utanenbutsu*, featuring Onatsu and Seijūrō, is known as his masterpiece" ("Upon Reading *Utanenbutsu*" 84; emphasis mine). One may wonder what exactly the "pure environments" are. We are reminded here that the Purity Campaign, pursued with fervor in the Meiji period against the sanctioned prostitution endorsed by the Edo system of sexuality, was not a simple call for the demolition of the prostitution; it was a call for chastity.[12]

Furthermore, as Tōkoku correctly points out, it is part of romantic love ideology, but not of *iki*, that true love should be intense (this statement may be redundant since romantic love ideology requires love to be "true," too). Then, the decision to see "intensity" or "truthfulness" as cores of «Love» is another ideological one. When the theory of *iki* is criticized by such standards, they are challenged by the Western conceptions, but not by the essentials, of universal "human" love, which transcend the cultural and ideological specificities.

A signified in a certain linguistic/ideological system may have a core of some kind, effective only temporarily and locally. But I argue against the belief in a core for a number of signifieds from various languages, that is, the "metaphysical" idea of a certain "transcendental" core, serving as a center of signs across the boundaries, both synchronic and diachronic. On the plane of synchronicity, it assumes a certain general Ur-signified that functions as a core of related concepts, including foreign ones; on that of diachronicity, an eternal thread of meaning that unites changing signifiers is presumed.

Such a core is suspect. To begin with, a core for a certain signified may not necessarily be singular. For example, as has been mentioned, the meaning content of the Edo sexual ideology of *iki* has a highly aesthetic dimension as well as the "sexual." Then, is its core meaning a (hetero) sexual sentiment between two human beings, or is it refinement of taste that demonstrates a "cool" sense of beauty? While Tōkoku treated *iki* as a term basically referring to a heterosexual relationship, the current usage of it (and the nineteenth-century usage) depends heavily on its aesthetic dimension. The modern Japanese philosopher Kuki Shūzō, in his phenomenological analysis of *iki* in its Edo usage, concentrates on the aesthetic aspects of the term, rather than the sexual dimension. What, then, is the core meaning of *iki*?

Perhaps, though, there is nothing wrong in presuming plural cores, or rather, kernels of meaning. *Iki* may be thought to possess two (or more) core meanings. The one related to the aesthetic dimension may form a constellation with other concepts, around the core of, say, «chic», or more broadly, around «the beautiful». On the other hand, within this theoretical framework, English «love» (and also «*iki*») may fall into the category of, say, a «tender sexual feeling». Then again, «love» may be a subcategory of «human compassion», the order to which such concepts as «kindness», «charity», «*ninjō*», and so on, may belong, but not «*iki*». Given this theorization, these higher, more general, categories are shared by all human societies, regardless of whether perfectly happy phrases for these concepts are found or not.

However, by resorting to a higher order of cores, or categories located at a higher rung of generalization, we only face a new difficulty in place of the old one. Suppose we think of two cores or original meanings for *iki*: sexual passion (which relates it to "love") and the aesthetic (which relates it to "chic"). We are, then, challenged with the question of the legitimacy of the supposedly ideal, original categories of the sexual and the beautiful. Are they not also culturally specific signifieds? (In fact, I shall try to historicize the concept of "sexuality" in the fourth chapter.) We have merely substituted one problem for another. In a quest for original, more general, senses for love and *iki*, we arrive at the "sexual" and the "beautiful," which are, after all, another pair of linguistic formulae equally liable to be historicized and culturally specified. The concept of plural cores, in trying to recuperate idealist thinking, after all makes those cores appear more indeterminate.

Such problems, involved in constructing basic core concepts by supposing plural cores, are, once again, silenced by a tacit Orientalist presumption. That *iki* involves "two" significative axes, one on the sexual plane, the other on the aesthetic plane is, probably, a vision transparent only for the observer whose language segregates the sexual and the aesthetic on different planes. On one hand, as Kuki points out, *iki-goto*, that is, what is *iki*, is synonymous with *iro-goto*, or what pertains to sex (21); *iki* here is used to refer to the sexual dimension. On the other hand, it can be applied to an aesthetic judgment alone when it refers, for example, to clothes. However, the two dimensions seem to be inseparable in the following example from Tamenaga Shunsui's *The Plum Calendar*, one of the most successful representations of late Edo erotic culture: "I learned, upon persistent inquiry, that he has a sexy (*iki-na*), beautiful (*utsukushii*) wife at home" (49). Is the wife not only sexy, but also beautiful? Rather, we are to understand that the wife is aesthetically refined because she is sexually attractive. The "two planes" of *iki* are interrelated without any differentiation.

Such a close interrelation is unavailable in European languages, endorsing Kuki's insistence, cited as an epigraph, that no term in Western languages can replace *iki*. As Saussure argues, the meaning of a signified is articulated only in paradigmatic relation with other signifieds, that is, within a closed synchronic structure. If so, a comparative analysis of a core meaning is a suspicious action. When, however, it is done, the extraction of a core, the differentiation of the levels of meanings, their hierarchization, must depend on the conceptual system of either one of the languages compared. *Iki* is considered a combination of the two dimensions, the sexual and the beautiful, only because these two are basic categories of Western criticism. A project of searching for a core (or cores) across cultural/linguistic boundaries is, thus, suspicious. A comparison is an act of breaking open the closed structure with, however, political, and not necessarily favorable implications.

From these observations, it appears that neither the idea of Ur-signifieds, nor that of a core meaning, can give supposedly related signifieds of various languages a determinate point of reference. If signifieds are indeterminate, so are their alleged cores. If «love» and «*iki*» are radically different segments of human activity, «Love», whatever it is, is also one historical formula, susceptible to changing segmentation.

A "core meaning" of «Love» that is supposed to relate those two terms, making them "comparable," is not only highly indeterminate, but also interpretation-dependent. From a standpoint that foregrounds romantic love ideology, one set of related signifieds to be compared would emerge, all having «Love» (or, in truth, [romantic] love) as their core. From a different ideological standpoint, a different set of signifieds would emerge: «*iki*», «*iro*», «*sui*», «*tsū*», «chic», «coquetry», and similar concepts. We do not start from a constellation of obviously related terms, existing outside our perspective, in order to deduce from it a certain core. We do not perceive a group of signifieds: «love», «*amour*», «*Liebe*», «*ai*», «*iki*», and so on, which leads to the discovery of «Love». When such a constellation is perceived, a core that has determinate denotations has already been presumed. I have written earlier that discovering what all cultures regard as the basic meaning of «Love» is a complex task. As a matter of fact, once an attempt has been made, it is not complicated at all. For, with the presumption that all cultures know something of «Love», expressed in local terms, the presumed terms of «Love», referring to that core, have already solved that task in advance.

To conclude this section, the theory of a core meaning, supposedly substituting a metaphysical notion of ideal «Love», does not restore the humanist belief in universal "love," which is expected to relate all the relevant signs of the world languages and point to one of the essential features of humanity.

Sign and Reality

The above speculation leads us to view with suspicion a metaconcept of "love" that can serve as a universal point of reference, that is to say, "love" that exists beyond the immediate cultural/linguistic expression. The belief in "love" existing in a linguistic void, from which signifiers of various languages only afterwards spring forth to represent it, appears rather suspicious now.

This conclusion has serious implications. Put in more general terms, it suggests that the ontological status of any entity, existing independent of, or prior to, its linguistic formulation, is questionable. The very distinction between ontology and epistemology needs to be reexamined.

We are not, though, questioning "realties" themselves, which obviously exist outside the human activities, but merely categorized "entities" that are, nonetheless, supposed to exist unconstrained by language. We do not, for instance, doubt that there is a certain act or passion of sexuality which is represented by /love/. In the same vein, we do not doubt the existence of a phenomenon referred to by

/*iki*/ or /*iro*/, two representative notions of premodern Japanese sexual ideology. (We will closely examine these concepts in the next chapter.) It is the noncritical concept of the "referent" that is at issue, a referent such as "love," which, according to the claim of ontological realism, exists prior to language, subsequently begetting the signifieds «love», «*iki*», «*iro*», and so on. It is such a belief in solid referents (rather than concepts), each possessing a stable position in the "real" world, that makes "love" and "*iki*" comparable. For, given a belief that a certain physical/mental feature "love" exists unmediated by human conceptualization, an Ur-signified «Love» that represents the referent "love" can easily be derived from it. And, finally, from the original signified its culturally varied formulae, /love/, /*iki*/, and so forth, can be derived with only a slight difference in nuances.

Actually, some of the concepts (and hence the relevant human faculties as their referents), including "love," are normally believed to transcend linguistic relativism. Among them are physical objects in nature and categories of humanism: even if a "snowman" is a human product, and therefore, the concept «snowman» is culturally specific, "snow" is a natural entity whose being-in-the-world is not affected by a culture or a language; "snow" is a tangible object, existing beyond the boundary of language. If French "esprit" is a parochial notion, a "fighting spirit," or more evidently, "spirit," is a universal human feature, independent of its cultural forms. In this section we will seek to deconstruct such ontological realism, or a belief in translinguistic/transcultural referents, by exploring the theory of Benjamin Whorf.

I do not, however, refer to the so-called Sapir-Whorf hypothesis, which is more or less regarded with suspicion today, that a language determines the nature of a culture in which it is spoken. My position is rather that a linguistic system per se is culture, that is, culture as a text. I shall, therefore, simply use those of Whorf's insights that are relevant to my discussion of linguistic relativism.

The well-known Whorfian example of conceptual differences is given in terms of "snow" in English and in an "Eskimo" language: the latter has three different words (falling snow, fallen snow, used snow) for the single English "snow" (Whorf 210).[13] It follows that there is no referent "snow" in the natural world that has nothing to do with human conceptualization. In other words, "snow" is a referent in the real world only from the perspective of the English-speaking observer. We can generalize Whorf's example and argue that not only "snow" but all other supposedly natural phenomena and entities are nothing more than concepts uniquely articulated in various cultures.

From an antithetical view, however, one may counter such a relativistic idea by resorting to the more comprehensible category of "Snow," writ large: English snow and Eskimo snows are merely subdivisions of "Snow," just as one can conceive of Love in place of various "loves." If this is so, the linguistic relativism involved in Whorf's theory can be circumvented: we do have a natural category "snow"; it is just that its linguistic renditions can differ.

Not to mention that such a view is simply a revision of the model of nomenclature, which had long been uprooted by Saussure, the model under which we give different names to things in nature waiting to be named. Whorf himself is not free from the nomenclaturative conception in spite of his apparent challenge to it. For, precisely by comparing English "snow" and Eskimo "snows," Whorf presumes a higher scheme of "Snow." In part, it is an inevitable result of his writing (and, perhaps, thinking) in English.

The same can be said of his other examples. He compares the English sentence "He runs" and its versions in various tenses to the corresponding sentences in Hopi, a language which he argues is timeless (213). His aim is to demonstrate the radical difference in constructing an event in the two linguistic systems. However, by comparing, he establishes the ultimate identity of those sentences. In other words, he shows them as different renditions of the same action referred to: "Running." A follower of universalism, therefore, would be able to undermine Whorf's relativism by insisting that the example merely shows two different ways of grammatically reconstructing the same event, which has already been conceived in a universally human way.[14] Once again, in trying to construct radically differentiating hermeneutics, we can, paradoxically, only cite an instance of identity, which has already been conceived to be an identical phenomenon in accordance with a certain paradigm. To show that the concepts of "running" are variously formulated, we need to first identify them as belonging to the category of (English) "running" in the last instance. We cannot talk from two different paradigms at the same time.

In a similar vein, by presenting a different way of articulating "snows" taken from a non-SAE (Standard Average European) language, Whorf's discovery questions an original referent "snow" which exists independent of linguistic formulation. Yet "Snow" (and English "snow") remains a foundational concept as a larger framework. We would still be presuming a general category of "Snow," supposedly corresponding to the situation of the physical world outside human activity. With such a theorization, the human faculty interferes only at a subsequent level, at which the English language adopts one signifier and Eskimo, three.

Now, is such a foundationalist conception, that is, the belief that English "snow" and the three Eskimo "snows" are all kinds of "Snow" writ large, tenable? To explore this issue, let us turn to the Chinese writing system. It categorizes snow, rain, sleet, hail, mist, fog, thunder, and so on, under the same heading (radical) of "rain (雨)": 雨, 雷, 雪, 霙, 霰, 雹, 霧, and so forth. Given the Chinese system of articulation, the comparison of English "snow" and three Eskimo "snows" appears arbitrary. If "Snow" is a transparent scientific category, having nothing to do with the human linguistic faculty, we should be able to find in the Chinese vocabulary one or more signifiers covering the larger "Snow," rather than a genus of "Rain" (unless we suspect some perceptual problem on the part of the Chinese people). However, such a correspondence is not discovered in Chinese. For, as the shared radical demonstrates, Chinese "snow" is a subdivision of not so much "Snow" writ large as "something that falls from heaven." In this sense, it can be associated with *lei* 雷 (thunder) and *dian* 電 (lightning), an association which is by no means available in English. A noun *yu* 雨 (rain) can be used as a verb, too, in the sense of "to fall down."[15] Therefore, *yuxue* 雨雪 may be rendered "Snow is falling," or "It is snowing." *Yu* (rain) can, then, convey even the sense of snow (falling). The Chinese scheme of "snow" overlaps that of English and Eskimo only in a very partial and fuzzy manner.

Thus, arrangements of the concepts in the coordinates of "natural" meteorological phenomena are achieved at various levels in most varied ways. Conceiving a category of "something that falls down from heaven," we will get: rain, snow, sleet, thunder, lightning, Eskimo's "falling snow," and so forth. Conceiving a category of "frozen flakes," we will find: snow, *xue*, Eskimo's three "snows," and so on. In any case, a core concept "snowness" is nowhere to be found.

Such a problem of comparative study of categorization is already suggested by Whorf's explanation. Whorf gives three Eskimo "snows" (falling snow, fallen snow, and cutout snow) for one English "snow." The Japanese scholar of Eskimo languages, Miyaoka, gives four, adding *pirtuk* (snowstorm). Now, is "snowstorm" a kind of snow or not? Miyaoka thought so, while Whorf did not. This already demonstrates the fuzziness of a category of "Snow" writ large which, in turn, can be subdivided into linguistically different categories.

Lucien Schneider's *Dictionnaire français-esquimau du parler de l'Ungava et contrées limitrophes* gives some twenty different Eskimo words for "snow." According to Miyaoka, four of these are basic terms, the rest being reducible to other roots. For instance, miŋuliq, fine snow that blows in through an opening, is based on the root miŋuy-, which means "dust"

(*Languages* 6). Then, it is, however, the conception of French, English, Japanese, and so on, but not the Eskimo language itself, that sees as "snow" what the Eskimo language perceives as "dust."

Of course, we may still resort to science, that is, to the vindication of the concept of snow as a meteorological phenomenon. It will be assumed that in spite of various categorizations and articulations, there must be "snow" at the root of all cultural and linguistic formulations, which is an unquestionable physical phenomenon, susceptible to scientific description.

The claim to scientificity can be, however, equally arbitrary and contingent upon a cultural paradigm. Whorf, along with the example of snow, gives different ways of articulating "water": the Hopi language distinguishes water in nature and that in everyday life (210). Once again, Whorf, in spite of his relativism, leaves the general framework of "Water" intact. From his perspective, it is just that Hopi divides this larger category into two, a division which may be considered meaningless in "scientific" terms.

The Japanese language has such "scientifically" insignificant subdivision, too, distinguishing hot water and cold water, respectively represented by (*o-*)*yu* and *mizu*. However, in spite of the Japanese people's knowledge of the relation between the two (that cold water turns to hot water when heated), these two are mutually independent physical objects to them. From the perspective of the Japanese, *yu* (hot water) cannot be considered part of water that has accidentally been heated. For there is no comprehensive concept "water" in Japanese that can either be hot or cold.

Speaking from my own experience, I, a speaker of Japanese, will try to draw cold water from the faucet when my American wife asks me in English to get her "water," by which she means the boiling water, singing in a kettle right in front of me. I would never associate it with "water." Such a response is, probably, the result of my having learned the

English word "water" as a translation for *mizu* (cold water). My response also shows that the way I segment the continuum is modeled on my native language, Japanese, even when I am speaking English.

Therefore, strictly speaking, translating *yu* as "hot 'water' " is already open to question since, to repeat, there is no comprehensible category of "water" in Japanese that comprises cold and hot water. *Yu* and *mizu* are mutually exclusive. Questionable also is the usual translation *mizu* for "water."

Such problems for the Japanese probably have roots in bilingual dictionaries. They list plural meanings for one term only as observed within the source language. Kenkyū-sha's dictionary of English-Japanese, the one widely considered standard and authentic dictionary of English-Japanese, tells us that "water" means (1) transparent liquid consisting of two hydrogens and an oxygen; (2) part of sea, rivers, lakes, and other bodies of water; (3) solution, and so on. The given categorization obviously follows the division of dictionaries in English. This is largely because a bilingual dictionary itself is usually a translation of English dictionaries. One of the most standard dictionaries of the early Meiji period, *Satsuma jisho*, for example, was a translation of Webster's *World Dictionary*. Kenkyū-sha's dictionary apparently relies heavily on the Oxford dictionaries. However, I know of no English-Japanese dictionary that defines "water" as "either *mizu* or *yu*," that is to say, a dictionary that gives not the Japanese words made to represent the English lexical system but the Japanese paradigmatic order. In other words, the multiple definitions of a bilingual dictionary are given only upon the basis of a one-to-one correspondence of an original signifier for another foreign signifier, thus tautologically reproducing the paradigm of the source language. Accordingly, in this case, "water" (1) is rendered *mizu*, "water" (2), *kasen*, and "water" (3), *yōeki*, and so forth. The fact that the content of «water» becomes ambiguous and indeterminate from the perspective of the Japanese lexicographical system, and, conversely, that *mizu* is not unequivocally and nonproblematically definable in the terms available in English, is ignored.

The Japanese example does put into question the higher category of "Water" comprising hot and cold water. "(Comprehensive) water" in English is merely one variety of segmentation of the natural world. *Mizu* and *yu* of Japanese is another.[16] However, such an idea is often challenged by the alleged scientific knowledge that both hot water and cold water are, chemically speaking, the same substance; "Water" writ large does exist as H_2O (0°C–100°C). Hence, the tenability of the general category of "Water." Hence, also, the frequently encountered discourse that the English language is more logical and scientific since it is closer to the natural categories, while Japanese is illogical and unreasonable.

Yet no natural language completely coincides with scientific language. H_2O is not equal to "water" as the former includes ice and vapor, too. Nonetheless, while "water" deriving from the distinction of vapor, water, and ice, is still within the order of science (chemistry), the Japanese distinction of hot and cold water, or the Hopi distinction of natural water and "human" water, have no legitimate place in a so-called scientific language. Is it that English and other SAE languages more faithfully represent the "natural" categories? Or is it that contemporary science more or less reproduces the structure of SAE languages? Whorf thinks the latter is the case, and calls for the creation of new science that is based on wider varieties of languages.

While it is not my intention to claim that so-called "scientific" categories are entirely arbitrary, or that the categorizations of English (or SAE languages) are made identical to so-called scientific categories, we should note the general ideological function of scientific discourses to confirm the categories of Western languages. Before us is a profound question: Is it that science gives a clearer and truer understanding of the objective world, inexactly articulated by the natural languages, or is it that science unwittingly reproduces the categories of the natural (Western) languages? Is there no possibility of constructing a science that allows for the meaningful differentiation of *mizu* and *yu* of Japanese, of three snows of Eskimo languages, or of the American native categories describing physical movements, the kind of science which Whorf called for?

Now, the above observation, challenging "scientific realism," as it were, suggests that a referent as well as a signifier and a signified exists only as a specific, but spatially and historically changing, sociocultural code. Put differently, the distinction between a referent and a signified is open for reconsideration. Obviously, a referent *is* a tangible object, but an act of reference is language bound. Therefore, a referent is already contaminated by a signified.

Perhaps, Derrida implies a similar problematic when he insists that there is no outside to texuality. In contrast, Saussure, despite his apparent criticism of a nomenclaturative theory, leading him to the distinction of a signified and a referent, in the last instance reestablishes a realistic belief in natural entities, which can ultimately reduce a signified to a referent, independent of cultural/linguistic distinction.

This is, ironically, an inevitable outcome of his triangular model: referent-signified-signifier. First, Saussure distinguishes an "idea" from a "thing":

> For some people a language, reduced to its essentials, is a nomenclature: a list of terms corresponding to a list of things. . . . This conception is open to a number of objections. It assumes that ideas already exist independently of words. (65)

Expanding and reinforcing this criticism, he contends that ideas are nothing but sociolinguistic segmentations of reality, differing from language to language:

> No ideas are established in advance, and nothing is distinct before the introduction of linguistic structure. (110)

In contrast to the arbitrary nature of a signified, a referent, for Saussure, has an ontologically stable condition, transcending contingent cultural/linguistic realization. The "sun" as a word is a linguistic value, realized only through social coding. But the sun as a physical object is unquestionably out there (114).

The out-there-ness of the sun as a referent is, however, no less questionable, as our foregoing analyses suggest. For the referent "sun" exists only as a result of distinguishing it from other stars, from planets, from a solar system, or from an entire universe, something which Whorf might name "Arupa," a chaotic continuum. Without such a distinction, there exists only "Arupa," but not the "sun" as a real object. Choosing as an example the physical object that appears most irrelevant to human conceptualization, that is, the sun, Saussure underwrites his belief in solid natural entities, obscuring his own critique of the nomenclaturative perspective. For even if a referent is nonlinguistic while a signified is a linguistic construct, are we not grafting "a list of terms" onto "a list of things" if behind a signified one can always find a referent, or a physical object, upon which an idea relies?

More problematic, however, than Saussure's obscure distinction between a referent and a signified is the way the transcendent status of a referent permeates a signified. A signified ontotheologically becomes an object of fetish because of the alleged unquestionable out-there-ness of its referent. In arguing the arbitrariness of the sign, Saussure contends:

> There is no internal connextion, for example, between the idea "sister" and the French sequence of sounds s-oe-r which acts as its signal [signifier]. The same idea might as well be represented by any other sequence of sounds. This is demonstrated by difference between languages, and even by the existence of different languages. The signification [signified] "ox" has as its signal [signifier] b-oe-f on one side of the frontier, but o-ks (Ochs) on the other side. (68)

As Saussure and structuralists who have developed his ideas argue, the signified, as well as the signifier, is a linguistic value that operates in relation with, and in differentiation from, other signifieds in the vicinity, that is to say, only within the paradigmatic system of one language. If so, /boeuf/ should in no way be able to replace /Ochs/ (nor / ox/, as the quoted English translation tacitly assumes by substituting English "ox" for German *Ochs*. A transcendental status of a referent as a "natural" objective entity, independent of linguistic articulation, must be assumed by Saussure in this passage: the signifier /ox/ may be arbitrary, and so is the signified «ox», but not the referent "Ox." In the above quotation, such a status is passed on to signifieds. Hence, the reinstated nomenclature of referent-signifier.[17] An ox as a referent is supposed to be identical to *un boeuf* or *ein Ochs*. We are required to believe that its existence is as self-evident as the sun; that even beyond the cultural boundary, it does not change its substance in spite of Saussure's claim that every signified is a social construct. An ox remains an ox regardless of its contingent name, just as the sun shines on every human being. When he relates the two signifieds (*boeuf* and *Ochs*; in fact, three [*boeuf, Ochs,* and ox], if we rely on the English translation) taken from the two independent linguistic systems to one physical entity, that is, the referent "ox," the French linguist is treating these signifieds and the referent as complete equivalents. With a one-to-one correspondence of a signified and a referent, Saussure's becomes a surreptitious revision of a model of nomenclature.

Now, the implicit nomenclaturative presumption of Saussure conveniently ties into humanist essentialism. The ontotheological status of a referent secretly endows the signified with a like status. The arbitrariness of the sign is reduced to that of a signifier, and of the relationship between a signifier and a signified, while the arbitrariness of a signified is circumvented.

In spite of many recent attempts at subverting Saussurean nomenclaturativism, such a tacit fetish of signifieds and referents seems to be at the bottom of transcivilizational comparative literature. With this fetish, the Etiemblean scheme of comparativism and metalanguage can easily be confirmed: "Love," an Ur-signified whose universality is guaranteed by the existence of a natural entity "love" out there, can, therefore, be called /amour/, /Liebe/, /ljubov'/, /ai/, and so on, the choice of which is completely arbitrary and, in fact, of little importance. Conversely, the theory of the contingency of a signified and of the cultural constituency of a referent is in total contradiction to humanist essentialism. For, from the perspective of universalism, things that may have various names, or at least, their core, have to be identical, whatever their changing names are.

Louis Hjemslev revised Saussure's model in order to remove the remnants of the nomenclaturative conception, by pointing more explicitly to the sociocultural formulation of the signifieds. His celebrated example is the segmentation of «Baum»—«Holz»—«Wald», which, he writes, is specific to German alone (54). The concept «Baum» can be signified neither by /arbre/ nor /tree/ precisely because «Baum», «arbre», and «tree» are not identical, for «Baum» depends on the triangular arrangement of «Baum»— «Holz»—«Wald». The French and the English languages are lacking in this arrangement, having instead «tree»— «woods», «arbre»—«bois». Whorf's example of Eskimo snow attests to the same, although he was not aware of its relevance to semiological considerations of reality.

Again, however, Hjemslev's revised theory about the segmentation of a continuum does not necessarily question the universality of larger categories. A more general framework of "wood(s)" or "snow" as a "natural" entity (and, therefore, as something that can naturally be conceptualized accordingly in a human mind) can still be, and actually is, deemed nonproblematic. Given this framework, one would simply think that the German and the Eskimo languages make further divisions to the original, more general categories. "Wood(s)" and "Snow" writ large, thus, remain as fetish referents, transcending linguistic differences. A semiotician would simply insist that human beings belonging to different systems segment continua in various manners, but not completely at random, for signifieds must more or less correspond to the original referents in the physical world. Fetishism in referents thus persists.

The example from Chinese that I cited earlier in this chapter puts the ontologically solid status of a referent "Snow" into question. As we have been analyzing, a larger category of "Snow" is already culture/language specific. In conceiving "Snow," the continuum in a semiological sense is already segmented to some extent even before finding a signifier (or signifiers). In other words, although being tangible objects, "Wood(s)" and "Snow" exist only as sociocultural constructs within a specific linguistic milieu.

Once again, such problems of ontological realism can be, and are, circumvented by virtue of Orientalist theorizing, namely, by retaining "snow" as a higher category, for which an Eskimo language happens to have subcategories, each represented by three signifiers. The universality of the meteorological phenomenon (and a concept) of "snow" is thus allegedly recovered. However, as we have seen, the categorization does not necessarily overlap this way, namely, "(English) snow" = "(Eskimo) snows" = a meteorological entity "Snow." If the Chinese language groups rain, snow, thunder, and other concepts, under the same rubric, which frame are we to propose as a larger category?

Consequently, it must be a concealed Eurocentrism, a generality of the categorizations of SAE languages, and geographical proximity, that allows the Saussurean version of nomenclaturativism to emerge. A farmer who takes his "ox" across the frontier and sells it to a foreigner has the same referent at hand, whether it is called *"un boeuf"* or *"ein Ochs."* The more remote the linguistic communities are, however, the more suspicious such a transparent correspondence of a signified and a referent becomes. The nomenclaturative argument of Saussure, cited above, would have very easily collapsed, or would not even have been conceived, if his choice of the example had been from, say, Japanese, which does not have a distinction between an ox, a bull, a cow, and a calf.

The last statement holds true except in the forms of compounds, by means of which the Japanese language, so it is held, can offer the given distinctions: *o-ushi* (male-bovine) for ox (or bull), *me-ushi* (female-bovine) for cow, *ko-ushi* (child-bovine or little-bovine) for calf, and so on. Based on this, some linguists contend that the physical world is not arbitrarily segmented by different languages. Even if a certain term is absent in one linguistic system, it is argued, that gap can be, and is, filled by other means of expression in that system: the contingent lack of a word "ox" in Japanese does not result in a different worldview because the same concept can be expressed by virtue of a compound. Such an argument tacitly presumes the higher categories, in this case, those of a species "bovine," a male-female distinction, and a parent-child relationship. Hence, the meaning analysis: ox = bovine + male; cow = bovine + female; calf = bovine + child; and so forth. Since these monemes (minimal units of meaning [Ducrot, *Encyclopedic Dictionary*]) are universal, they can be expressed somehow in any language, whether in the quality of one signifier or compounds.

The argument collapses when one thinks of such an example as the concept of *shusse-uo* in Japanese. Some species of fish change their name in the course of their growth. For instance, a yellowtail has four different names, starting from baby *tsubasu* via *hamachi, mejiro,* to adult *buri,* which is also used as a general term for the species.[18] What are their monemes? Shōgakkan's *The Great Japanese Dictionary* defines *mejiro* as "a slightly grown *buri,* having the length of about 60 centimeters." (A fully grown *buri* is about 100 cm long.) Is *mejiro* then *buri* + 60-cm-ness? Does not this demonstrate the radical contingency of the formation of signs, and hence, categories in the "real" world?

Thus, we reconfirm the conclusion that a referent as well as a signified is culturally specific, or rather, that the referent/signified distinction is debatable. By moving from the plane of a signifier to a signified, to a more general signified, to a transcendental Ur-signified, or, finally, to a signified endorsed by a referent, one does not arrive at the translinguistic field. We still find "realities" language-bound and articulated in drastically contingent manners.

If this is the case, comparativism proves dubious. For comparativism relies on the identity, or the fundamental similarity of the signifieds of different languages. However, the fetish of an ontotheological entity, that is, a referent, and the denial of its constructedness can work as a principle to reinstate and substantiate comparative literature. Even though, it will be held, a concept of love may be variously formulated as its signifiers: /love/, /aimer/, /ai/, /iki/, and so on, what it refers to, namely, the ontotheological object of «Love» (or simply "Love" since it is not considered a linguistic value any more), is out there. Hence, the legitimacy of giving it a symbol 愛, a meaningless icon for Westerners. Also, the legitimacy of comparing various "loves," all referring to the identical "Love." The task now is to analyze in what way it is subsequently rendered in linguistic constructions and in literature. Yet, if, as we have argued, the status of an original signified, or a referent, is contestable, so is comparison.

The play of ever-changing signifiers and signifieds that seems to permeate our cultural scene, defying a "referent" and an original signified, thus problematizes comparativism. Signifieds are linguistic, therefore culturally specific, categories, just as much as signifiers. By marking a signified with some neutral symbol, namely, by, for instance, giving «love» a code X which is internationally accessible even without the knowledge of specific signifiers, /love/, /amour/, and so on, a comparativist would not do away with the specifically linguistic structure of «love». The quest for a translinguistic code X representing human values is the implication of Etiemble's proposal, a code for which Etiemble, in a deceptively non-Orientialist gesture, proposes the use of a Chinese hieroglyphone. Be it a code X or a Chinese character 愛, however, we are still segmenting a continuum of reality according to the Western paradigm, the concept of «love».

But this illusion, created through doing without Western signifiers, functions to surreptitiously legitimize the Western signified as an international standard. This has been the way the transcivilizational comparison operates. Even if the radical method proposed by Etiemble of using the Chinese writing system is not adopted, a comparativist can safely claim that, by comparing expressions of «love», his or her comparative research is based on the transculturally shared signified, and that, therefore, the particular signifier chosen for convenience's sake does not constitute a problem. The choice of English /love/, it will be argued, is strictly contingent. With this move, comparativism turns into an Orientalist discipline.

Let us proceed to another problem. Starting, as we have, to question the semiotic model of referent-signified-signifier, we now call into question the ontological status of referent/reality and the universality of an original signified. We may slightly expand this hypothesis to include the notion of representation. A model of reality as an ontologically stable entity that then finds representation to mirror it becomes questionable, too. Is it not that what we conceive as "reality" is already represented, and is, therefore, linguistically constructed?

In the Meiji history of love, "reality" was obviously constructed according to the linguistic/discursive model. It was a representation of Western love that enabled Tōkoku to conceive his betrothed as a "friend" and to actually address her as such. We have here a mutual determination of literary production and "real" life. In other words, he "lived" his own discourse.

Thus, the case of the importation of romantic love ideology in early Meiji Japan supports the textualist assumption: one desires and puts that desire into practice following the recipe prescribed by the language and by the cultural paradigms which are actualized in various discourses. More crudely put, "love" is a verbal construct, hence, a text. Early Meiji literati had access to Western sexual mores only through literary, philosophical discourses, by virtue of which they reconstructed their own ideology of sexuality. Their sexual behavior in real life was modeled on European writers', and their own, verbal products.

Given this textualist move, a distinction between "reality" and "representation" becomes significantly subverted. As the modern Japanese example of the shift of sexual paradigm shows, we find these two entities, representation and the represented, determining and displacing each other. The result will be the radical questioning of the essentialist notion that a human being "loves," according to the instinct termed "sexual desire," and abiding by the "human" sentiment of tender affection; this innate passion, it is contended, is essentially human though expressed in various forms within varied cultural vocabularies; it may or may not be poetically represented in literary discourses.

I view such a model with skepticism. I would rather argue that discourse on sexuality, which is not so much the representation of sexual activities in real life as human sexuality per se, is a paradigm encoded in cultural texts. So-called reality for human consciousness is, as we have argued in the previous section, nothing other than a system of such codes. Hence, Marx's thesis: "Language is as old as consciousness" (51). "Love" for Tōkoku is at once the representation and the represented.[19]

Of course, one can still argue in protest against my ongoing arguments that texts Kitamura Tōkoku had an access to were "representations" of the Western practice of "love" in reality, and that, therefore, "reality" precedes representations after all. Thus, the fear of nominalism is rejected, and ontological realism is reinstated. It is, to the relief of a positivist, the words, the text, or the language, that only subsequently mirrors the reality. The problem with this objection is its implicit and expanded Orientalism. It implies that Edo Japanese culture was lacking both in the consciousness of love as mutual respect, friendship, and spirituality, and in expressions to represent it. Edward Said's critique of

Orientalism is directed against the West's project of representing the Orient in place of Eastern cultural vocabularies on the ground that the means for representation of the East are meager. In the above objection against the nominalistic/textualist theory, which turns out to be a typical expression of such Orientalist thinking, Eastern culture is devoid of both reality and representation. All we see there is a barren field, without a signifier /love/ or signified «love», awaiting to be filled and represented by Western cultural tenets.

The doctrine of humanism expects signifieds to exist prior to signifiers. Admittedly, in the cultural history of modern Japan, the signified «love» preceded the signifier /ren'ai/. The latter, in turn, however, preceded the concept «ren'ai». The new signifier /ren'ai/ was distributed before that which it could represent was crystallized. It came into circulation in three stages:

1. As a (half-)empty signifier, which was the case in *The Characters of Modern Students*, where a student's affair was imagined to be "love" regardless of its content. At this point, the definition of love was not particularly clear to the user.

2. As an expression for the traditional idea, simply adding some new nuances. In this case, too, a signifier circulated without a supposedly proper signified.

3. As a fully established sign with a signified roughly identical to «love», although by the time the signification of /ren'ai/ was achieved, it could not be completely synonymous with "love."

Historically speaking, then, the primacy, or the precedence, of the concept «love» over the neologism /ren'ai/ is undeniable. On the international scale, a new signified, taken from a foreign vocabulary, must always precede its signifier, created afresh. This fact appears to support the humanist belief that signifieds concerning human values exist prior to obtaining signifiers.

Orientalist humanism, however, makes a further claim: that it is always an original (Western) signified that precedes other non-Western signifiers. «Love», it will be emphasized, preceded /*ren'ai*/ in the Japanese language as it must have preceded all the other cultural/linguistic embodiments of it. Problems of a political nature, thus, arise when one conceives the general, essential primacy of the concept of «love» over other (non-SAE) signifiers. This is a natural consequence of univeralist humanism. It must presume the universal human essence of "love," which precedes concrete linguistic expressions. In such a manner, the humanist belief and the notion of the primacy of signifieds tie into each other. It supports, however, a hidden Orientalist presumption since although non-SAE signifiers are reduced to «love», the English word /love/ alone is not. A search for a signifier preceding the notion of «love» is not pursued, either. The chain of significations breaks here, establishing "love" as an origin. «Love» thus surreptitiously gains the position of the original signified, passing for the "human," not Western, essential.

This brings us back to the issue of translation that we touched upon in the previous section. Translation is essentially the act of giving identical meaning, namely, the act of replacing one signifier in a certain language with another in a different language, both representing the same signified.[20] However, if not only the signifier, but also the signified, is an arbitrary, historicocultural construct, such a project is untenable from the very beginning. To render "water" *mizu* is not an act of selecting the nearest equivalent with an inevitable (therefore, permissible) loss of some meaning content, as is usually thought. It is a projection of the paradigm of the source language, opening up infinite sets of different segmentations in the target linguistic system. In this case, we now have a new segmentation originally absent in the lexical system of Japanese. Conversely, at the heart of any theory that endorses the commensurability of translation is a belief in a basic correspondence of signifieds in various cultures, not to mention the inevitable distortion that takes place in the act of translation whether the source language is SAE or non-SAE. The problem, however, is that it is normally the Western categories that are believed to possess higher generality and universality. If translating "water" as "either *mizu* or *yu*" is considered to be unnecessary dilettantism, the rendition of *yu* as "hot water" is regarded as sufficiently accurate concerning the parochial structure of the Japanese lexicon. Does this double standard not reflect Eurocentrism?

The Comparative Frame of Don Juan as a "Lover"

The above description of the history of /*ren'ai*/, in light of the theoretical reconsideration of the segmentation of reality, demonstrates the indeterminacy of both signifier and signified, and their ever-changing relationships. While signifiers replace one another frivolously, new signifieds emerge and then disappear. The change appears to be extremely contingent and arbitrary. "Love" can be called /love/, /*Liebe*/, /*rabu*/, /*airen*/, /*ren'ai*/, or even /*houdini*/, if you will, as the epigraph to this chapter suggests. The signifieds of love can be as varied as the signifiers. In this sense, the definition quoted in the epigraph is legitimate, too, that is, the definition that Handey mischievously quotes and then denies: "Love is (not) something to put chains on and throw into a lake." There is no reason to reject this definition. For Handey is either making a subtle reference to some extreme form of "love," or metaphorically speaking of its intensity. He can pass judgment that love is *not* something to put chains on and throw into a lake precisely because love *could* be. It is the radical difference between what he terms "Houdini" and an ordinary idea about "love" and, at the same time, their similarity, that makes his "deeper thought" rather humorous.

Conversely, the gist of «Love» in the humanist conception is the stability of the signified as an ontotheological essence that stands and remains out there. Such a belief in
the primacy of the signified functions to perpetuate a belief
in so-called humanitarian values. The comparativist Edward
Seeber writes that "humanitarianism was a familiar sentiment before the word itself came into being" (42). This belief entails a doctrine that a signified can precede a signifier,
a nonspoken signified existing without a material signifier.
I do not gainsay the possibility of a humanitarian sentiment's preceding the word /humanitarianism/, for a
signified «humanitarianism» could have very well been represented by another signifier, or other signifiers, awaiting a
felicitous encoding by virtue of the signifier /humanitari-
anism/. This, perhaps, is not quite the way Seeber conceives
the situation, though, since, for humanist thinking, a humanitarian value exists independent of its coding at some
point in history. Thus, "humanitarianism" transcends the
materiality of a sign. And if "humanitarianism" is a human
sentiment that transcends history, "love" is also a humanitarian sentiment par excellence.

Such a humanistic idea is closely connected with the
idea of language as a tool. Seeber, calling for discrimination
in literary terms, quotes the philosopher Harold Lee: "When
words are used as words should be used, they are tools of
thought. When the proper usage is neglected, they tend to
become the masters of thought" (qtd. in Seeber 50).

Thus, the thought "humanitarianism" obtains the status of a master who uses words as mere tools. The same
model is projected on "love." An idea of «love» dominates
over a word /love/. It is, however, a suspicious gesture to
conceive of "love" before it is even so called simply because
it is considered an important tenet of humanity. The fact
that, in modern Japanese history, the signifier-tool, /ren'ai/,
preceded the signified, «ren'ai», is a sufficient refutation of
the domination of the signified. Unless, that is, one, in an
Orientalist move, bestows upon «Love» the position of the

master-signified. The idea, then, that romantic love is an essential and universal quality of human nature that, though it can be distorted, suppressed, or dormant, is nonetheless omnipresent, is, finally, dubious.

Such an ontotheological status of signifieds, which, I hold, is a theoretical consequence of humanist ideology, is naturally more easily conferred on the concepts cherished in humanism. They are the so-called humanistic categories: "humanitarianism," "love," "humanity," "maternity," and so forth. «Love» is part of the parcel of humanism, if «snow» is not. In other words, if «love» is relevant to what it is to be a true human being, «snow» is not. There is, thus, a certain circle of terms that are unquestionably considered as master ideas. This is explained by humanist philosophy from the fact that "love" concerns a human activity or a feeling while "snow" is a physical phenomenon external to us. However, "masturbation" does not constitute a tenet of humanism although it is undoubtedly a human activity, most prevalent at that. Neither does homosexual love. It is heterosexual desire alone which is endowed with the title of human passion shared by every human being. An inventory of humanism is, then, an ideological formulation, reflecting a specific outlook on life and a conscious choice of constitutive elements.

If such a critique of ideological content of humanistic values sounds too crude, one should be prepared for the even more shocking problematization of the distinctions of external/internal, physical/metaphysical, material/spiritual, and so on. (We will explore the recent theories of culture that consider "internality" as a product of modern discursive practice in chapter 4.) They are, probably, also parts of a particular parcel of thinking which is prone to deconstruction. We do not have to automatically assume that physical, material, and external realities cannot be part of "human essences." If rice is the spirit of the Japanese (*Nihonjin no kokoro* or *tamashii*), as is too often claimed, there is no reason why we should not imagine "snow" as part of our human souls.

Now, we need to address the claim that the stability of certain "human" categories is required in order to speak realistically about "love" in premodern Japan. This brings us back to the issue of comparativism. If love was absent from the Japanese cultural vocabulary, would it be permissible to speak of "love in Edo Japanese literature," and then go on to the comparison between "love in Edo" and "love in such-and-such literature"? Probably not. This notwithstanding, under the pretext of "humanitarian" values, signifiers in European languages are tacitly considered to be more neutral, transparent, comprehensible, and therefore, applicable terms. Whereas speaking of "Hikaru Genji's love" would not arouse suspicion, a formula *"Torisutan no iro-gonomi* (the *iro-gonomi* [an ideal of sexual activity in ancient Japanese courtly culture] of Tristan)" would instantly sound awkward, and be censored. The general identity of what the Shining Prince executes as "love" and Tristan's "love" independent of their characters and contexts is presumed without challenge. Consequently, /love/ is used as a critical term to discuss heroes in premodern Japanese literature. Likewise, the formula *"Hikaru Genji no ren'ai"* (*ren'ai* of the Shining Prince) is acceptable since *ren'ai* merely replaces and translates "love." For contemporary critics, *ren'ai* has universal applicability. On the contrary, the parochiality of *iro-gonomi* makes it inapplicable to European heroes. Translators are discouraged to render /*iro-gonomi*/ as /love/ precisely because «*iro-gonomi*» is a parochial concept, lacking the generality of «love» and applicable only to Japanese heroes. In contrast, English /love/ is translatable into an appropriate Japanese signifier for «love», which happens to be /*ren'ai*/. The assumed universality of the Western words parallels their alleged translatability. As a matter of fact, this translatability is guaranteed not so much theoretically but historically, that is to say, by the historical fact that the signifier /*ren'ai*/ was created in modern Japan to translate «love». However, if /*ren'ai*/ is a neologism, coined to express «love», we are, in fact, not speaking of translation, but redundance. The universality of Western cultural tenets is, then, tautological: the Western is universal since it is everywhere, or rather, it has forced its way in everywhere.

In the same vein, susceptibility to translation is more or less believed to be guaranteed with respect to the metalanguage or theoretical language. If translation of a *haiku* appears a complicated task, the choice of the language of its criticism is considered to be facile. In fact, whether the criticism is done in Japanese, English, or French is presumed to be more or less irrelevant. A critical language is a transparent tool, open to substitution. Also, the terms used in criticism such as "epic(al)," "lyric," "drama(tic)," "poem," "type," "theme (of 'love,' 'seduction,' 'indecision,' 'procrastination,' and so on)," are expected to transcend linguistic difference, and are applicable to the genre of *haiku* as well.

My foregoing arguments contradict such a view. I have tried to show that the metalanguage of criticism, which is ostensibly universal, is basically confined to Western terminology. Normally, if we can and do legitimately speak of "lyric" aspects of some Japanese *haiku*, we feel that we should in no way discuss *sabi* features of English poems (*sabi*: poetic ideals foregrounding loneliness and tranquility, developed notably by the *haiku* master Bashō). If we are allowed to speak of a "character" in *The Tale of Genji*, we are not encouraged to think of Western novels upon the standard of *katagi mono* (a species of story dealing with humbler people and their doings [Miner, *Princeton Companion*], featuring exaggerated descriptions of character-types [*katagi*]), which is supposed to lack the universality necessary to a critical concept. If, finally, we can attempt to undertake a comparative theme study of "love" of the heroes of world literature, that of *giri* applied to Western literary tradition is considered untenable (*giri*: a sense of obligation, on which plots of Edo plays often hinge).

The above statement is not mere speculation. Because of such a double standard, a certain Horton, a teacher of English at Tokyo Imperial University, who taught English literature toward the end of the nineteenth century, felt such untenability of Japanese critical concepts in class. He thought his student Tsubouchi Shōyō's criticism of *Hamlet* pursued in the light of a Confucian principle, *kanzen chōaku* (didacticism; literally, the encouragement of good and the punishment of evil), one of the basics of Edo theatrical and narrative construction, was irrelevant and inappropriate, giving him a humiliating grade (Tsubouchi, *Recollections* 345). Conversely, the British teacher would probably have not been troubled if Tsubouchi had attempted a criticism of Chikamatsu's Kabuki plays, using Western terminology for theatrical conventions: characters, dénouement, climax, and so forth, a kind of criticism that Tsubouchi was, in fact, to engage himself in later. The double standard is not past history; it persists even today.

In any case, "Love" as a transparently translatable term, whether in the quality of an important tenet of humanism, or of the metaconcept of criticism, no longer appears to be so. The instability of the denotation of "love" puts into question the possibility, suggested by Etiemble, of speaking of an East/West Don Juan as "a man who loves." If "love" is as parochial a notion as *kōshoku*, *iki*, or *iro-gonomi*, what legitimizes translation of *Kōshoku ichidai otoko* (*The Man Whose Life Was Devoted to Kōshoku*) as *The Man Who Spent His Life in Love* (Hibbett xi)? Or, why is it acceptable to speak of Hikaru Genji's "love" for Murasaki?

Etiemble, however, in his definition of Don Juan, may be using the term "love" in quite a different way from the way early modern Japanese writers understood it, and from the common contemporary notion of it. He seems to mean by "to love" quite generally "to be passionate about women," rather than the more specific definition of (romantic) love which foregrounds spirituality, sincerity, morality, and so on.

In contrast, Gendarme de Bévotte evokes a distinctively "Western" concept of love, that is to say, love as a feat of sincerity and sacrifice. By adopting that sense, however, he ultimately has to declare that Don Juan does *not* love: "In reality Don Juan does not love if to love is to be attached to, to sacrifice oneself, to forget one's self in that of another" (8).

Nonetheless, Gendarme de Bévotte, to display even more clearly the instability of the meaning of "love," immediately betrays his own statement by adding: "Don Juanism is that form of love which feeds solely on change. . . . Don Juan has no other goal in life than to love. To love is his vocation" (8). Now, Don Juanism regains its status of being an expression of "love." But, as a final twist, this status begins to crumble at his next comment that "[i]t is the opposite of true love, which is constant" (8). Love is redefined as constancy, expelling Don Juanism into the dark periphery one last time. It is the dialectic of "true" and "false" that allows this game of definitions about Don Juan, and finally gives the concept of love precarious stability. The ideological/ significative system remains intact when all inconsistencies are named "false."

Thus, even within a Western conception, the signified of "love" is enormously flexible and changeable. With these varying definitions, Don Juan now becomes a lover, now ceases to be. Now you see love, now you don't. East/West comparison is, naturally, a trickier business. A different definition of "love" can bring to the fore a different candidate for comparison, that is, a different "Japanese Don Juan." For "an eternal lover," one may think of Hikaru Genji. For a more epicurean type, Yonosuke may appear suitable for comparison. For an inconstant, unfaithful lover, Tanjirō becomes a true Japanese Don Juan. Now, do they love? Now they do, now they don't.

3 the emergence of don juanism

He [Don Juan] is all man, all appetite; that is to say, all phallus.

—Lawrence Lipking, "Donna Abbandonata"

Don Juanism is found in the human nature as deeply rooted as Don Quixotism: even more deeply; this demand is much more innate.

—Ivan Goncharov, The Precipice

The Erasure of the Don Juan Theme in Early Modern Japan

In the first chapter, I referred to some of the definitions of universally acknowledged Don Juan "types": Etiemble's "a man who loves," Guillén's "a man who seduces," Ortega y Gasset's "*the* Man," and so forth. In chapter 2, I attempted to demonstrate the untenability of love as a universal concept; hence the problematic of the comparative scheme of a "Don Juan who loves." As a matter of fact, a definition more commonly held than Etiemble's, one that Gendarme de Bévotte seems ultimately to endorse, specifies Don Juan as a man who does *not* love. In this more popular conception,

Don Juan is he who seduces, without any affection, for the sole purpose of satisfying his carnal pleasure. We have here Don Juan as a symbol of sensual lust, defying spiritual love. Etiemble's scheme allows us to see Ariwara no Narihira of *The Tales of Ise* and the Shining Prince of *The Tale of Genji* as possible Don Juans. They are untiring lovers. Conversely, Gendarme de Bévotte's Don Juan is a perverted, insincere lover. The Japanese hispanicist Ōshima, whom I cited in chapter 1, shows a similar idea in his definition of a Don Juan type as a "man who arouses a swirl of lust."

In this chapter, I will examine the tenability of this latter definition as a basis for comparison: Don Juan as a lustful man who does not love, who seeks only carnal pleasure and power over women; in other words, an interpretation of Don Juan as a "human prototype of debauchee" (Gendarme de Bévotte 6). In doing so, I will attempt to historicize the concept of "lust," and question its universality as a point of reference. For this purpose, let us return to early Meiji Japan.

Futabatei Shimei, in one of his interviews, told a reporter that his celebrated first novel, *Drifting Clouds* (1887–89), was entirely an imitation of Goncharov's *The Precipice* (1869) ("Turmoil of a Writer" 162–63). In confirmation of this, *Drifting Clouds* displays, in fact, many features which suggest that it is a loose adaptation of *The Precipice*. First of all, both novels describe a conflict between the older and the younger generations. Secondly, both focus on a passion that is attempted and fails in this setting. Thirdly, the general scheme of the main protagonists is quite similar: the hero Bunzō, his cousin Osei, and Osei's mother Omasa in *Drifting Clouds* correspond, respectively, to Raiskii, his cousin Vera, and Raiskii's grandmother Tat'iana Markovna in *The Precipice*. More importantly, the characterizations of the heroes of the two novels share many features. Both are self-conscious, intellectual young men. Both represent the ideal of the new age, which they try to convey to the women they love. Their passion is in a sense part of their effort to express their new philosophy.

In spite of such similarities, however, the characterizations of the two heroes differ in one major point. Bunzō of
Drifting Clouds strives to establish a chaste love with the
heroine. He consciously avoids physical intimacy:

> In front of Osei he maintained his self-control and con-
> tinued to treat her with proper ceremony. One day they
> had been chatting pleasantly together, becoming more
> and more relaxed, when he suddenly felt almost over-
> whelmed by desire for her, and had to close his eyes
> and stop speaking to steady himself. Still laughing, she
> coyly tried to coax him out of his silence and reached
> out and tickled him. He pushed her away angrily. "I
> must control myself. Please go downstairs, Osei." Osei
> was furious about this. (220)

Bunzō's statement that their emotions are still "slaves of the
'custom' (*shūkan*)" (and, therefore, he must control himself)
is not rendered in Ryan's translation. It echoes Osei's words
from earlier in the same chapter: "[We are trying to break]
the traditions [*shūkan*] of two thousand years" (215). "The
traditions of two thousand years" is an exaggeration. Osei
refers more specifically to the marital system and sexual
practices of the directly preceding Edo period. As we have
seen, the sexual (or erotic) activities of this age were more
or less confined to the pleasure quarters. Men and "ordinary
women" were supposed to associate according only to the
semifeudal hierarchy without any sense of affection or mutual respect. This is why Bunzō criticizes his rival in love
and career, Noboru, for treating his cousin Osei as if she
were a geisha (300). The old system, as Bunzō and Osei hold,
is one that foregrounds immoral playfulness and uncon-
trolled desire. In contrast, their goal (at least, at this point)
is to destroy those traditions and refrain from any sensu-
ous activities.

At the same time, they aim at the moral perfection of
their personalities through a love relationship that takes the
form of a quasi-comradeship. Osei says to Bunzō: "[N]ow

that I've made friends with you I feel much more confident about my ideas" (216).

These are some of the features of romantic love as understood by the modern Japanese literati that we examined in chapter 2. Their actions are best comprehended within the context of the model of love advocated by the early Meiji poets and critics who were influenced by European literature and the Western cultural ideals in general, and who harshly criticized the premodern notion of loving in Japan. In the novel, the couple conceives such an ideology, which echoes the Western idea of romantic love, as "Occidentalism." Consequently, Bunzō is seriously offended when he is addressed mockingly by Noboru as a modern version of Tanjirō, the hero of the classic erotic story of the former era, *The Plum Calendar*, representative figure of a libertine at that time, embodying the Edo sexual ideology of *kōshoku* or *iki*.[1] For libertinism à la Tanjirō is precisely what Bunzō is struggling against.

On the contrary, Bunzō believes that it is this rival of his, who teases and eventually seduces their common object of love, Osei, without any sense of moral discipline, that actually epitomizes the licentious and concubinal attitude of the preceding age. In Bunzō's mind Noboru is the one who deserves the title of Tanjirō.

In contrast with the moralism of Bunzō, the hero of *The Precipice*, Raiskii, is a self-professed Don Juan. His Don Juanism appears to be modeled on that of Byron's *Don Juan*, whom he mentions in the novel, and that of E. T. A. Hoffmann's novella, *Don Juan or A Fabulous Adventure that Befell a Musician*. Raiskii reproduces the Hoffmannesque concept of Don Juanism: a search for an ideal woman:

> My enthusiasm for women is always sincere and spontaneous. It is not philandering. . . . And when my ideal, even in one single feature, approaches the ideal that my fantasy creates in me at this moment, the rest will be achieved automatically, and then the ideal of family happiness will arise. (5: 13)

Raiskii's Don Juanism, however, is unique in that it is consciously associated with artistic concerns: "Can I really enjoy feminine beauty (in real life) as I would enjoy it in the form of a statue? Don Juan appreciated such a demand foremost aesthetically" (5: 13). Therefore, Raiskii boasts of being a connoisseur of feminine beauty: "Except beauty!? It is everything" (5: 14). Beauty, woman, and Don Juanism become one in him. He unabashedly admits that he prefers love of the flesh to a chaste, spiritual relationship: "I bow down before beauty, I love it,—he gave a tender look at the portrait [of Sophie]—with my body and soul, and I confess . . . —he sighed comically,—I love more with the body . . ." (5: 132–33). So saying, he goes on seducing his young female relatives.

In this manner, the heroes of the two novels, in spite of facing the issue of libertinism alike, take an almost diametrically opposed attitude toward Don Juanism: the Japanese hero strictly rejects it, while the Russian enjoys it and even seeks after it.

The hero of *The Precipice* is not a simplistic Donjuanesque figure, though. He knows that he loves both spiritually and carnally. When he fails to seduce one of his cousins, he says with a sigh of relief that his soul has overcome the temptation of lust, which would have disgraced her, and that he should now remain instead a gentle protector and a "knight of friendship" to her (5: 261). Thus, being a modern amalgam of a supporter of "courtly" sentiment for a spiritual relationship and of a hedonist of carnal pleasure, Raiskii embodies within himself one of the central dichotomous frameworks of Western sexuality: carnal lust versus spiritual love; Don Juanism versus "chivalry"; desire versus morality.

In contrast, Bunzō, as we have seen, incarnates only the latter, that is, the abhorrence of sexual pleasure and a longing for spiritual enhancement through love.

Does this mean that he is not involved in the dualistic regime of sexuality? Quite the opposite. Only in the different kind of dichotomy. But, before we locate it, let us further examine the "disappearance" of Don Juanism in modern Japan.

In the previous chapter we examined the nature of the idea of spiritual love. In the context of Meiji literature, moral love was generally attributed to the ideal of newly introduced Western romantic love, or what Meiji writers termed *ren'ai*. For the most part, this ideal was to dominate conceptions of sexuality among the Meiji literati. This was especially so in the first half of the Meiji period when the new idea of love was fashionable and was associated with the rising generation. Thus, in the case of Bunzō of *Drifting Clouds*, written in the nineteenth and the twentieth years of Meiji, the new ideology completely overshadows and erases the promiscuous aspect of the original Russian model, and establishes a unilateral aspiration for morality and purity.[2] Bunzō's professed desire is monolithically chaste. For "love" is now nothing other than chaste sentiment for a "respectable" (nonprostitutional, that is) woman.

This change in the characterization from the protagonists of Goncharov's novel to those of Futabatei's is an example of the curious disappearance of the Don Juan theme throughout Meiji literature. After encountering modern European literary discourses, Japanese "men" of letters appear to have emphasized only the elements of spirituality and courtesy in the Western tradition of passion, and to have ignored its Donjuanesque aspect altogether. For example, a prominent advocate of the ideology of European romantic love, Kitamura Tōkoku, refers in an essay to Byron's *Manfred* as a most remarkable work of literature; a work that expressed the author's fury toward "a vulgar, licentious society" ("*Manfred* and *Faust*" 64). A dramatic poem based on *Manfred* by Tōkoku features a type of the Eternal Woman. The hero considers love for her maddening but sacred (*The Song of Fairyland* 35). In an essay "On the Inner Life," Tōkoku contrasts what he conceives as Byronic abhorrence for licentiousness with the vulgar form of sensual passion expressed in Edo Japanese literature: "Most of them [Edo literati] depicted vulgar human emotions. . . . Their stories were about affection, but they could not understand the essence of this sentiment. The tender feelings described by them were no more than sensual. They had no other means to express romantic sentiments than to depict carnal lust. They could not even dream of the kind of love portrayed by Plato, Dante, and Byron" (144). In another essay, Tōkoku eulogizes the "wonderful power of love" that a true poet like Byron could describe, while deploring the lack of it in the history of Japanese literature and the abundance of bestiality in its place ("Upon Reading *Utanenbutsu*" 85–86).

Nonetheless, in none of his plentiful writings on the English author did Tōkoku ever mentioned another of Byron's major works, *Don Juan*. Probably, for Tōkoku, Byron's poems had to be nothing but a description of true love, pure and ennobling. How could Tōkoku cite *Don Juan*, or adapt it as he adapted *Manfred*, if Byron's poems were supposed to be "the fire that raged at lewd, vulgar society"? Although *Don Juan* does show indignation at political injustice, when it comes to the issues of passion, the epic, with themes of extramarital affairs, seduction, transvestism, and so forth, displays a rather significant diversion from the ideals of spiritual, or romantic, love. We know very well Byron's sexual adventures in his private life were not necessarily chaste, either. We also know that these adventures of the author were not unlike those of his Don Juan. How could, then, Tōkoku have mentioned the Donjuanesque aspects of Byron's life which the Byronic version of *Don Juan* may represent, even if he had been aware of them? To Tōkoku, Byron was supposed to be a paragon of Western romantic love, an ideal exactly opposite to the "beastly desire" of Edo Japan that he had devoted his life to criticizing.

Tōkoku is not the only one who deliberately ignored the theme of Don Juan. Reference to Don Juan in the critical discourse of the Meiji period was considerably less frequent than reference to other major figures in literature.[3] This fact contradicts Leo Weinstein's statement:

Whenever during a literary discussion the participants are asked to pick out the four greatest heroes in modern literature, their choice is most likely to include Hamlet, Faust, Don Quixote, and Don Juan. All four have enjoyed universal renown and given rise to innumerable studies, commentaries, and interpretations. So vast is each of them that together they seem to encompass the greatest problems and aspirations of mankind. (1)

Even when the name of Don Juan *was* evoked in Meiji literary criticism, it almost always referred to Byron's *Don Juan*, a rather exceptional figure in the entire tradition, which demonstrated merry hedonism more intensively than the themes of seduction, betrayal, and corruption, and which entailed the interplay of sexuality, philosophy, and religion. Translations and adaptations of other Don Juan versions were either much fewer or almost nonexistent in early modern Japan. To the best of my knowledge, the only Japanese Don Juan version written to this day is Yoshiyuki Junnosuke's *Fake Don Juan* (1963). The first Don Juan legend in Japanese translation was Tsubouchi Shikō's translation of *Dom Juan ou le Festin de pierre*, which appeared as late as 1920. In contrast, translations of the other major literary figures of Europe appeared much earlier: Hamlet (1886), Romeo (1886), Don Quixote (1893), Faust (1904), Odysseus (1904).

Why was it that European Don Juanism was paid so little attention by the Japanese intellectuals of Meiji? Why was it that many early Japanese writers dismissed the voice in the Western tradition that supports "promiscuity" and, rather, preferred to describe almost exclusively the puritanical world of chastity as depicted in modern European literary discourses?

Perhaps, the larger context of Western "cultural colonization," as it were, of early Meiji Japanese discourses has to be taken into consideration here. In the Meiji period, especially during the second decade (called "the age of

Rokumeikan," the peak of Westernization), cultural resources of the West, represented in its discursive formation, invoked admiration and invited imitation as long as they marked a difference from existing Japanese cultural assets. Masaoka Shiki, the leading poet of the era, spoke of this "cultural colonization" in quite a crude manner, grudgingly reporting his experience of having his own story taken for translation:

> Even with literature a fetish for the West has plagued us. An intelligent person should acknowledge and accept the virtues of foreign cultures. So that the [Japanese] literature may develop, it is important to learn from the strengths of foreign literatures. Nonetheless, if we speak in terms of nations, it is to our shame that our literature is inferior to foreign literatures. . . . I once wrote a short story. Some people wanted to know whose work I had translated. Others suggested that it was an adaptation of an English novel. My story excels neither in its plot nor in its rhetoric. But I devised it all by myself. Still people suspect that it is a translation. In fact, they say this as a compliment, not as a criticism. Maybe I should feel honored. However, shame on our literature, shame on Japan, and shame on me, that my story is suspected to be a translation all the more because it is no good. My ambition in literature is (I am serious!) to surpass foreign literatures. (60)

The Japanese, probably including Masaoka himself, were no longer so confident in their cultural heritage (although, of course, there were nationalistic reactions, too), largely due to the politico-economic threat of Western colonization. The West was a difference that marked a positive value.

Now, "promiscuity" had abounded in Edo literature, especially in the literature of the period that immediately preceded the Meiji Reformation. However, the idea of purity and morality in love, proposed in Western literary tradition, was quite new to the Japanese reader. Thus, while representations of chaste lovers in European literature highly appealed to the Japanese, Don Juans were in general left unnoticed. In other words, only differences from the traditional values, and positive differences at that, fell into the perspective of the Japanese who were devouring modern cultural paradigms and building on the premises of the hardly reversible sociocultural hierarchical relationship that was developing between Japan and the modern West. During the process, when residual Edo sexual morality was consciously marginalized as being premodern and uncivilized, anything that resembled it in the Western vocabulary had to be either downplayed or ignored.

The effacement of Don Juanism was, therefore, part of the systematic reconstruction of sexual ideology that took place in early Meiji Japan. As was clearly seen in Tōkoku's essay, the Western dichotomy of spiritual love versus physical love was now reread as a dichotomy of the European concept of romantic love versus the Japanese notion of *kōshoku*. Western literature was conceived by Tōkoku as symbolizing only the spiritual beauty of love, while the premodern Japanese ideal of love in literature was simply considered to be bestial.

In an interview, Futabatei Shimei related his experience of visiting brothels in his youth. He described it as corruption and an expression of lustful "animal appetite" ("Confession" 271). Such an experience would have been an ordinary act of (male) love-making in the Edo period. The repentance of this major translator of Russian literature now sounds much like the confession of Pozdnyshev in Tolstoy's *The Kreutzer Sonata*, who, after the visit to a brothel, terribly regrets his losing innocence and purity, and his turning into a "libertine" (sect. IV). Involvement with prostitutes is deplored not so much for its general inhumaneness as for its fleshly, animal nature, which typically does not concern spirituality. With the advent of the spirit/body dichotomy, prostitution becomes "merely" carnal, devoid of the courtly sense of "love." The activities based on the principle of *kōshoku* are thus reread and reduced.

Futabatei's recollection illustrates that he was now perceiving sexuality according to a new ideology acquired through the reading of Western literature. Thus, for the first time in history, the consciousness of lust, bestiality, and promiscuity arose in modern Japanese culture.[4]

The Making of "Lust"

The early Meiji writers' superimposition of a spirituality/carnality dichotomy upon the binary opposition of Western spiritual love/*kōshoku* was problematic in many ways. Foremost, it resulted in the transformation and distortion of the original concept of *kōshoku*. Edo sexual ideology of *kōshoku* primarily referred to the comprehensive idea of passion, for which the distinction of love/bestiality was irrelevant. The term was now restrictively transfigured into a concept signifying nothing more than sensual lust. This distortion was, however, legitimatized, or rather dismissed, as "progress" from a barbarian "tradition of two thousand years" toward civilization on a par with Western societies.

In his criticism of the lust and eroticism implicit in Genroku (mid-Edo) literature, Tōkoku conceived the Edo sexual ideology of *kōshoku* as the antonym of *ren'ai*, or the Meiji Japan version of Western romantic love ideology:

> Bear in mind how apart love is from lust (*kōshoku*) in literature: lust is a liberation of the basest brutality of mankind while love is a developer of the spiritual beauty of mankind. To describe lust is to expel mankind into the beastly world of corruption. To describe true love is to equip a human being with beauty and spirit. Any author who is an encourager and an interpreter of lust thus drives mankind into the state of a lesser creature and impairs love, which ought to be most beautiful and most wonderful in literature.
> (*"Kyaramakura* and *Shinhazueshū"* 72)

Although Tōkoku's understanding may be too schematic, the opposition of spirituality and carnality has a conspicuous thematic significance in the Western literary tradition and in some Japanese literary works written under its influence. Conversely, Edo literature dealing with sexual passion, on which European conceptions exerted hardly any influence, is seemingly ignorant of so-called spiritual love and, therefore, of the distinction between spirituality and carnality. The introduction of the Western sexual paradigm created a dichotomy within a unitary field of signification of the premodern Japanese ideology of sexuality. Promiscuity emerged only when the notion of chastity and virginity arose, and chastity, on the other hand, emerged with the inception of the concept of promiscuity. In other words, it was the boundary that separated the two entities which created these categories and, therefore, such "realities."

Only with the advent of the spiritual love/carnal lust dichotomy did a sexual relationship without affection become meaningful. Such a dichotomous structure of sexuality explains the nature of Don Juan's desire. The Donjuanesque task of depriving a woman of chastity alone without necessarily winning her heart was finally conceivable. Hence, the opening seduction of Don Giovanni where he, feigning the identity of the fiancé Octavio, has sex (or, at least, attempts to) with Donna Anna, and then flees. In this maneuver, Don Giovanni's sole object is Anna's sexuality, not love, whatever his "real" motivation or hidden desire may be. The Hoffmannesque interpretation that Donna Anna is the ultimate goal of Don Giovanni's spiritual craving, driving him to a series of futile carnal adventures in which he seeks Anna's ideal love in vain, does not contradict the basic construction of Don Giovanni's desire. Either way, his desire is shaped by a dichotomous structure of love/lust. Don Giovanni is after the flesh alone, either because he is not interested in the spiritual, or because he is not able to attain it.

Such a scheme of desire, that is, desire solely after the flesh, is not the task of *iro-otoko*. He may, just like Don Juan, play a trick on women, and can deceive them badly. But his deceit should enable him to win the total devotion of women. His deceit has to be successful, too. Don Giovanni's rape and subsequent escape, with his real identity revealed, would be a clumsy failure for *iro-otoko*. The hero who represents *iro-gonomi*/*kōshoku* is never a rapist. Instead, he should be the kind of man that every woman wishes to make love to.[5]

Again, it is not that the Tokugawa Japanese culture knew of no repressive sexual politics. "Ordinary" women (*jionna*) of Edo society were in fact ordained to be chaste, and not promiscuous. On the other hand, men and prostitutes were largely exempted, or forced to be exempted, from this requirement. In contrast, Western ideology essentially made the stigma of carnal pleasure applicable to all. Bunzō's criticism of the philanderer Noboru, or Tōkoku's fury at a "lewd society," were all applications of this concept of sexual "stigma." As a result of "modernization," every woman could now be the target of erotic activity, and yet, paradoxically, was now required to be chaste and moral as well. Conversely, prostitution became a marginalized field of sexual activity because of a new emphasis on spirituality. One of the basic platforms of the Purity Campaign, conducted by the Salvation Army of Japan, was that prostitutes should lead a "pure" life. Spirituality, or the lack of it, made sexuality either chaste and pure, or lustful and promiscuous. This was when "lust," which had been largely absent in late Edo Japanese culture, appeared in its full sense when *kōshoku* was reduced to mere promiscuity, with spiritual love serving as the opposite pole in the conceptual framework. The ideal of chaste love required an idea of carnal lust to complete and activate the dichotomous frame.

If *kōshoku* thus changed its signified, a similar transfiguration occurred in Western conceptions after they were imported. As has been examined, the author of *Drifting Clouds* deliberately obscured the Donjuanesque phase of the hero of *The Precipice*, turning him into a chaste lover. Likewise, the Western tradition of passion, which entailed the dichotomy of love and lust, was given a wrong conception, and was reduced to mere spirituality. Negotiation of the conflict of desire and morality that marked the thematic of Goncharov's novel and propelled its plot was thus lost in the characterization of Bunzō.

Nonetheless, the dichotomous nature of the structure of Western sexuality was introduced to Japanese culture after all, and was to be firmly established. Only now the ostensibly negative item of the binary opposition was not Don Juanism, as in the European cultural vocabulary, but *kōshoku*. It was represented to the Western-oriented writers in Meiji as an unfavorable sociocultural heritage that needed to be discarded in order to accept the "enlightened," "progressive" Western concept. Now the dichotomy became Western spiritual love, which ennobled, versus the Edo notion of *kōshoku*, which disgraced. In Tōkoku's polemic: "Western 'chivalry' [Tōkoku uses the English word] has enhanced the value of love. Chivalry and love in cooperation have created a graceful and noble taste. 'Chivalry,' which arose in (Edo) Japanese lay society, has, in its fake 'gentlemanship' [Tōkoku's use], already made woman a toy to play with, and destroyed the value of love" ("Democratic Ideals" 92).[6]

At this point, the term *kōshoku* changed its denotation and connotation quite parallel to the change displayed by the concept *ai* (fondness), described in the previous chapter, only in the opposite direction. *Ai*, after the inception of the signifier *ren'ai* and the concept of romantic love, ceased to denote the condescending, patronizing affection of a man toward a woman (often a prostitute), which represented the semifeudal hierarchical male-female relationship. Instead, it came to signify the sincere, respectful sentiment between two equal partners. The word *ai* thus retained the status of one of the most favored terms in the sexual vocabulary, and even acquired the connotations of a progressive concept representative of the "new civilized" epoch.

In contrast, *kōshoku* lost that position. The term *kōshoku* had seldom been used in a derogatory sense before the onset of such a dichotomy, especially in later Edo literary discourse, from and in opposition to which the conceptions of Meiji literati more or less directly sprang. In the post-Reformation discourse, however, *kōshoku*, came to mean "lustful," whereas it had previously meant simply "sexually active," because the new paradigm stigmatized active sexuality. Sexual lust was now to be distinguished from chaste love and, therefore, to be recognized.

Such a shift in the signifieds of *kōshoku* is confirmed by its changing definitions in bilingual dictionaries. One of the earliest standard English-Japanese dictionaries, *A Pocket Dictionary of the English and Japanese Language* of 1867 (the second and revised edition), generally known as *Kaiseisho jisho*, basically reproduces Edo sexual conceptions, explaining "out of love" as "(a courtesan's) losing favor (*chō-ai otoroe te*),"[7] and "loving" as "patronizing (*hiiki ni shite kureru*)." The dictionary thus translates the term within the paradigm of sexuality standard in the Edo period, and conceives of "love" as a favor that a man bestows upon a prostitute. English "love" is identified with *ai*, used here in the traditional sense (that of patronizing affection) before it changes its meaning in conjunction with the introduction of romantic love ideology, and before the new signifier *ren'ai* is invented. In other words, the new significative system has not been discriminated yet. Consequently, it (mistakenly) recognizes an Edo sexual ideal in Western conceptions, something that actually is not there. This is why it gives *kōshoku* as the translation of "love-suite" (*sic*; probably, meaning "courtship"). On the other hand, English "lust" is not translated *kōshoku*, but is simply rendered "greed (*yoku, gōyoku*)." If English "love" and traditional *ai* are identified, *kōshoku* is not yet reduced to "lust," but still retains its original meaning and the comprehensive denotation of sexual passion.

Quite different nuances are offered by *An English and Japanese Lexicon* (1898, seventeenth printing), edited by Yamada Yutaka and published nearly twenty years after the above dictionary and after the publication of a series of articles that advertised the ideal of romantic love. First of all, its definition of "love" centers on the newer area of signification foregrounding romantic love (although it gives traditional meanings, too). "Love" is defined *ai-suru-koto* and *ai-jō* before being rendered as the more traditional *chō-ai, kenren, renbo,* and so on. Like *ren'ai,* the compound *ai-jō* is a new invention with fairly explicit Christian connotations. The scholar in modern Japanese language, Matsushita Teizō, associates it with the Christian concept of agape (226-27). Consequently, we have to understand that *ai* in the compound *ai-jō,* which is given as a translation for love in this dictionary, has the modern sense of love. It denotes not a condescending but a respectful affection that aims at spirituality and morality. Also, for "lover" it gives *ai-suru-hito* (a beloved one) and *tomo* (a friend) before rendering it as *jōjin* (a mistress), a term more relevant to Edo sexual ideology. Thus, a new field of the meaning of love is reflected in the translation. As if to correspond to such a change, the Edo tradition of *kōshoku/iro-gonomi* is now associated with "lust." "To lust" is rendered *iro o konomu* (to be fond of amorous activities) along with *hossuru* (to want) and *musaboru* (to devour), the latter two being standard renditions which we observed in the earlier dictionary. "Lustful" is translated into *iro-o-konomu* (fond of *iro,* absorbed in *iro-gonomi*); "one who lusts," into *kōshoku mono* (one who is devoted to *kōshoku*). The association of *iro-gonomi/kōshoku* with lust is thus firmly established. Sexuality is no longer what one happily consumes abundantly, but what one devours in defiance of decorum. It is an act of deplorable excess and an expression of Don Juanism. But, oddly enough, this new concept is represented not by the Western term /Don Juanism/ but by the indigenous /*kōshoku*/ or /*iro*/.

The introduction of romantic love, the segmentation of sexuality into spiritual and carnal, the creation of *ren'ai,* and the shift in the content of *ai* to express spiritual sentiment took place in a systematic manner. These changes were in exact proportion to the emergence of lust, to the shift in the content of *kōshoku*, and to its relegation to the carnal aspect of sexuality in the newly created dichotomous significative field. This was the moment when *kōshoku* and its earlier version, *iro-gonomi*, were turned to a certain excess (but not abundance), an uncontrollable sexual desire; the moment when "lust" emerged as something to be controlled due to its tendency to overflow; and when "love" was established as something different from *kōshoku*.

However, it is not my contention that a Western sexual paradigm with the conception of lust brought in hitherto unknown repression in the liberated field of sexuality in premodern Japan. The regime of sexuality had been achieved in various other forms. In fact, during the Edo period, there were several subtraditions which were opposed to the appreciation of excessive sexuality, embodied in the ideology of *kōshoku*. One was Confucian didacticism, which was expressed in moralistic, educational writings. It tied in with the semifeudal political system that frowned upon sexual licentiousness. This is why the author of *The Plum Calendar*, in an obviously false excuse, advertised in the preface to the sequel to it that his previous publication was "a teaching to warn against the lewdness of man and woman" (*The Pleasure Quarters in the Northeast* 242). In spite of such efforts, he was to be put to chains later.

However, the Edo Confucian ascetic tradition was neither essentially nor categorically anti-eros. For instance, the concept of *ta-in* (excessive erotic desire) in Confucian writings was predominantly associated with women, and "ordinary" women (*jionna*) at that. In other words, it was more or less gender-specific immorality. "Lust" was, then, not a universal sin. Or, more exactly, it was a basic sin only for "ordinary" women who were not allowed to be sexual except as a performer of the reproductory function.[8] As we saw in the previous chapter, such a system was well encoded in Books of Conduct (*Onna daigaku*, or *Women's Learnings*). We also saw, in what came to be known as the first version of *Women's Learnings*, how the author Kaibara Ekiken explicitly enjoined *jionna*, "ordinary" women, to wear no makeup and remain as sexually unattractive as possible. Since an "ordinary" housewife's sexuality was an offense, her expression of it had to be prohibited. In contrast, prostitutes were encouraged to be sexually active. Men were allowed to be so if they had material means to pursue the activity. This is precisely why these Confucian teachings of the Edo period ordained wives not to be jealous: wives should not discourage their husbands' amorous activity outside the household even if they might choose not to encourage it.

Another anti-erotic tradition in the Tokugawa period foregrounded Buddhist ideology. It theorized that sexual involvement was an ephemeral pleasure and a categorical obstacle to religious enlightenment. As mentioned above, just like a Judeo-Christian conception, it had the connotation of bestiality, that is, the association of sexual passion with animal nature. However, the Buddhist admonition against sexual desire covered, at least theoretically, the entire field of sexuality. The Buddhist view saw no distinction between spiritual love and carnal lust. Any involvement with a woman was essentially sinful even if it was purely platonic. Hence the extreme form of misogyny in Buddhist theology. The *Lotus Sutra* triumphantly predicts: "[When the Buddha's way is fulfilled,] [t]here will be no evil ways and no womankind, [for] all living beings will be born transformed and have no carnal passion [or better still, *in'yoku*, sexual desire]" (Katō et al., trans. 172). Actually, a chaste (heterosexual) relationship is an oxymoron from the Buddhist perspective. In its clear differentiation from the Christian-oriented romantic conception of love, the possibility of spiritual love is excluded here.[9]

With the newly introduced paradigm of spiritual love, the goal of purifying one's sexual desire into chaste love was, for the first time, recognized and valorized. This explains Tōkoku's ultimately reserved evaluation of Chikamatsu's plays. He admires them on the ground, somewhat eccentric according to the contemporary standard of criti-

cism, that some heroines in Chikamatsu demonstrate a passion that, though originating in "sensual" desire, has been
elevated via "affection" to sacred "love" ("Upon Reading
Utanenbutsu" 85; the words in quotation marks are given in
English in the original). In the final analysis, however,
Tōkoku censures Chikamatsu. He contends that Chikamatsu's *Utanenbutsu*, which displays one of the few representations of "sacred love," fails to give any sense of hope
or life, leading finally to the hero's despairing that it has all
been "a play of a dream." Tōkoku ascribes this failure, as
he sees it, of Chikamatsu to grasp the essence of love and
to understand the ideal of spirituality, to Buddhism, wherein
the choice is either to be sinfully engaged in sexual acts in
the present world, or to abandon them all together as a
"dream" in order to awake to religious truths. In contrast,
Tōkoku's Christian-oriented philosophy of love dichoto-
mizes sexuality. It creates the possibility of redeeming it by
changing it into a sacred, spiritual love, which, then, does
not contradict religious sentiment.

Thus, sexuality and "love" are articulated in quite a different manner by Buddhist and Christian ideologies even if
both are superficially similar in their abhorrence of carnal
pleasure. It follows from this that in the Buddhist tradition
we do not find the conceptions of "lust" and "promiscuity"
as formulated in Western ideology within a dualistic framework. As I tried to demonstrate in chapter 2, differently segmented categories are different realities. "Edo Japanese lust"
is a fallacy in conceptualization.

Moreover, ascetic connotations derived from Buddhist
and Confucian discourse were often co-opted by the more
dominant tone of eroticism found in Edo urban cultures. For
instance, *The Great Mirror of the Art of Love*, the Bible of love
in the mid-Edo period, is modeled on the *Lotus Sutra*. From
it derives Saikaku's *The Life of an Amorous Man*, who is able
to embody the goals presented in *The Great Mirrors*. The author sums up the thoughts of the hero of the tale Yonosuke
at the end of his career: "He had never prayed consistently

for salvation in the next world, accepting resignedly the in-contestable belief that, after death, he would willy-nilly be torn by the punishing demons of hell. Even if he were to embark on a change of heart now, it would not be easy, he knew, to be saved by Buddha's mercy" (230). So reasoning, he embarks on a journey to "the isle of Nyogo, an isolated body of land inhabited solely by women" on a boat he

Figure 2. Yonosuke on his way to the Isle of Women.
Courtesy of Osaka Nakanoshima Library.

names *Yoshiiro-maru*, *yoshiiro* being another pronunciation for the Chinese characters *kōshoku*.[10]

We now return to the hegemonical concept of *iro-gonomi/kōshoku* as a festive excess of sexuality. In his essay *The Structure of "Iro-gonomi"* the novelist, Nakamura Shin'ichirō, proposes a reevaluation of this powerful, rather "carnivalesque" tradition of passion that demands greater and greater consumption. He quotes the episode from *The Tales of Ise* in which the hero, Narihira, makes love with a ninety-nine-year-old woman as a favor; an act that the author of the story applauds as a feat of *iro-gonomi*. Further, Nakamura argues that in contrast to modern sexual morality, *iro-gonomi* was the affirmation of erotic adventures, excessive sexuality, and playful curiosity (26–27). He sees the same ideal operating in the Shining Prince of *The Tale of Genji*.

Nakamura's rereading of the erotic tradition leads to the subversion of the popular view of *iro-gonomi* that sees it in a more somber light. Such a viewpoint merely finds in the concept an unhappy compensation for political failure. Hence, the exile of both Ariwara no Narihira of *The Tales of Ise* and Hikaru Genji (the Shining Prince), which leads to their sexual adventures with local women. In protest against this kind of view, Nakamura points to the lavish sexuality of emperors and empresses, and suggests the compatibility of *iro-gonomi* with political plots.

Of course, Nakamura is only writing about the ancient/medieval ideal of sexual activities, *iro-gonomi*, and not about Edo sexual ideology of *kōshoku*. However, a similar line of argument is taken by Teruoka Yasutaka, a distinguished specialist of Saikaku and Edo literature in general, in *Love and Sex of the Japanese*. He also evokes the positive aspect of the Hikaru Genji's sexuality, whose exorbitance was admired by both contemporary audiences and later critics such as Yoshida Kenkō (41–42). In other publications, Teruoka insists on the signification of *kōshoku* (as an Edo notion) more or less similar to *iro-gonomi*, with affirmative nuances and meaning-content that includes the larger field of sexuality (See, for instance, *Kōshoku*). At any rate, *iro-*

gonomi and *kōshoku* share the common feature of valorization of active sexuality and the nondualistic perspective toward it, thus, not differentiating "lust" from "love."

These positive views on *iro-gonomi* are, however, fairly
recent. More traditional theory deriving from Motoori
Norinaga's reading of *The Tale of Genji* associates the term
with *mono no aware* (the deep feelings inherent in, or felt
from, the world and experience of it [Miner, *Princeton Companion*]). *Iro-gonomi* has thus been understood as part of
these "sadder and even tragic feelings." There is also a
strong tradition of criticism which relates *iro-gonomi* to Buddhist pessimism. In any case, however, *iro-gonomi/kōshoku*
differs from the devouring sexuality of Don Juanism, the
power of lust that corrupts and destroys women. This is,
of course, the reason why Yonosuke, the Amorous Man
(*kōshoku ichidai otoko*) is a positive hero through and
through.[11]

Now, such a shift in the meaning of erotic behavior
from the profuse *kōshoku* tradition to the modern notion of
mere sensuality is imbedded in the contour of the term
jōyoku ("desire"). In the pre-Reformation era, *jōyoku* had
been used in two senses. One meaning denoted a wish or a
desire in general, usually worldly and ephemeral: "When a
man is young he has such an overabandunce of energy that
his senses are quickly stirred and he has many desires
(*jōyoku*) [for beautiful clothes and possessions]" (Yoshida
148). The other sense referred specifically to erotic desire:
"Although he thus felt a surge of (sexual) lust (*jōyoku*), he
had no means to overcome his age" (Takizawa 45).

Such ambivalence was to be gradually lost in modern
usage. *Jōyoku* has come to mean monolithically "sensual
lust," its ordinary denotation today. The sense of "desire in
general," however, remained in force for some time after the
Reformation. This can be proved by the fact that in early
Meiji philosophical discourse "passion" was sometimes rendered *jōyoku*.

The ambivalence of the term *jōyoku* and at the same
time, its reduction to one single sense of "lust," which

slowly took place in the early years of Meiji, is recorded in an episode concerning the translation of an English novel by Tsubouchi Shōyō. He recalls with a touch of indignation the way his translation of Walter Scott's novel was corrected by the editor: "I rendered the passage that said Mrs. Aston's character was 'passionate' as 'possessing tempestuous *jōyoku.*' I admit that the translation was neither smooth nor happy. Mr. Kobayashi, however, corrected it, misunderstanding the Japanese phrase as meaning 'lustful (*tain tajō*).' If I make a thorough investigation, I could probably find more such silly mistakes" (Introduction iii). For Tsubouchi, translating "passionate" as "possessing tempestuous *jōyoku*" was acceptable, if not graceful, since it was one of the meanings of the word recognized in the year 1880. In fact, Inoue Tetsujirō's influential *The Dictionary of Philosophy* (1881) gives *jōyoku* as the translation for "passion" in its general sense. The editor's correction, however, to make Tsubouchi's translation conform to the other meaning demonstrates that the sense of "sensual desire" was beginning to dominate the significative field of the word. Desire was reduced to lust. Lust was now associated with having excessive sexual desire (*tain tajō*). A gradual shift of the meaning of sexual activity from "full of passion" to "too much sensuality" was thus slowly but steadily taking place.

Iro-otoko as a Lustful Man Enters

A similar case is found in connection with a Don Juan legend. I refer to the first, unfinished translation of Molière's comedy into Japanese: Kusano Shibaji's translation of *Dom Juan ou le Festin de pierre*, entitled *Onna tarashi (A Libertine)*.

A translator of English and French literatures, Kusano actively translated a number of Molière's plays that he published in several journals and, later, in *Complete Works of Molière* (1908). *Complete Works* included fifteen pieces which Kusano had published in such journals as *Kabuki, Shirayuki,* and *Myōjō. Onna tarashi,* his translation of *Dom Juan,* also appeared in *Kabuki* (1908) but apparently was abandoned after the translations of only two scenes were published in two successive issues.[12]

The reason why the translation was not completed is unknown. However, the translation as such displays a certain awkwardness and even contradictions as a text written in Japanese. The piece is meant to be performed, at least theoretically, as a Kabuki play. All the characters are given Japanese names: Dan Jūza for Dom Juan, Ryōji for Sganarelle, Tamaki for Done Elvire, Shichisuke for Pierrot, and so on. Dan Jūza, an obvious play on the name of Don Juan, and Tamaki are aristocratic names for members of the samurai class, thus giving the piece an appearance of a Kabuki *jidai mono* (plays dealing with subjects in earlier periods [Miner, *Princeton Companion*]). The genre of the play thus defined, such Western names as Aristotle and Alexander, which are used carelessly in the translation, stand out awkwardly. (Anachronism and "anatopism" are fairly common in *jōruri/* Kabuki plays, though.) The term used for the commander, *shireikan*, sits clumsily, too, being the only name of a character taken from the modern glossary. *Shireikan* is a word derived from translation of the Western military vocabulary. (*The Dictionary of Meiji Terms* notes that it is a neologism of the Meiji period, citing a provision of a naval regulation revised in the fourteenth year of Meiji [1881].) In other words, the play *Onna tarashi* is a somewhat unwieldy product, hanging loosely in between the original comedy and a Kabuki play. These are a few of the reasons the translation was not completed.

A similar awkward, ambiguous position is observed in connection with sexual ideology. For instance, for the word "passion" the Japanese translation gives 情欲.[13] The expression 情欲 ("lust"), usually pronounced *jōyoku*, appears with a gloss that it be read *kokoro* (feeling). Kusano does seem to be attributing the concept of lust to the word *jōyoku* by virtue of its association with Don Juan. However, the sense of *jōyoku* as lust, which was destined to become the standard denotation of the word, is circumvented by translating it by the far more neutral term *kokoro*, meaning heart or feeling. As a matter of fact, for the French *désir*, appearing shortly after this passage, Kusano gives 心 (heart), but not 情欲 (*jōyoku*; "lust"), with the same gloss that it be read *kokoro*. Thus, the text ascribes as well as dissociates Western concepts of lust and (sensual) desire to and from the Japanese conception of male sexuality.

Such ambiguity and ambivalence would disappear in subsequent translations of *Dom Juan* made by other translators. For instance, one of the standard contemporary translations by Suzuki Rikie almost invariably uses *jōyoku* for the French *désir*. In the revised translation *Dan Jūza* (1912), Kusano, too, renders *désir* as *jōyoku*, a standard contemporary translation.

The shift of the denotation of the term *jōyoku* from passion in general to (sexual) lust is thus parallel to the shift of *kōshoku* from the ideal of energetic, erotic activity to Don Juanism. As Nakamura Shin'ichirō and Teruoka Yasutaka argue, *iro-otoko*, that is, heroes of *iro-gonomi/kōshoku*, such as Ariwara no Narihira, Hikaru Genji, and Yonosuke seduce not to corrupt but to bestow. Their excessive desire is a bliss, not an evil, at least from the male perspective (*Structure* and *Love and Sex*). This understanding clearly contrasts with the excessive sexuality of Don Juan, whose desire is selective in the last instance: in spite of his wide interests, he particularly prizes and craves young and beautiful women. Leporello's observation that "he [Don Giovanni] does not persist, be she rich, be she plain, be she pretty; if only she wears skirts, you know what he does" (Da Ponte 19) is a caricature, not to be taken at face value. For, after all, "the predominant object of his passion is the young novice" (19). Don Giovanni's own self-justification that "[any one of my adventures] is all out of love. He who is faithful to one woman is cruel toward the others" (54) is a purposeful falsification, soon betrayed by his mockery of Leporello, who, he says, does not know what feminine beauty is. Unlike *iro-otoko*, Don Juan seduces for the sole purpose of depriving, but not conferring, that is, depriving women of their values of chastity and purity. On account of which, however, his existence, as Lawrence Lipking convincingly argues in his article "Donna Abbandonata," ironically becomes poorer and poorer. Don Juan's desire is ultimately centripetal, not centrifugal. In contrast, if the Edo *iro-otoko* deprives at all, it is not the value of chastity that he demands.[14] For, prostitutes, his main objects of desire, do not possess it from the very beginning.

Incidentally, the reader might perceive that I am engaged here in the comparison of Don Juans East/West; precisely the kind of comparison that I have been consistently arguing against. I am most definitely comparing. In order to undo the comparison, I must refer to the already existing comparisons. In more general terms, one can problematize an issue only from within the paradigm in which one is already trapped. I shall return to this issue again later in this chapter.

Now, excessive desire, infidelity, animal lust, impiety, and polygamous passion form a constellation of meanings associated with Don Juanism. They function in a dichotomous scheme, at the other end of which are constancy, spiritual love, awe of the sacred, and monogamous passion.

As is most obvious in both Tirso di Molina's and Molière's versions, Don Juanism is defiance against the spiritual order. Don Juan performs a sexual deed defying religious principles just as chaste lovers strive to love according to the standard of sacred love. The association of sexual love with religious "love" and other forms of moral passion is a feature of Western "love," which is not, as we saw in chapter 2, a prerequisite in the segmentation of sexuality within the Japanese language.[15]

The romantic poet Tōkoku highlights this contrast in an essay "Upon Reading *Utanenbutsu*": "[Chaste male-female] love (*ren'ai*) is the beginning for all kinds of love. Any love (*ai-jō*) from filial love (*ai*) to amity (*yū-ai*) that bears the name has arisen on the basis of [heterosexual] love (*ren-ai*). Pure love (*jō-ai*) that leads to the heavenly height is also closely related to this love (ren-ai)" (85). Such an ultimate identification of sexual love with other human emotions such as filial sentiment, friendship, and especially religious love, is obviously a Western conception, inconceivable within the paradigm of the Japanese language. The term *ai* for "love" now offers a network of various kinds of "love" which had not been necessarily transparent.

The difference in the conceptualization of "love" between Japanese and European languages underwent an immense change in the Meiji period. Sexuality was now rearranged according to the Western model, and a hitherto unknown binary opposition was established: *ren'ai* versus *iro-gonomi*, or spiritual love versus carnal lust.

The creation of this new dichotomy can be observed in the use of qualifiers. In the early years of Meiji, Japanese terms representing sexuality could be applied to various European literary figures who exemplified romantic love. Romeo is a case in point. In his translation of *Crime and Punishment*, Uchida Roan footnotes that "Romeo is a playboy (*en'yarō*) from a Shakespearean play. A figure similar to our Tanjirō [the hero and *iro-otoko* of *The Plum Calendar*]" (252). In the twenty-fifth year of Meiji (1892), it was still permissible to call Romeo *en'yarō*, a "libertine" of Tanjirō's kind. Of course, such a description is unthinkable or even absurd today, when Romeo is counted among the epitomes of the romantic lover. One can no longer speak of the *iro-gonomi*, *kōshoku*, or *iki* of Romeo, precisely because a rupture took place some time around the turn of the century, evoking an ideology in which (romantic) love is not synonymous with *kōshoku* but, on the contrary, antithetical to it. After the break, one could no longer see Romeo as embodying *kōshoku*.

This break also created a certain imbalance in the application of critical language. As we have already seen, while it would be impermissible to describe Romeo in terms of the achievement of *kōshoku*, it became perfectly acceptable to speak of Hikaru Genji's (*ren-)ai*, or "love."

This analysis entails the problem of an epistemological power struggle, that is, the issue of the relevance of
politico-economic conditions to the formulation of discourses. When two cultures of considerably disproportionate political and economic forces meet, first, the alien
conceptual framework of the culture of the greater power
is imposed on the culture of the lesser power; second, what
is important to be known in the former is grafted onto that
of the latter, to the distortion and the deletion of aboriginal
significations; third, the paradigms thus imposed become
objectified and reified. The way of knowing is culturally
specific, and deserves equal rights. An Eskimo reader of
Kawabata Yasunari's *Snow Country* is free to attempt to
know which type of snow out of the rich Eskimo vocabulary of "snow" is implied in the title, a task that would immediately arise if a translation of Kawabata's novel into
Eskimo languages were to be made. The problem is, however, that the epistemological horizons of the politically and
economically less powerful culture are bound to be considered irrelevant and rendered subordinate. Whereas an Eskimo critic's effort to find out the specific type of snow
would be considered meaningful only locally, "love" in *The
Tale of Genji* is normally regarded as universally significant
and worthy of being known to all. Likewise, after the establishment of the Western paradigm of sexuality (achieved,
or encouraged, by virtue of the political, economical, and
military superiority of the Euro-American powers), Japanese
readers were soon discouraged from perceiving Romeo as
en'yarō, a hedonistic playboy fond of courtesans, yet encouraged to speak of the Shining Prince of *The Tale of Genji* as a
version of Don Juan.

Such a problem of hermeneutics is relevant to the issue of comparativism. As I have repeatedly insisted, one
cannot see, know, or speak of a phenomenon from two different paradigms at once. That is to say, when one compares
two objects belonging to two different cultures, one of the
two is perceived according to the code familiar to the
comparativist, while the other is understood through a para-

digm different from the original. For instance, when Tōkoku "compared" *ren'ai* (love) and *iki* (or *kōshoku*) to the detriment of the latter, he decoded both cultural phenomena according to the paradigm entailing the former. *Ren'ai* found a full signification, whereas *iki* was distorted to fit the ideology of romantic love (as a negative term, deprived also of its aesthetic dimension). He was, then, "comparing" and posing the problem as a result of, not to the effectuation of, the paradigm shift (from *iki* to *ren'ai*), speaking only from the code complying to the ideals of (Western) "love." Not only was the poet describing *kōshoku* in a way unimaginable for Edo citizens, but also his usage of *kōshoku* itself had by then been transformed because of the newly accepted paradigm: *kōshoku* was now mere "lust" that forms a binary opposition to "spiritual love." Furthermore, *kōshoku* in Tōkoku's new coding was deprived of its once common homosexual connotations, and was confined to the usage foregrounding only the heterosexual relationship. *Kōshoku* was now lust for women, not for boys. The homosexual dimension was removed precisely because he was comparing it with (heterosexual) romantic love. Thus, when Tōkoku described the Western notion of love as the only moral way to love (a woman), in light of which *kōshoku* was viewed as impediment to it, the issue was, overall, contaminated by modern Western sexual ideology.[16]

I am not arguing that such a (mis-)reading is essentially wrong. A problem arises only when the objects thus known are given an ontotheological status, that is, when they are considered independent from the points of view of the observers belonging to one or the other paradigm. By virtue of such an absolutist belief alone, however, comparativism gains an illusory neutrality.

The title of my book, *Don Juan East/West*, is, then, obviously problematic. For what is an "Eastern Don Juan" other than a form of appropriation and subsumption? However, changing the title to *Don Juan and "Iro-otoko"* does not solve the problem. This title is similarly problematic since such a framework may give the impression that it presumes the possibility of comparison, leading to an essential identification of these types. To justify the identification, a comparativist must rely on some "critical" concept, taken almost invariably from the paradigm that has substantiated Don Juanism but not *kōshoku*. In this comparative criticism, *iro-otoko* simply is a paraphrase for an "Eastern Don Juan."

My book was, or had to be, originally conceived as one such comparative criticism. It was meant to be an attempt to compare conceptions of sexuality from which, so I presumed, both Don Juan and *iro-otoko* have sprung. Although I am now problematizing this kind of a universalist proposition, I have retained, in the title of the book, the sense of comparison (Western Don Juan and Eastern Don Juan) in order to show that I was, and still am, embedded in the paradigm that the above-mentioned epistemological break involved, and that I can problematize it only from within, in an awkward, limited manner. The attribution of "Western and Eastern" Don Juans to a single category of "Don Juan" was evoked only after the acceptance of a Western ideology of sexuality: a concept of lust that was differentiated from chaste love. In spite of my critique of and objection to comparative projects, I am already within the field of comparison when I criticize it. The discourse that sees *iro-otoko* as a man of lust just like Don Juan is my critical heritage and I can in no way feign ignorance of this. The knowledge of it inevitably binds me. As Derrida correctly remarks, "[O]ne does not leave the epoch whose closure one can outline" (*Of Grammatology* 12). Nevertheless, the fact that I am trapped in the epoch holds the very possibility of my breaking out.

While engaged in comparison of various "Don Juans," a comparativist might believe that the universal type of "lustful man" is at issue. However, "lust" is, as has been demonstrated in this chapter, a culturally specific concept of the West, which is actualized only as one of the items within the dichotomy of spiritual love versus carnal lust. It is the dichotomous nature of the Western ideology of sexuality that causes lewdness to emerge. In contrast, since Edo *iro-otoko* is free from such signification, to think of *iro-otoko* in terms of "libertinism" is to read in a meaning that is not originally built in the conception of *kōshoku*.

The moment of such a shift, when it became possible to see *iro-otoko* as a libertine, is recorded in *Drifting Clouds*. When Noboru, the hero's rival, mocks Bunzō, by saying that he is "a revival of Tanjirō, the representative *iro-otoko*," he is half-serious. He does feel envy toward Bunzō, who is very close to Osei, their common object of love and Bunzō's virtually promised bride. To be a Tanjirō and to exploit women's affection and sexuality is Noboru's own goal. He says to Osei: "In fact, you [Osei] protect him [Bunzō] all the time. I'm so envious. He's the Tanji [Tanjirō] of the Meiji era, a veritable Don Juan. What I wouldn't do to be like him" (298). This sense of grudge is completely lost on Bunzō, who no longer shares the conception. Their failure to communi-

Figure 3. A representative "libertine" of the late Edo period, Tanjirō, with a courtesan, Yonehachi, on whom he depends for living.

cate represents the gap between the two paradigms wherein reside, respectively, Japanese premodern *kōshoku* and Western lust.

A comparative explanation "a veritable Don Juan" in the above-quoted passage is added by the English translator. In fact, however, protection by women and the total dependence on them, for which Noboru is envious of Bunzō, are remarkable features of Tanjirō, but not Don Juan. Such features identify Bunzō with Edo *iro-otoko*, but differentiate him from Don Juan.

Standards of *iro-otoko* are illustrated in Santō Kyōden's *Grilled Playboy Edo Style* (1785), the story of a wealthy but unattractive man who dreams of establishing for himself a reputation as an *iro-otoko*. As one means to achieve this, he maneuvers in vain to pretend that he is under the devoted protection of the courtesans while in truth he is patronizing them. If dependence is antithetical to conquest, *iro-otoko* and Don Juan are paradigmatically opposite figures. Another of his unsuccessful attempts is to hire rogues and have himself beaten in an effort to conform to the standard that an *iro-otoko* is physically powerless. This feature, too, considerably differentiates *iro-otoko* from Don Juan, who is a paragon of masculine violence.

As we have seen, the newly created dichotomy of love/lust was a hierarchical one. Moreover, the hegemony of Western cultural tenets required that the items in the binary opposition be reassigned from "spiritual love versus carnal lust" to "Western romantic love versus Edo Japan *kōshoku*," so that the latter items of the dichotomies might represent a negative value while Western culture was to be endowed with purely positive values. The reconstruction of ideas about love and sex was part of the "colonization" of Japanese culture by the West in the sense that European discourses appropriated positive semantic areas, and that the ideological agenda of the West became naturalized and hegemonical, having marginalized the indigenous values. Such is the new paradigm of sexual ideology that was established around the turn of the century, and since then has continued to articulate the sexuality of the Japanese.

As a result, *kōshoku* has ceased to be a meaningful category today. The word has become almost obsolete, and has simply been replaced by Don Juanism. Consequently, the binary opposition within contemporary Japanese cultural paradigm of sexuality has become *"ren'ai* versus Don Juanism." In a French-Japanese dictionary published in Tokyo in 1914, one finds the term "Don Juan" defined as *yūyarō*, another term for *en'yarō*, representing a Japanese "libertine." In a Russian-Japanese dictionary published in 1928, Don Juan is defined as "a man like Don Juan," a tautological definition which demonstrates that "Don Juan" has entered the common lexicon. Nowadays, Don Juan is by far the more familiar term than *yūyarō* (*en'yarō*, or roughly, *iro-otoko*). With Don Juan finding a footing more firm than *iro-otoko*, the Western dichotomy of spiritual love versus Don Juanism finds a full articulation in present-day Japanese culture.

As Foucault remarks, however, the shift in the epistemology obscures its own origin. When the paradigm of sexuality changes, according to which notions such as "love," "lust," "chastity," "purity," *kōshoku*, *jōyoku*, and so forth, are constructed, the new conceptual framework and new terms begin to appear natural, universal, and transhistorical. It then gains a powerful legitimacy, making the earlier conceptions incomprehensible. Japanese today find it hard to believe that the word *ren'ai* is a translated coinage which originally represented the European concept of love. Similarly, to culturally "colonized" eyes, the realm of signification that divides sexuality into the dichotomy of spirituality and promiscuity appears only universal, common to all humanity. Romantic love now claims the status of the essence of "human nature." If, for Meiji observers, Edo literature seems to be representing "lust" and "promiscuity," categories that were actually hardly meaningful within the semantic field of late Edo literary discourses, the "observed" fact (of "lust" and "promiscuity") is attributed to the aberration and distortion of the essence of (common) "humanity" in the Edo society. The corruption of "humanity" is then explained by the repression imposed by "the barbarian, feudalistic regime," which hindered the achievement of an authentic form of love that was spiritual, chaste, and moralistic.

In contrast with such a view, Futabatei Shimei, who early in his career himself joined in the creation of the new conception, in his later works offered an oppositional perspective that challenged the "naturalness" of this new meaning and attempted to undermine the rigid dualistic thinking that had been introduced from the West. His last novel, *Mediocrity* (1907), was meant to be a refutation of Tolstoy's scandalous work, *The Kreutzer Sonata*. In this novel, Tolstoy insisted that sex was a categorical sin, and that the prevalent notion that love was a poetic sentiment that elevated morality and consecrated the marital union was a hypocritical illusion. Thus arguing, he typically foregrounded the Judeo-Christian dichotomous conception of sexuality. Futabatei Shimei furiously opposed this view. He wrote in the novel:

> In the conclusion of "The Kreutzer Sonata," [Tolstoy] says that . . . purity is the ideal of Christianity . . . that Christians ought to pursue this ideal all their lives and advises the married people of the world to live as nearly as possible as brothers and sisters.
>
> What does this mean? I cannot understand it at all. . . . The substance of our love is always sexual desire. Sexual desire is not a noble thing, nor can I think it a mean thing. It is neuter [*sic*] and indifferent. (*Mediocrity* 126–29)

So insisting, in the same novel Futabatei launches into a description of love that relies on idioms taken from Edo erotic narratives such as *The Plum Calendar*. Futabatei may have evoked in his Japanese (male) readership a sense of nostalgia for the "neutral" field of sexuality that Japanese men possessed before encountering the all-powerful Western culture. Futabatei's passage reminds of what the Japanese have

lost, along with what they have gained through the aboli-
tion of the restricted quarters and through the acquisition
of romantic love ideology. The latter endorsed the idea of
companionate marriage as opposed to the "feudal" marital
institution. Instead, it dismissed (or changed) the concept
of *kōshoku*, and opened up a bifurcated vision of sexuality.

In this chapter, we have critically examined the tenability of a comparative scheme of Don Juan as a paragon of lust
and inconstancy, as a seducer who corrupts by temporarily
satisfying carnal pleasure but not sustaining his passion. As
we discussed, however, an apparently similar act of *iro-otoko*
of "seduction" and "inconstancy" is not an expression or a
result of his "lust." Therefore, we should reject the use of
"lust" as a point of reference for comparison, just as we abandoned "love." We have yet another rung to climb since a
comparativist might ultimately resort to the most general of
comparative frames, a schema of Don Juans as "sexually energetic personages." This framework remains to be subverted
in order to complete our critique of universalism. For, if it is
maintained that Don Juan is a paragon of active "sexuality,"
the above difficulty of comparativism can be evaded: even if
"lust" is a culturally specific phenomenon, "sexuality" is a
neutral, analytical term by which one can speak of the similarity or the difference between modern Western sexuality
and Edo sexuality; even if an *iro-otoko* is not "a man of lust,"
he and Don Juan equally display powerful sexuality. Within
a framework such as this that can include both Don Juan and
iro-otoko, a comparativist is subsequently authorized to proceed to explore the scholarly "interesting" cultural differences
in the ways in which "lust," "seduction," "inconstancy," and
similar terms, are formulated.

Is "sexuality" a natural, scientific category, applicable
to any human society? Or, is it as historicizable and culturally specific as the concept of "lust"? Can it serve as an axis
for comparison of Donjuanesque figures, or no? I shall try
to answer these questions in the next chapter.

4 sexuality as a historical construct

If the term "normality" is to refer either to what is anthropologically fundamental or to what is culturally universal, then neither it nor its antonym can be meaningfully applied to the varying forms of human sexuality.

—*Peter Burger*, The Social Construction of Reality

All objects are made, and not found.

—*Stanley Fish*, Is There a Text in This Class?

Sexuality as a "Natural" Fact

In *Speech Acts* the linguist John R. Searle makes a distinction between what he calls a "brute fact" and an "institutional fact." The latter, such as marriage, depends on the "existence of certain human institutions." The former is reducible to "physical or psychological properties of states of affairs" (51).

I have, in the previous chapters, tried to present "love" and "lust" as examples of "institutional facts." They are, however, commonly considered to be less tangible and therefore less institutionalized aspects of human nature

117

than, say, marriage. It remains to be seen whether I have succeeded in showing "love" and "lust" as sociolinguistic constructs, thus putting in question some of the fundamental tenets of "humanism." However that may be, the cultural relativism implicit in my arguments might easily be co-opted into the scheme of essentialist thinking in another form. This can be done by resorting to a certain, more basic "fact" that transcends the difference of conventions endorsing various kinds of "love" and "lust," and whose ontological status cannot be historicized.

One candidate for such "brute reality" is sexuality. In this view, "love" and "lust," which may be contingent on varied cultural formulations, are expressions of the fundamental human feature, "sexuality," common to all humanity.

The hypothesis that I have tried to validate, that "love" and "lust" are arbitrary cultural constructs, would prohibit a comparison of various Don Juan figures of the world. Even so, given the above theorization, a comparativist can have resort to a "bruter," more natural fact: the fact of human sexual behaviors. If sexuality thus attains the status of a neutral, analytical entity, shared by every human being as an essence, on the basis of which one can speak of cultural differences, a comparative scheme of Don Juans as "sexually active men," or that of Don Juanism as vigorous sexuality, becomes legitimate.

To complete my critique of universalism, essentialism, and ontological realism, concerning the possibility of comparing Don Juans East/West, I will attempt in this chapter to dismantle the concept of "sexuality" as a "brute," "natural," and transcultural "reality."

It is significant that Searle invokes, in the above quotation, "physical and psychological properties" in formulating what he calls a "brute or natural fact." A "fact" can be typically established beyond cultural modification, and becomes "brute and natural" when it is "physically and psychologically" substantiated. What sustains Searle's argument is the combination of an idea of the physical world, scientific principles (physics, psychology, biology, and so on), and the concept of nature, a triad that he considers as meta-ideological and unquestionable.

The word "natural," as used by Searle, is a metaphor to invoke the binary opposition between things as they are and things as constructed. It is a means to privilege empirical, physical "reality" as opposed to historical, cultural constructions. However, as we saw in the second chapter, allegedly "natural" categories often do not have an essence in "nature," but are human constructs after all.

The labels "natural" and "nature," however, conceal such constructedness. This is hinted by the linguist George Lakoff when he writes in the spirit of Saussure and Hjemslev against the concept of nomenclature: "In moving about the world, we automatically categorize people, animals, and physical objects, both natural and man-made. This sometimes leads to the [unfounded] impression that we just categorize things as they are, that things come in *natural* kinds, and that our categories of mind *naturally* fit the kinds of things there are in the world" (6; emphasis mine).

We are, together with Lakoff, invited to question the categories which appear to be "natural," those that seem to be out there, independent of human categorization. This eventually leads to the question as to whether "sexuality" may also not be "natural." Is it not another sociocultural category which only appears to be "natural"? A case from literary history, namely, the issue of naturalism, may prove to be a breakthrough. Let us turn again to early modern Japanese literature, especially Mori Ōgai's sexual semi-autobiography, *Vita Sexualis*.

Ōgai's *Vita Sexualis* in the Context of Naturalism

Naturalism in Japan is usually thought to have reached its peak in the last years of the Meiji period, when some of its representative works were published. Among them were Shimazaki Tōson's *Broken Commandment* (1906), and two works by Tayama Katai, *The Quilt* (1907) and *A Country Schoolmaster* (1909). Ōgai's *Vita Sexualis* (1909) was published when naturalism was the predominant mode of literary discourse. As a matter of fact, the novel possesses many features of Japanese naturalism: a semi-autobiographical narrative structure, vivid description of the themes concerning sexuality, and application of medico-scientific categories. For this reason, it was largely considered to be a work of naturalism by its contemporary readership.[1]

However, Ōgai himself insisted on distinguishing it from naturalist writings. For instance, the hero of the novel, Kanai, who exhibits a resemblance to the author, expresses his doubt about naturalism in the following way:

> Each time he read a naturalistic novel, he discovered that the author never failed to use every occasion in daily life to represent his hero in reference to sexual desire, and that the critics themselves acknowledged these novels accurately depicted life.
>
> At the same time he was wondering if such representations were actually true to life, he suspected that perhaps unlike the rest of the human race he might be indifferent to such desires, that he might have an extraordinary natural disposition which might be called frigiditas. (25–26)

Then, why does Kanai himself join in this discourse, and how can he do so? Because he believes that his "frigidity" allows him a necessary critical distance toward the object in question.

So reasoning, Kanai decides to write a history of the development of his sexuality. He is hoping to find out which is normal, his "frigidity" or the naturalists' excessive concern. Is his sexual temperament "normal" or "anomalous"? It is, however, already quite clear from these opening passages that Ōgai believes that his is the normal, and the naturalists' is the anomalous representation of sexuality. For, *Vita Sexualis*, as opposed to naturalist novels that demonstrate unduly obsessive interest in sexual matters, takes a cool, sober scientific attitude. In spite of superficial similarities in the intense attention paid to the subject, Ōgai thinks, his novel completely differs in spirit from naturalistic writings. Such a reading (that *Vita Sexualis* is not only non-naturalistic but totally opposed to naturalism), supported by the author himself in the novel, apparently has been well respected by later critics, and constitutes a critical heritage. For instance, the medical doctor Kawamura Keikichi, who is also one of the leading critics of Ōgai, argues:

> Whereas Ōgai constantly tried to enlighten the general public with the knowledge on sexuality, he was furious and intolerant with these novelists [naturalists]. A writer should be knowledgeable. But, they were completely lacking in an accurate idea about sexuality. . . . Naturalism originally adapted the spirit and the method of natural science to literature. When you see a human being as a physical object, sexual desire becomes the major aim of description. This led to the common mistake that naturalism consisted in depicting sexuality [thus, incorrectly subsuming *Vita Sexualis* under the naturalistic writings]. . . . His *Vita Sexualis* was a challenge to naturalism. (*Sorrows* 57–58)

One of the representative scholars of Mori Ōgai, Hasegawa Izumi, has more or less the same view. He insists that, although *Vita Sexualis*, being a sexual biography, demonstrates striking resemblances to naturalist writings, the author presents essentially different perspectives deriving from his research on sexological discourse, and that as a hygienist and writer, Ōgai achieved an original history of his sexual development that naturalism could not accomplish (105). The poet Satō Haruo writes in a postscript to *The Complete Works of Mori Ōgai* that the administration that banned *Vita Sexualis* concluded, judging from the subject matter, that it was an erotic novel (*seiyoku shōsetsu* [a novel describing sexual desire]), not realizing that it was a work of philosophy (iv). All these criticisms proclaim the fundamental difference of *Vita Sexualis* from naturalistic novels, and the reason for this claim is that Ōgai's descriptions are based on the principles of science (medicine, hygiene, sexology, and so forth) and philosophy. Such a claim appears to be justified in light of the abundant references in the novel to medical and philosophical authors such as Krafft-Ebing, Jerusalem, Schopenhauer, and Nietzsche. Of course, it is also endorsed by the authority Ōgai has as an established army surgeon and leading thinker of his time.

Ōgai's rejection of naturalism is typically expressed in the word *debakame-shugi* (*debakame*ism, or peeping-tomism), with which Ōgai labels naturalistic writings in *Vita Sexualis*:

> Meanwhile, the Debakame affair came to light. A workman by that name had the habit of spying on women in their section of the public bath, and one day he followed someone on her way home from the bathhouse and raped her. . . . It was linked with the so-called naturalist movement. A new term, debakame-ism, was used as a pseudonym for naturalism. (26–27)

For Ōgai and the critics who have read *Vita Sexualis* in the wake of the author's own reading of it, naturalism with its crude description of sexuality without the perspectives of a doctor or a philosopher is nothing more than peeping-tomism.

The reference to *debakame* (normally pronounced *debagame* today), taken from a true story, is of a highly journalistic nature. The incident took place in 1908, only a year before the publication of *Vita Sexualis*. Ishii Kendō's *The Origin of Things and Practices That Began in Meiji* gives a concise narrative of the affair:

> The Etymology of *Debakame*
>
> A twenty-five-year-old gardener, Ikeda Kametarō, had protruding teeth, bringing him a nickname of *Debakame* (Kame[tarō] with buckteeth). He was a pervert (*shikijō kyō*) who was fond of "peeping through a hole."
>
> On the twenty-second day of March in the forty-first year of Meiji, En, wife of Kōda Kyō, was murdered by an unknown hand in front of a public bath.

On the fifth of April, Kametarō was ascertained to
be the murderer. Since then, peeping into public baths,
and so on, has been commonly called *debakame*. (122;
slightly abridged)

The Origin of Things and Practices That Began in Meiji is an
encyclopedia of customs, businesses, institutions, concepts,
and so forth, which originated in the early years of Meiji,
largely on account of Westernization. Here, however, the
editor, Ishii, speaks of the *etymology* of *debakame*, not the *origin* of it. Are we, then, to think that, in this instance, Ishii is
concerned with the origin of the expression "debakame,"
signifying an act of "peeping into public baths, and so on,
with a perverse motive," an act which has been as familiar
to premodern Japanese society as any other?

This is, to me, a rather doubtful hypothesis. After all,
public baths before the Meiji period had commonly been
mixed. It is quite obvious that under the social circumstances in which female naked bodies are not concealed, an
act of peeping at them cannot take place. A Japanologist and
professor at Tokyo Imperial University, Basil H. Chamberlain, writing in *Things Japanese* (originally published in 1890),
cites the editor of *The Japan Mail* and expresses his agree-
ment with the view that "the nude is seen in Japan, but is
not looked at" (60). Moreover, he is referring not to the
mixed bathing in public baths but to the practice of taking
a bath in a tub placed outside individual houses. In Japanese society during the Edo period and earlier, female nudity was not only easily viewed in public baths, but was as
open to the public gaze as to be presented on the street. Under conditions like this, peeping at women's bodies must
have been meaningless.

Furthermore, it could not be an issue of shame or
morality. As an anthropologist, Edward Morse, in the
recollections of his stay in Japan in 1877, remarked:
"[N]akedness . . . in Japan for centuries has not been looked
upon as immodest. The exposure of the body in Japan is
only when bathing and then everybody minds his own

business" (97). Asked by his colleague Dr. Murray to measure the temperature of a hot spa, Morse unwittingly sights two young girls in the bath whom he has met earlier in the day. To the surprise of Morse, they do not scream for shame or anger. Instead, they greet him with a cheerful "Ohayo (Good morning)" (98). In this instance two significations are involved. The signifieds of the nude bodies are totally different for Morse and those women. Morse's was a meaning that modern Japan was destined to learn: a secret zone that has to be concealed and shuttered from the public/male gaze. That of the girls was a signification, or the non-signification of the nakedness, that was to be prohibited soon.

Of course, the fact that the inside of public baths of the Edo period had generally been quite dark has to be taken into consideration. For this reason, female nudity was more or less out of the sight of onlookers even when the hall was mixed. To be sure, there were also baths that provided a fence between men's and women's sections, especially in the capital city of Edo. Shikitei Sanba's classic story *The World at the Bath-House* (1809–1813) has two sections, treating respectively men's and women's baths. With its Confucian moralism, the Tokugawa Shogunate government frowned upon the custom. It issued many statutes to prohibit mixed bathing, the first of which was issued in the mid-Edo period (1791). The main object of these regulations was to encourage segregated bathing according to the days of the week. However, such an effort on the part of the Shogunate testifies, on the contrary, to how widely spread and how tenaciously observed the practice of mixed bathing was.

The Meiji administration continued an attempt to enact the prohibition that the Tokugawa government had in effect failed to achieve. Under the heading "Prohibition of Mixed Bathing," *The Origin of Things and Practices That Began in Meiji* records that, in the second year of Meiji (1869), the Tokyo metropolitan government issued an injunction similar to those of the Shogunate. It was twice reissued in the third and the fifth years, suggesting the difficulty in eliminating the custom. The Meiji period, however, eventually saw the installation of segregated bathing, which has remained in practice to this day except for a small number of spas in rural areas. *A New Guide to Metropolitan Tokyo* published in the seventh year of Meiji (1874) has a chapter entitled "Recent Bath Houses" in which they are described as having "two chambers and two baths for men and women, separated by a glass partition" (224). If a glass partition was the latest trend in the new capital, so was segregated bathing.

This being the case, we are invited to think that the *debakame* phenomenon was a culturally specific one that, having become meaningful, emerged only at a certain historical stage. In other words, we are probably not to assume that an act of sexually charged peeping at female nudity, universal to any human society, just happened to be termed *debakame* in Japanese in 1908. At least, nudity in public baths (if not female nakedness under other circumstances, or female nakedness in general), and the surreptitious gaze toward it, became sexually charged at a certain historical point on account of a change in the system of culture, that is, prohibition, implemented anew, of the display of nudity in public. If so, we can say, after all, that *The Origin of Things and Practices That Began in Meiji* records the origin, not the etymology, of *debakame*.

It becomes, then, easier to understand why the Meiji administration succeeded in enforcing the new practice that the Shogunate had found difficulty in imposing. One of the reasons may be sought in the new pressure from Western countries. Mixed bathing, it seems, was one of by far the most conspicuous aspects of Japanese culture that struck Westerners who first started visiting Japan toward the end of the Tokugawa regime and at the beginning of the Meiji period. Almost all the records of Japanese society of the late Edo to early Meiji period by foreign visitors mentioned this custom with amazement. Many saw it as a sign of a lack of civilization, morality, and spirituality.

Commodore Matthew Perry, who voyaged to Japan from 1853 to 1855, aired a most critical comment on this, based on his observations there:

> A scene at one of the public baths, where the sexes mingled indiscriminately, unconscious of their nudity, was not calculated to impress the Americans with a very favorable opinion of the morals of the inhabitants. This may not be a universal practice throughout Japan, and indeed is said by the Japanese near us not to be; but the Japanese people of the inferior ranks are undoubtedly, notwithstanding their moral superiority to most oriental nations, a *lewd* people. (Hawks 469; my emphasis)

Perry did not have a chance to figure out whether the practice was universal or not. However, his conviction that the Japanese people were *lewd* was so unshakable that, to conclude the topic of mixed ("promiscuous," that is) bathing, he added an observation about the lasciviousness of Japanese popular culture:

Figure 4. A (mixed) bathhouse in Shimoda. From Heine's *Reise um die Erde nach Japan* (*A Journey Around the World to Japan*).

> Apart from the bathing scenes, there was enough in the popular literature, with its obscene pictorial illustrations, to prove a licentiousness of taste and practice among a certain class of the population, that was not only disgustingly intrusive, but disgracefully indicative of foul corruption. (469)

Judging from this additional comment, he may well have suspected the universality in Japan of mixed bathing in spite of information to the contrary.

Such an opinion about the "barbarism"[2] of Japanese society, especially coming from a high-ranking diplomat like Perry, must have been extremely unwelcome to the new Meiji government. (Perry himself visited toward the end of the Shogunate, not during the Imperial regime, though.) At the time, it was trying hard to impress the Western nations with Japan's achievements of "modernization" and "Westernization," which, the Meiji administration hoped, would lead to the revocation of the unequal treaties that the Edo Shogunate had been compelled to sign. The pompous but superficial demonstration of accomplishments of "Westernization" at the new, Western-style guesthouse, Rokumeikan, was typical of such efforts. Naturally, the Japanese government was anxious to annul customs such as mixed bathing that struck the Westerners as barbarian, immoral, and uncivilized. In spite of the record in *The Origin of Things and Practices That Began in Meiji*, the first effort by the Imperial government to prohibit mixed bathing actually materialized in the first year of Meiji (1868) in Yokohama and Osaka, a policy that was obviously influenced by the number of foreign residents (Westerners, that is) in these cities. In the same year, a strict order was given in Tokyo to forbid mixed bathing and to install a panel to screen the second floor (which was often a locus for prostitution) of the bathhouses in Tsukiji, a part of Tokyo that was to be developed into a residential area for foreigners.

If such was the external pressure, there functioned an internal pressure, too. The Japanese probably started to internalize the European sense of morality as regards nudity in response to the foreigners' gaze. Such a shift is recorded by Morse. First came the recognition of the Westerners' eyes which had hitherto been unknown:

> [The Japanese] are wholly lacking in appreciation that nakedness is immodest, and, utterly lacking it, you [a Westerner living in Japan] are no more abashed by it than are the Japanese, and therefore conclude that what would be immodest for us is not for them. The only immodesty displayed is the behavior of foreigners in looking at nakedness, and this behavior the Japanese resent and turn away from. (100)

To demonstrate the point, he then relates one of his own experiences. On their way home in rickshaws, he and Dr. Murray came across a woman bathing in a wooden tub on the street who in no way reacted to them by trying to hide or to cover her body: "Not one of our jinrikisha men turned his head to look, nor would any other of the thirty millions of people have done so" (100). But then something went astray:

> I could not resist calling Dr. Murray's attention to her in a hurried way, and the woman, noticing my gestures, turned partly away from us, probably taking us for country bumpkins, or barbarians, as, indeed, we were. (100–101)

Perhaps, incidents of this kind led to the reorganization of the paradigm of sexuality in the Japanese culture, in response to a new conceptual system that foreigners presented. The embarrassed (or lasciviously curious or somehow charged) gaze of a foreigner changed an act of bathing in public (as if in a vacuum) to the act of being looked at, and eventually to having to feel shame. After an encounter with, and a recognition of, a charged stare, nudity became charged, too. It is exactly this gaze that changed a female body in Japan from "something seen" to "some-

Figure 5. "An amorous man," Yonosuke, peeping
through a spyglass at a maid (see note 3).
Courtesy of Osaka Nakanoshima Library.

thing to be looked at." The step from this to "something to
be peeped at" was very short.[3]

Such a shift in sentiment may have encouraged the notion that mixed bathing was a custom to be frowned upon.
The emergence of bathhouses with segregated chambers and
tubs, in turn, promoted the consciousness that nudity was

sexually charged. If the act of peeping was meaningless when nudity was omnipresent, a naked body became worthy of attention with the setting up of partitions to screen it.

Mori Ōgai himself writes in *Vita Sexualis* about the maneuvers Ōgai-Kanai contrived in order to take a look at the genitals of a girl in the neighborhood. Kanai had to be strategic because: "[i]n those days there were no public baths in castle towns [such as Ōgai's home town, Tsuwano]" (42).[4] In Ōgai's childhood (toward the end of the Edo period and at the beginning of the Meiji period) public baths normally offered a chance to observe female nude bodies. One's desire to see would have been aroused only without such an institution.

The material condition (divided bathhouses) and the consciousness (of lust, shame, sexuality, and so on) constituted one and the same phenomenon, comprising a system of sexuality in which bathing women were now erotic and, consequently, mixed bathing was shameful.

Only then was female nudity relegated to the private field and cut off from the public gaze. One of the ordinances issued by the Tokyo district government in 1871 to prohibit mixed bathing has this additional remark: "A curtain or a screen should be hung at the entrance and the windows of the second floor *so that it may not be visible from outside*" (*The Origin of Things and Practices That Began in Meiji* 126; emphasis mine). The prohibition of mixed bathing segregating female sexuality from the male sexual gaze thus meant the creation of private space that was supposed to be "not visible from outside."

What is private emerges only by its segregation from what is public. The case of prohibition of mixed bathing was, then, one aspect of the creation of the privacy and the inner space (of an individual) in Japan, which, some hold, took place in the early years of the "modernizing" process. Karatani Kōjin argues in his *Origins of Modern Japanese Literature* that the genre of I-novel,[5] by virtue of its confessions, created the human interior, and that Tayama Katai's *The*

Quilt, a representative I-novel, discovered "sexuality" as interiority in the same way: "Although Katai was seen as confessing what had been hidden, it was the reverse. The institution of confession led Katai to discover 'sexuality' " (79). It is the literary apparatus of confession that realized what was to be confessed, that is, sexuality as something deeply personal and private. Likewise, it was a fence that separated men and women that created the nudity as a private entity.[6]

Vita Sexualis adopts the same structure of narrative as *The Quilt*. It closes with the following passages:

> After reading his manuscript, he wondered if he could show it to the public. It would be quite difficult to. There are things which everyone does but which one does not mention to others. Since he was a member of the educated circle governed by the law of prudery, it would be difficult for him to bring out his book. . . .
>
> He picked up his pen and wrote in large letters in Latin across the front cover of his manuscript, VITA SEXUALIS. He heard the thud of his manuscript as he hurled it inside a storage chest for books. (152–53)

In spite of, or rather precisely because of, the last sentence to the effect that "he hurled it inside a storage chest," *Vita Sexualis* had to be published. It was the insistence of its being private that endowed it with significance for it to be made public. Also, it was the claim that at stake here was something to be (or not to be) confessed, that demarcated the field to be concealed and hence confessed. Ōgai's consciousness that the novel in question was about what normally has to be kept secret, created sexuality as a private, inner area of personality.

Naturalistic writing thus inevitably combined sexuality with its narrative mode of confession. The method of naturalism is usually conceived as the sensational revealing of, and the scientific description of, a personal life. One of the major theorists of Japanese naturalism, Hasegawa

Tenkei, lists things to be urgently revealed by naturalistic writings, among which are "something physical (*niku teki*)" and "something sexual (*seiyoku teki*)" (180). But, why does it have to be "something physical and sexual," of all the personal data that can be laid bare, that has to be revealed? Why is it matters pertaining to sexuality that need be confessed? Precisely because sexuality is formulated as nothing but what is concealed, or confessable. Naturalism, therefore, is a method of revealing what is meant to be revealed.

What is sexual thus emerges exactly as something that is private, that which has to be concealed and, therefore, to be revealed. The scheme of confession, which is shared by naturalism, the I-novel, and *Vita Sexualis* alike, segments sexual desire as private. The critical heritage to distinguish *Vita Sexualis* as a scientific description of sexual life from naturalistic writings as a mere expression of voyeurism is a gesture to conceal the origin and the nature of "sexuality."

The function of confession articulating "sexual" interiority in naturalistic writings is analogous to that of peeping. If privacy exists as something to be made public, sexuality arises as something to be peeped into. *Debakame* represents a kind of gaze in which naturalism segmented privacy and sexuality. In this sense, *debakame-ism*, which is sometimes considered to be an unfair title for naturalism, may in fact be appropriate.

"Sexuality," then, emerged only sometime during the second half of Meiji (around the turn of the century) along with naturalism, segregated baths, voyeurs, and, as we will see, sexological discourse, all of which appeared at approximately the same time.

The emergence of such a paradigm and the related discourses coincides with the creation of the Japanese signifier for sexuality. The most common translations for "sexuality" in contemporary Japanese are *sei* or *sei-ai*. The examples that *The Dictionary of Terms in the Meiji Period* (1868–1912) cites, however, are limited to the usages in the senses of "born nature" and "(grammatical) gender." This probably suggests that the use of *sei* in the sense of sexuality does not go back much earlier than the Taishō period (1912–1926). Shibata Shōkichi's *Eiwa jii* (*English-Japanese Vocabulary*), published in the nineteenth year of Meiji (1886), a reprint of the 1868 edition, defines "sex" as *rui* (species) and *sei* with a note in parentheses: "both in respect to male/female distinction." For "sexual," it gives *jinrui no* (human, probably meaning, "pertaining to the human categories of male/female") and *nannyo no* (male/female); for "sexuality," *sei no kubetsu* (gender distinction). The dictionary thus evokes only the sense of male/female distinction.

It seems to have been the compound *sei-yoku* (sexual appetite, desire) that first conveyed the meaning of sexuality in the modern sense, and it was soon widely used. The first example from Shōgakkan's *The Great Japanese Dictionary* dates from 1907: "A thing of this kind should be called the awakening of sexual desire (*seiyoku*) and not love" (Futabatei Shimei, *Mediocrity* 128). The first example in the General Index to *The Complete Collection of Meiji Literature* (*Meiji bungaku zenshū*) is a passage from Tayama Katai's *The Quilt* (1907), which appeared in the same year as *Mediocrity*: "Frustration caused by sexual desire (*seiyoku*) oppressed his heart with an overwhelming force" (92). Ōgai's *Vita Sexualis* (1909) is also among the earliest to record usages of *seiyoku*. This demonstrates that it was the naturalistic literature that promulgated the term *seiyoku* (sexual desire) and the concept of sexuality (although the relationship of naturalism to Futabatei's *Mediocrity* is as complex as that between naturalism and *Vita Sexualis*).

Naturalist discourse, however, was not the first to use *sei* in the sense of sexuality. It was the medico-scientific discourses of sexology, hygiene, psychology, and so forth, that appear to have initiated it. This is no wonder, since naturalism is a mode of literature based on an interest in the laws of science, the laws of nature. Consequently, the medical discourse of sexology and the literary discourse of naturalism demonstrate a close interplay.

As a matter of fact, it was the author of *Vita Sexualis*, Mori Ōgai himself, who opened up such signification in a series of articles he published in the journal *Public Medical Affairs* (*Kōshū iji*), of which Ōgai was editor-in-chief, around the thirtieth year of Meiji (1897). For example, in *The New Theory of Hygiene*, he writes:

> There is no doubt that the central nervous system controls the sexual life. Budge (1811–1888), Eckhard, and Goltz (born 1834) demonstrated by experiments that the nerve center for erection and ejaculation of animals is located in the pelvic spinal cords. Probably the same holds with human beings. (Kawamura, *Mori Ōgai's Miscellaneous Writings on Sexual Desire* 103)

Sexuality is a physical phenomenon, associating humanity with the animal world.

Although Ōgai's study relies on various sexological sources such as Hegar, Loewenfeld, Grimonde, and Freud, it seems that his major source of information was Krafft-Ebing's *Psychopathia Sexualis*, which was to become very popular and influential after a Japanese translation appeared in 1913.[7] In this way, it was the sexological discourse that first brought in the concept of sexuality into Meiji culture.[8]

Afterwards, the concept of the sexual further spread from the more specific term *sei-yoku* (sexual desire) to a broader arena, creating a new sense of *sei* as sexuality in general. It was again Ōgai who demonstrated one of the earliest occurrences of the usage:

> I received a report from Germany on the sexual education [literally, education concerning sexual desire (*sei-yoku teki*)]. "Concerning sexual desires" is not an appropriate expression. "Sexual" can be translated into *sei teki* [concerning *sei* (sexuality)], but not *sei-yoku teki* [concerning *sei-yoku* (sexual desire)]. The character *sei*, however, is so multivalent that unfortunately I have to add "desire." (*Vita Sexualis* 90)[9]

Thus, Ōgai uses *sei* in the sense of sexuality in general. However, he also demonstrates here that this usage was not firmly established yet. If in the contemporary use "the Chinese character for 'sex' (*sei*)" means primarily "sexuality," it was at the time multivalent; other connotations such as "human nature" were more immediate. Consequently, in order to pin it down to the field of sexuality, the doctor-writer had to evoke a more specific concept of sexual desire, *seiyoku*.[10] A similar reservation is expressed in the Japanese translation of *Psychopathia Sexualis*, published in the second year of Taishō (1913). The translator does use the word *sei* along with *seiyoku* (sexual desire). However, *sei* in the sense of sexuality always appears with quotation marks. Two glosses attached to *sei-teki tokushitsu*: *geshurehitsukara-kuteru* and *Geschlechts=charakter* (*sic*; sexual feature), demonstrate that *sei-teki* itself could not signify without the original German phrase.

Such a medicoscientific rendition of the concept of sexuality and its emergence was not a phenomenon restricted to Japan alone. According to Raymond Williams, "it seems unlikely that the sense of *sex* as a physical relationship or action is at all common before [the nineteenth century]. . . . *Sexuality* followed the same line of development. It is scientifically descriptive from [the last third of the eighteenth century]" (*Keywords* 284–85). The new medicoscientific conception of sexuality thus originated more or less simultaneously in the West and in Japan.

Jeffrey Weeks in his *Sexuality and Its Discontents* also points to what he perceives as a shift in the concept of sexuality that took place in the last century, spurred by sexological knowledge: "What was, however, new to the nineteenth century was the sustained effort to put all this on to a new, 'scientific' footing: to isolate, and individualize, the specific characteristics of sexuality, to detail its normal paths and morbid variations, to emphasize its power and to speculate on its effects" (65–66). In a like manner, what was new about *Vita Sexualis* was its combining sexual themes with scientific discourse. The vivid description of sexuality had been a common feature of Edo literature, which a romantic poet of Meiji, Kitamura

Tōkoku, appropriately called "erotic literature" (*inbun-gaku*). Ōgai's novel marked a departure from "premodern" erotic literature in its anatomical approach and its pronounced seriousness. Sexuality was now something to be analyzed and seriously discussed.

Sexuality as a "Root" of Human Nature

Another feature that arose with the incipient sexological discourse was the idea that sexuality was the fundamental aspect of human nature, a first principle placed deep within: "The gratification of the sexual instinct seems to be the *primary* motive in man as well as in beast" (Krafft-Ebing 2; emphasis mine). It is here that the notion of sexuality opened the possibility of relating a human being to an animal, considered to be a lower creature: "The term 'sexual instinct' may be said to cover the whole of the neuropsychic phenomena of reproduction which man shares with the lower animals" (Ellis 1: 1).

Subsequently, however, sexuality must proceed into the "higher" psychological arena of humanity, and attain the status of "love": "Having entered the higher brain, or organ of mind, and become modified, complicated, and combined with the different branches of psychic activity, the sexual appetite takes the name of love, properly so-called" (Forel, *Sexual Question* 104). Attribution of sexuality to a lower physical function relates it to the concepts of "nature" and "instinct." Sexuality is relegated to the lower rung both within an individual organism and on an evolutionary ladder. Such a connotation of sexuality ties in with a notion that we have examined, that the sexual is what is the innermost part of a human being, internal, hidden, and private. Sexuality is an essence, an origin. This is clearly different from the Edo *iki* ideology, where sensual desire can, and should be, distanced as mere play in which you are advised not to get overly absorbed.

Thence arises the close tie of the sexological discourse with naturalism in literature. For instance, since sexuality is a physioneurological basis of human beings, it is closely related to the idea of heredity. That is why Krafft-Ebing does not fail to add, to each of the cases he has studied, information as to the physical/mental problems of the relatives of his patients-clients as a relevant piece of information. This obsession within sexological discourse is largely shared by naturalism in literature.

Since sexuality is a facet of humanity that relates it to the physical, natural world, and since the new conception of sexuality defines it as a basic aspect of a human being, naturalism has to turn to it to demonstrate the reality of "human nature."[11] Hence the above-cited comment by the doctor-critic Kawamura on naturalism and *Vita Sexualis*: "When you see a human being as a physical object, sexual desire becomes the major aim of description." We may, however, stop to wonder whether sexual desire is so transparently the central feature of humanity as Kawamura suggests, "if you see a human being as a physical object." Is it not, rather, the ideology of medicine and sexology that renders sexual desire "the major aim of description" of a human being?

As sexuality is considered to be one of the most basic aspects of humanity, sexology has this view: "Sexual feeling is really the *root* of all ethics, and no doubt of aestheticism and religion" (Krafft-Ebing 2; emphasis mine).[12] Then, a metaphor such as the following naturally arises: "The sublimest virtues *spring from* sexual life" (2; emphasis mine).

However, the "root" does not necessarily possess a positive connotation of being the first principle, but often that of an inferior starting point that has later to be developed and sublimated. This results in an immense ambiguity in the notion of sexuality in sexological discourse. Krafft-Ebing's concern is mainly with the dark side of sexuality. It is no accident that *Psychopathia Sexualis* is subtitled *A Forensic Study* (*Eine klinisch-forensische Studie*). The German psychopathologist notes: "[Sexual desire may] degenerate into the lowest passion, *basest* vice" (2; my emphasis). Sexuality is a base which can be "base." From time to time, however, Krafft-Ebing speaks of sexuality as an absolutely positive source of power and human greatness, from which derive art and religion. Conversely, another sexologist, Forel, sees "human nature," including sexual instinct, as essentially "indifferent," something "that has nothing to do with morality" (*Sexual Ethics* 13). Forel emphasizes its being a moral issue in the last instance, though:

> The word "moral" is commonly used to mean sexually pure, that is to say, continent; while the word "immoral" suggests the idea of sexual incontinence and debauch. This is a misuse of words, and rests upon a confusion of ideas, for sexuality has in itself nothing to do with morality. It points, however, to the undoubted fact that the sexual impulse, since it has other human beings as its objects, easily leads to moral conflicts within the breast of the individual. (*Sexual Ethics* 13)

In such a manner, the concept of sexuality as formulated by early sexology[13] becomes closely intertwined with that of immorality and delinquency. Sexuality is a basic, cruder aspect of humanity, an animal part of it, which eventually has to be domesticated and moralized. In the words of Ōgai-Kanai, "[h]e had tamed his tiger of sexual desire and controlled it. . . . It was certainly tamed, but its power to terrify and awe was not at all enfeebled" (*Vita Sexualis* 152). When this process fails, it leads a human being to vice and crime. Sexuality is potential delinquency.

As a matter of fact, Krafft-Ebing's concept of sexuality also vastly exploits the traditional dualistic system of the Western moral consciousness, grafting a new dichotomy onto the older one, that is, the dichotomy of animality versus purity. Conventional Judeo-Christian notions of corruption, lust, and sensuality are associated with modernized notions of instinct, nature, and pleasure, phenomena pertaining to the "physical" order. Conversely, the concept of "mentality" is now annexed to purity, chastity, love, sublimity, beauty, and so on. The pattern of dichotomous thinking is clear when he argues about the "mental and physical merits [of sexual acts]" (3).

This ties into the moment that I outlined in the previous chapter—the emergence of "lust." Sexuality emerges as potential lewdness where too much passion and desire is a problem. Therefore, Forel speaks of "a monstrous superabundance of feeble, sickly, mentally perverted, criminally disposed, idle, treacherous, vain, crafty, covetous, passionate, capricious, and untrustworthy individuals" (*Sexual Ethics* 40) who have degenerated because of the failure to moralize their sexuality. Passion is now a moral problem on a par with idleness, vanity, caprice, and treachery. It is a crime and disease.

When such a paradigm of sexuality was introduced to Meiji Japan, *kōshoku* became lust, *iro-otoko* became a libertine, and mixed bathing became "promiscuous" bathing.[14] Peeping in public baths and at naked women became a crime, and hence a lure only then. Female nudity (in public baths) became a potential trigger for a crime as in the case of Debakame.

As mentioned earlier, such were new dimensions of the phenomena of "sexuality" articulated by sexological discourse. The writer Futabatei Shimei seems to have been as familiar as the doctor Ōgai with works of sexologists such as Forel and Krafft-Ebing.[15] In his last, semi-autobiographical novel, *Mediocrity*, the narrator compares himself to one of "the mentally perverted, passionate individuals that Forel and Krafft-Ebing list in their works." As we have seen in the previous chapter, Futabatei's *Mediocrity* is an account of a moment in Japanese cultural history when the bifurcated structure of sexuality, which has thereafter distinguished spiritual, noble love from carnal pleasure, was formulated. It was also a moment when "lust" was created. Futabatei Shimei, as I argued, attempted to annul the Western dichotomy of "noble love" and "sexual desire." Paradoxically, the novelist could not escape from this dichotomous structure precisely by protesting against it. Once he has known it, his horizon is loaded with it.

> [F]orcing into an unnatural and pathological thing the
> neutral and indifferent sexual passion I would have

had, had I remained an ordinary man, I assumed in
imagination that satyriasis which appears in the books
of Krafft-Ebing and Forel and felt very noble all by
myself. (*Mediocrity* 132–33)

Of the two sexologists mentioned in the passage, Futabatei
relies more on Forel's thoughts than on those of Krafft-
Ebing. For, Futabatei, just like Forel, postulates sexuality as
"indifferent" per se, whereas Krafft-Ebing takes it to be
value-laden, whether it be a root of all human powers or a
dark, degenerating force. Following Forel, the novelist differentiates "perversions" from "indifferent sexuality." As a
matter of fact, however, it is precisely Futabatei's regarding
"sexuality" as "neutral" and "indifferent" that speaks of
the vast hidden field that is *not* neutral, and therefore
"satyristic." The status of being "unnatural" and "pathological" emerges only when the "natural" and "normal" field
of sexuality is articulated. In other words, sexuality is a normality, demarcated only in contrast to the potential abnormality and criminality.

Thus, Futabatei, along with Mori Ōgai, introduced the
notion of sexuality as pathology and promiscuity. The spirit
in which Mori Ōgai wrote *Vita Sexualis* was diametrically
opposed to that in which Futabatei wrote *Mediocrity*, however. The latter accuses himself of having been indulged in
perverse satyriasis when his sexuality should have remained
"indifferent."[16] Conversely, the former asks himself in the
novel if he is frigid. However, Ōgai's implicit criticism appears to be more directed toward naturalist writers than toward himself. He asks whether "people in general had
become erotomaniacs or he [Mr Kanai] himself was abnormally frigid" (27). Quite obviously, he thinks the former is
the case. Ōgai's judgment notwithstanding, just as Futabatei
introduces a paradigm of "sexuality" by invoking dichotomies of neutrality/abnormality and indifference/pathology,
Ōgai evokes it by suggesting a certain field where sexuality is absent. For such a suggestion is possible solely on the
basis of a binary opposition of frigidity/erotomaniac, that

is, of lack/abundance of sexuality. By declaring himself frigid and ultimately normal, he places himself in the realm charged with the same signification as the one occupied by the naturalists.[17]

In the previous chapter, I cited another passage from *Mediocrity* to show Futabatei's critical attitude toward the Western conception of love and his nostalgia for the Edo paradigm of passion. However, nostalgia is felt only for something one has lost and for a position in which one is no longer situated. Futabatei can only speak from the framework where "sexuality" is actively functioning, that is, where it is not indifferent, but unnatural and pathological. This is why sexuality is now capable of leading one to a status of madness (*shikijō kyō*). While *shikijō* (erotic desire) is a word probably originating in the Edo era, most notably in a Buddhist context, the use of *shikijō kyō* (sexual maniac) does not date back further than late Meiji, around the turn of the century.[18] This is the moment when sexuality was articulated, or more precisely, when it emerged as a potential mental disease, namely, *kyō* (madness).

Shikijō kyō is not a lack of morality, or an ethical defect, but a perversion and a disease. Put differently, it is an essential, not a contingent, problem. This is the second feature that makes a Japanese voyeur, *debakame*, fundamentally new besides the initiation of private, sexual space he substantiated. It was no accident that *The Origin of Things and Practices That Began in Meiji* (1908) had defined *debakame* as *shikijō kyō*. Voyeurism was established in modern Japan as a pathology when Debakame (a man named Kame with buckteeth) was arrested. It is his conspicuous physical, biological feature that marked him as a neurotic once and for all. His bodily deformity was a sign that symbolized his interior sexual pathology. If a "Peeping Tom" is a man who peeps just like everyone else can and may, a voyeur is one who is *compelled* to peep because of his uncontrollable inner desire to do so. Here the concepts of perversion, delinquency, nature, physical existence, and so on, are intermingled. His problem is innate and constituent. He is a criminal through and through precisely because his impulse derives from his perverse and insane nature, deep within him.

This demonstrates the moment when the notion of "perversion" was established. Krafft-Ebing explains voyeurism in the following way: "The same thing [the cases which stand in etiological relation with abnormally intense libido and defective virility or courage, or lack of opportunity for normal sexual gratification] must be assumed in the case of so-called 'voyeurs' " (499). The qualifier "so-called" and the quotation marks indicate the relative newness of the phenomenon conceptualized as voyeurism. Further, Krafft-Ebing shows reservation about the nature of this "perversion" when he footnotes the "voyeurs": "Dr. Moll calls this perversion (? [sic]) mixoscopia" (499). The reservation expressed by the question mark, however, is immediately mitigated by the strong comment that follows where he refers the readers "concerning this moral aberration" to Coffignon's book, in which "[t]he revelations, in the domain of sexual perversity, and also perversion . . . are horrible" (500).

The same moment occurred in Japan. In the Japanese context, the abnormal nature of this sexual perversion was more clearly marked by the bodily deformity of the original "pervert," Debakame (Kame with bucked teeth). Voyeurism is a physical feature just as projection of the teeth is, and hence, a fixed condition. In a queer departure from the spiritual, the mental in sexological conception gets sutured with the physical. At any rate, the sexological discourse of perversion in Japan is thus successfully and stably articulated by replacing deformity with itself.

As I mentioned earlier, since naturalism was on the whole considered to have an obsession with sexual matters, its nickname of *debakame-shugi* (peeping-tomism) was, in fact, highly appropriate. For, if the *debakame* phenomenon concerned the creation of an area of sexuality, it was to become a symbol for lust and perversion, broadly denoting "an abnormally lascivious fellow." Shōgakkan's *The Great Japanese Dictionary* (1975) defines *debakame* as "a man who performs a *perverse* action *such as* peeping into a women's bath; more broadly, a derogatory term for a lustful (*kōshoku-na*) man (my emphases)."

If so, what distinguishes *debakame-shugi* (or, voyeurism) from the traditional forms of "peeping" such as *kaimami* (a mere glimpse: occasional glimpses that princes and courtiers obtained of the courtly ladies who were enclosed by curtains and screens) is the ontological status the former gives to one who peeps.[19] While with *kaimami* the violation of the taboo is basically contingent, an act of *debakame* reveals the essential feature of the viewer. Kashiwagi in *The Tale of Genji* accidentally catches a glimpse of the rather incautious Third Princess, which leads to their fatal unforgiven affair. The act, if it can be explained from his fate, cannot be attributed to his physical or mental constitution. In contrast to such a construction of desire, an act of voyeurism is something that a voyeur by nature cannot do without. He is made to commit this act of perversion since it is an innate (and possibly hereditary) feature he possesses. In the modern Japanese context, such an ontological status is metaphorized by the buck teeth of the first voyeur.[20] Voyeurism (and perversion in general) is a feature of perverts' selves that they are born with, and that they cannot abandon as long as they live.

Such actually is the common feature of the concept of the "sexual" phenomena. For instance, Weeks writes concerning the sexological theory of onanism: "[Masturbation] determined what sort of person you were. Desire was a dangerous force which pre-existed the individual, wracking his feeble body with fantasies and distractions which threatened his individuality and sanity" (66).[21]

The peeping of a voyeur is an essential, not contingent, act. Voyeuristic desire determines his whole existence. Interestingly, the essentialization of voyeurism is in parallel with the essentialization of female nudity: a naked body of a woman is now considered *essentially* erotic, whereas, in reality, its "essence" takes form only through the essential gaze of a voyeur. These two forms of essentialization, however, took place almost simultaneously.

By the same token, Don Juan is *essentially* a seducer and debauchee since his lust is built in his nature. This is why Gendarme de Bévotte repeatedly evokes metaphors of "nature" and "instinct" in his treatise on Don Juanism: "Don Juanism is an *innate instinct*"; "Don Juan has answered and attacked religion and its dogmas in the name of *nature*" (8); "Egoism is merely a *natural* exercise of his force"; "Therefore, he is cruel out of not so much intention as *instinct*" (10; emphases are mine). For Gendarme de Bévotte, precisely because Don Juanism is human *nature*, but not a cultural construct, a comparativist should be able to find it universally, and therefore, to compare its expressions. For "Don Juan seeks happiness in love, which is an end common to *all* males" (12; emphasis mine).

The Emergence of a Sexual Life

In such a manner, "sexuality" or *sei* emerged as a sign foregrounding concepts of privacy, physical and physiological constitution, morality, delinquency, nature, mental disorder, perversion, and so forth, in the discursive practice of sexology and naturalistic literature. Sexuality was a conceptual framework that came into being as a specific significative constellation, hence as a historical construct, around the turn of the century. What we have here is not a *shift* in the paradigm of sexuality, but exactly the *creation* of it.

What took place together with the emergence of sexological writings and naturalism, however, is commonly described as sexuality altering its previous form. By virtue of this conceptualization, sexuality is given a stable existence. Karatani, as I quoted above, writes about its new form rendered possible by the confessional mode of I-novels. My contention is that sexuality per se emerged for the first time exactly in such a form.

In this sense, I do not agree with Weeks when he speaks of the culturally mediated forms of sexuality springing forth from the foundation of a fixed physiological condition: "We know that sex is a vehicle for the expression of a variety of social experiences: of morality, duty, work, habit, tension, release, friendship, romance, love, protection, pleasure, utility, power, and sexual difference. Its very plasticity is the source of its historical significance. Sexual behavior would transparently not be possible without physiological sources, but physiology does not supply motives, passion, object choice or identity. These come from 'somewhere else,' the domains of social relations and psychic conflict" (122). So arguing, however, Weeks gives an ontological status to the concept of "sex," which serves as "the expression" of, and the basis for, historically changing significances. The latter, in turn, must theoretically include, say, sexual ideologies of Edo Japan, when, if my foregoing arguments are valid, "sexuality" had not taken shape.

The Japanese reader might feel reservations about "sex" or *sei* functioning as a "vehicle" representing precisely the kind of constellation of significations that Weeks evokes: "morality, duty, work, habit, tension, release, friendship, romance, love, protection, pleasure, utility, power, and sexual difference." In the third chapter, we saw that "love" and "morality" in Edo Japan were two different agenda, whereas they were part of the same package in the Western romantic love ideology. We also found that the association of friendship involved in the "sexual" arena in the modern European literature was absent in Edo literature. These observations suggests that the constellation that Weeks roughly names "sex," making it stand for "sexual" phenomena, is untenable in the Japanese context. There is, then, no reason to assume, and to try to see, in premodern Japan, such a constellation as existing only in an incomplete fashion, allegedly lacking in some important aspects. It was, in fact, simply not there. In my view, it is not that "sex" is a vehicle of social experiences, omnipresent itself, and representing the structure of different cultures in a varied manner. "Sex" is a social experience par excellence that may or may not be found in a certain culture.

Of course, Weeks's arguments do not take into account the Japanese experience, or the transcivilizational comparative scheme of sexuality. However, the historicization of the concept of "sex" and "sexuality" in premodern Japanese culture, which I attempted above, leads us to regard with suspicion Weeks's formula of "a change brought to the earlier form of [ontologically unquestionable] sexuality by sexological discourse." If "sexuality" as a system of signs had not existed before the nineteenth century, what would legitimatize Weeks's concept of changing (but not emerging) sexuality, other than the metaphysical belief in the ubiquity of the phenomenon of "sexuality"?

Weeks does question the essentialist bent of the sexologists, namely, the idea that sexual desire is unquestionably out there, being central to human nature, by pointing to the fact that "we are no more able than those 'best authorities' [sexologists] were to define its ultimate essence" (80). However, by assuming the genealogy of sexuality, that is, by tracing the course of the changing signification from Plato and Aristotle, via St. Augustine, a Plymouth Puritan, and the eighteenth-century moralists, finally to Darwin and the modern sexologists (80), Weeks endorses the out-there-ness of "sexual phenomena," which take various historical forms but remain essentially identical. In the last instance, his is an essentialist theory that, in spite of the difficulty of definition, the ultimate essence of sexuality, that is, something that can be defined, traced down, and pinpointed somehow, really exists, forming an undoubted stream of human phenomena.

I do not question the "plasticity" of sexuality (or, "sex" in the modern sense) that Weeks evokes. Nonetheless, when we speak of its "plasticity," we have already made a step forward toward essentializing and universalizing "sexuality." This danger is all the more imminent when a transcultural comparison is pursued. By seeing a certain cultural phenomenon as an expression of "sexuality," which is highly plastic and which can take quite a different form, we are using the concept of "sexuality" as a neutral, scientific category representing a more or less static human physiological condition. Such exactly is the view in Western sexology of the nature of "sexuality."

Conversely, I argue that "sexuality" is historical just as medicine, biology, psychology, and the boundaries that cut them apart are historical. Our task, therefore, is neither to reduce the biological-physiological to the social-ideological, nor to reduce the social to the biological, nor even to create an accurate map in order to distinguish the biological from the social. It is this very distinction that I insist we problematize, that is, the complementary concepts of the ideally biological and the purely social, of which any physical phenomenon is a certain mixture. Modern biology and medicine have created such a scheme and a boundary. They have enabled the existence of the categories (the biological and the social), through the fissure of which could emerge the biological body and sexuality.

In other words, not only is the way sexuality was mapped historicizable, but also the map itself is historical. Failing to historicize the map, Weeks, in spite of his usual insights into "sexual" phenomena, ultimately affirms a humanist ideology. Initially, he undermines it in the following way: "The very concept of sexuality as biological necessity becomes possible, it has been argued, because of the new concept of man emerging by the eighteenth century, when human beings came to be interpreted as knowing subjects, and, at the same time, objects of their own knowledge" (121). But the succeeding passage reveals his embrace of humanist values: "A rejection of the enticing model of the bourgeois individual in all 'his' world-making glory should not necessarily involve an abandonment of what we have come to regard as 'humanist values.' Love, solidarity, trust, warmth are not inconsequential qualities; they are fundamental to the 'good life' on any interpretation. But it is dangerous to base these on a supposedly fixed, continuous and eternal, human nature" (121).

I fully sympathize with Weeks's proposal not to base "humanist values" on a "fixed, continuous and eternal, human nature." And I agree that "love" was, is, and can be necessary for the "good life" of human beings at some historical points in certain areas of the world. But I hesitate to think that "love" is a fundamental category, or is "consequential on any interpretation." It is true that Weeks disavows the continuity of "fixed, eternal human nature," from which traditional humanism derived the eternal value of "love" and the automatic relationship between human nature and love. However, he refuses to problematize "love." Then, "love" becomes an eternal value. Such an idea entails a belief that "love" or what may be translated as "love" represents what is humanly consequential beyond sociolinguistic and historical boundaries, a theory of which I made an extensive critique in chapter 2. Weeks thus valorizes the ahistoricism of humanism in the final instance.

We may return here to Searle's distinction between "a brute fact" and "an institutional fact." My foregoing arguments suggest that what may appear to be the statements of "brute facts" such as "Don Juan chases women" (Guillén) or "Don Juan loves" (Etiemble) are "in fact" what Searle calls "institutional facts." So are even statements like "Snow is falling," or "Water is boiling," if, as I tried to demonstrate in chapter 2, "snow" and "water" are not natural but cultural categories. The distinction between brute and institutional facts now appears ambivalent. Searle would consider sexual phenomena brute facts because they are "physiological and psychological" realities, that is, because they are "natural." We have established that sexuality is an ideological construct, defined by modern medicine, hereditism, sexology, criminology, naturalism, and so forth. "Kametarō was *debakame*, a sexually active man" is a fact that is only culturally, ideologically, and institutionally established. With the distinction between brute and institutional facts thus becoming fuzzy and pointless, an appeal to "nature" or "natural phenomena" does not confer on any entity ontological stability.

Yet my theory that "sexuality" is a historical, and hence contingent, category, may bring forth a serious charge against my own preceding arguments, namely, that in the analyses on the formation of "love," "lust," and "sexuality" in Meiji Japan, I myself have resorted to the concept of the sexual. By differentiating sexuality in premodern Japan and modern sexological discourse, by comparing (and refusing to identify) Don Juan and *iro-otoko* equally as "sexual personages," and by bringing into this study themes of desire, love, passion, reproduction, eroticism, and so on, have I not depended on the paradigm whose name is "sexuality (*sei*)"?

The answer to this charge would be in the affirmative. Just as the novelist Futabatei who criticized Tolstoy's dualistic conception of sexual love was not free from the dichotomous structure itself once he learned it, I, as a scholar who speaks modern Japanese, and whose subjectivity has been determined by contemporary Japanese culture, am not free from the modern paradigm that enables me to articulate both Don Juanism and *kōshoku* as "sexual phenomena." I offer feeble resistance by historicizing the concept, an attempt that, however, does not allow me to escape this trap.

Nor did Ōgai elude the trap. My earlier observations concerning the paradigm of "sexuality" formulated as a modern discourse locate *Vita Sexualis* within the boundary of naturalist literature in spite of the author's and the later critics' claim to the contrary. One of the major polemics of *Vita Sexualis* was, as we have seen, that it took a calm, suppressed attitude toward sexuality while then fashionable naturalist writings described a sexual aspect of a personal life as the essence of it. Kawamura Keikichi expresses his dissatisfaction with Ōgai's pretense as a show of hypocrisy ("Mori Ōgai's View" 8–9). Hasegawa Izumi defends it, evaluating it as part of the novelist's polemics against naturalism (96–97). Be it hypocrisy or a legitimate polemics, Ōgai attempted to de-pathologize himself. By de-pathologizing, however, the doctor-writer ironically subsumed himself in the paradigm, from which naturalism also spoke, namely, a place where sexuality was potential pathology.

Nonetheless, the view taken by Ōgai in *Vita Sexualis* and reiterated by later critics was that Ōgai demonstrated a profound difference from the naturalists in the way he saw sexual desire even if the subject matter was identical. Such a view endorses a positivist-objectivist realism: sexuality is out there, which is only subsequently observed, analyzed, described, and reacted to, in varied manners. Ōgai is considered to have assumed a neutral, scientific perspective concerning sexuality, while naturalists merely showed erotomaniac interest in it. In my opinion, just the converse took place: it is the naturalistic gaze that caused sexuality to emerge as a private, internal space. It is also the medico-scientific gaze that saw sexuality as a potential perversion that let it emerge. It is, in short, the gaze, not the object, that crystallized what was termed "sexuality." In this sense, this gaze was shared by Ōgai, Futabatei, and the naturalists alike. After the introduction of the concept of "vita sexualis," sexuality has entrapped everyone, including the author of this study, who lives the paradigm where the sexual is a meaningful category.

Don Juan as a Sexual Pervert Enters

In this chapter we have examined a new conception that inaugurated the new meaning of "lust" by virtue of the dichotomy of spiritual love and carnal desire, and that, therefore, reduced *iro-otoko* to a man of lust. It was now systematized by sexology. Sexological discourse, however, reinforced the dichotomy in a slightly different way. With sexology, *iro-otoko*, who had turned into Don Juan in his signification, further changed from an epitome of immorality to one of perversion. The dichotomy of spiritual love/ carnal lust was grafted onto that of normal sexuality/abnormal perversion.[22] Exit the libertine; enter the pervert.

Accordingly, *kōshoku* was given a sexological connotation, too. The Japanese translation of *Psychopathia Sexualis* (1913) identifies *kōshoku* as a morbid, excessive sexual desire. It is now a disease:

> Hyperaesthesia (increased desire, satyriasis). In this state there is an abnormally increased impressionability of the vita sexualis to organic, psychical and sensory stimuli (abnormally intense libido, lustfulness, lasciviousness [rendered *kōshoku* in the Japanese translation]). The stimulus may be central (nymphomania, satyriasis) or peripheral, functional or organic. (Krafft-Ebing 47)

We witness here the moment when *kōshoku* was equated with "abnormally intense libido, lustfulness, lasciviousness." The positive abundance implied in *kōshoku* was reduced not only to an abnormal excess, but also to a disease, or erotomania, a problem of a scientific, rather than moral, order. *Kōshoku* became a sexological notion.

At this point, the common Edo sense of passion that love was something one should seek in a prostitute, but not in a wife, was reversed and denigrated.[23] A man with an Edo ideology of love became pathological: "[T]here are men to whom sexual contact with their virtuous wives does not supply the necessary stimulus for an erection, but in whom it occurs when the act is attempted with a prostitute, or in the form of some unnatural sexual act" (Krafft-Ebing 45). The system of sexuality adopted by Japanese society that institutionalized extramarital relationships was now opposed to morality. It became a moral issue that could offend "virtuous wives." This judgment, however, was justified on a scientific ground: that it was an "*unnatural* sexual act." Now, a hunt of women beyond the marital bond was not only an immoral act, but also a certain form of perversion.

It is, then, significant that the following observation is added to the above quotation:

> Woman-chasers [*die Schürzenjäger*], or Don Juans, represent a subsequent stage, whose entire existence is

devoted to the indiscriminate satisfaction of their carnal desire, and who, their moral sense being obstructed, do not avoid seduction or adultery, nor do they even shy away from incest. (62; translation mine; pagination refers to the German original)

A chaser of women (*der Schürzenjäger*),[24] or Don Juan, seduces them, defying marital codes and sexual taboos, exactly because he is a mentally sick pervert with an insufficient sense of morality. Hence, the Foucauldian vision of Don Juan:

> Here [in the surging infractions against the legislation or morality pertaining to marriage and the family, and offenses against the regularity of a natural function of sexuality] we have a likely reason, among others, for the prestige of Don Juan, which three centuries have not erased. Underneath the great violator of the rules of marriage—stealer of wives, seducer of virgins, the shame of families, and an insult to husbands and fathers—another personage can be glimpsed: the individual driven, in spite of himself, by the somber madness of sex. Underneath the libertine, the *pervert*. (*History of Sexuality: An Introduction* 39–40; my emphasis)

Thus, according to Foucault, Don Juan emerged as an unnatural pervert, defying "lawful" marriage and "normal" desire. I do not see, though, with Foucault, "a likely reason for the prestige of Don Juan for the duration of three centuries" purely in his challenge to the marital and sexual order. Don Juan the pervert (in the sense of the degenerate) emerged with the advent of the new configuration of normality, morality, and sexuality prescribed by the sexological worldview that was opened sometime around the turn of the century. Don Juan underwent a drastic shift from a trickster via a playboy, an atheist, an outlaw, a libertine, to a madman. We do not find a continuous tradition of three centuries.

Now, Krafft-Ebing's term *"der Schürzenjäger"* reminds us of Guillén's definition of Don Juan: "an eternal woman-chaser." If, however, Guillén proposes the definition as a universal type which transcends historical and geographical specificity, Krafft-Ebing's *Schürzenjäger* is a newcomer, who chases because of the newly formulated "sexual" problem of "satyriasis." In this paradigm, Don Juan is a specific kind of the mentally sick, that is, a man who hunts women through suffering from "hyperaesthesia." As a matter of fact, the sexologist Forel, who follows Krafft-Ebing's classificatory system, has this explanation of "hyperaesthesia," combining it with Don Juanism: "Sexual hyperaesthesia, or the exaggeration of the sexual appetite: 'This anomaly may be congenital, for example, in the sexual paradoxy of children. Every one knows Don Juans and Messalinas with their insatiable appetites. These types of sexual hyperaesthesia are certainly less frequent and more abnormal in women than in men, but the intensity is as great or greater' " (*Sexual Question* 225).

We have here "a woman-chaser," driven by hyperaesthesia, or an abnormal desire, which sexological discourse has presented us. If woman-chasing is now considered a sexologically defined hyperaesthesia, it is clear that we have to differentiate it from *kōshoku* or *iro-gonomi*. For *kōshoku* is abundance, a bliss, a play, but not a disease. It did not necessarily defy the "legislation or morality pertaining to marriage and the family" or offend "the regularity of a natural function of sexuality." The twentieth-century version of Western Don Juanism as satyriasis thus calls into question its comparison with *kōshoku*. "A chase after women" can no more serve as a neutral, universal point of reference for Don Juans than "love" or "lust," but only as a historically specific one.

Nor can "active sexuality" be a comparative axis, which in the sexological system merely means incipient "hyperaesthesia." If in the emerging conceptual framework of "sexuality," a hyperenergetic sexual activity is nothing more than a potential perversion, where do we find a place for *iro-otoko* in this field of signification? Paradoxically, by defining *iro-*

otoko as a "sexually active man," so virile as to chase women who are not tied to him with a conjugal bond, a comparativist turns *iro-otoko* into a potential pervert, hence into a personage other than *iro-otoko*, a Foucaudian Don Juan. At this point, a claim to the category "sexuality," which has appeared an ultimate ground for comparison of Don Juan and *iro-otoko*, collapses. Our search for a comparative axis of Don Juans, East/West, from "love" via "lust" to "sexuality" thus exhausted in vain, we bid farewell to a "Japanese Don Juan."

5   politics of comparative literature

. . . the irrepressible human need for reducing the diverse to one.

—Henry Remak, *"Comparative Literature at the Crossroads"*

*What is that fear which makes you seek beyond all boundaries,
ruptures, shifts, and divisions, the great historico-transcendental
destiny of the Occident?*

—*Michel Foucault*, The Archaeology of Knowledge

"Love" and Its Connection with Humanism, Liberal Democracy, and Universalism

In the preceding three chapters, I attempted to demystify three concepts: love, lust, and sexuality, more or less regarded as basic features of human nature, and hence, likely candidates as points of reference for comparing Don Juans East/West. My intention has been to demonstrate that these categories, normally conceived to be so essential, universal, and abstract as to be applicable to non-Western cultures, are actually socioculturally and historically specific to the (modern) West. Consequently, an act of comparing Don Juan and

155

an Eastern Don Juan, say, a Japanese *iro-otoko*, is that of sub-suming the latter to the former in the name of common "humanity."

It is the humanist belief in a universal essence of human nature that has encouraged transcivilizational comparisons. Gendarme de Bévotte displayed this connection of universalism and humanism along the axis of Don Juan: "Don Juanism is inherent in human nature: the ancients knew it as much as the moderns, and non-European civilizations do not ignore it at all" (2). Since Don Juanism is "human," it is universal, and, consequently, it can be found among "les civilisations extra-europeenes."

It is, however, not clear at all what is the basis for the theory which Gendarme de Bévotte takes for granted, that the non-European civilizations have known "Don Juanism." Even up to this date, there has not been a global study of "Don Juans," by either an anthropologist or a comparativist, sufficiently systematic and comprehensive to confirm Gendarme de Bévotte's theorem. I have so far argued to undermine it. In any case, it remains, at best, an unfounded hypothesis.

As a matter of fact, Don Juanism may not be a particularly happy agenda for such a humanist/universalist belief. Gendarme de Bévotte himself displays an ambiguous attitude toward Don Juanism. Admittedly, his basic theory is that Don Juanism is naturally human and innate: "Don Juanism is so profoundly human and so widespread since love is after all the essential law of life. . . . Don Juanism is an innate instinct, primitively normal" (8). Then, why has Don Juan been an antihero? The French critic's idea is that Don Juan has merely been led astray by the religion, the marital system, and the moralism of the society. However, Gendarme de Bévotte then switches his attitude and directly stigmatizes Don Juanism, writing: "Don Juan's virility denaturalizes love" (9). In this statement, it is Don Juanism itself that is the unnatural, which in turn impairs love, the natural. Hence, his comment that "Don Juan has a perverse curiosity" (9).

Such an ambiguity leads Gendarme de Bévotte to another contradiction concerning Don Juan's ability to love. At one point he sees the essential character of Don Juan in his desire to love: "Don Juan has no other goal in life than to love. To love is his vocation. He reduces all his actions and thoughts to love" (8). At another, he refuses Don Juan the title of lover: "He cannot love: he would yield to a different realm" (10).

Thus, Don Juanism, as Gendarme de Bévotte conceives it, proves to be contradictory grounds for a comparison on the basis of a claim to "humanity": for comparison of Don Juans East/West do we turn to "lovers" or "nonlovers"? The legitimacy of the standard for comparison, however, does not appear to constitute a major problem for Gendarme de Bévotte. For, after all, as a comparativist of the French school, he does not allow himself such a comparison anyway. The French comparativist can, with a clear conscience, dismiss the issue of Don Juanism, which is supposed to concern all humanity, after a brief discussion in the introduction that occupies less than a tenth of the whole book, the project of writing a history of Western Don Juans.

Conversely, concern with such an issue haunts a critic like Etiemble, who defended the transcivilizational comparison of the American school. It is, then, significant that Etiemble quite simplistically defined Don Juan as "an eternal lover." For, "love" apparently (so is it normally claimed) entails far less ambiguity as to its universality than "nonlove" or "unnatural passion." If for Etiemble "comparative literature is humanism" (the title of a chapter from *The Crisis in Comparative Literature*), and is a means to achieve cosmopolitanism, a comparison of Don Juans must reveal something about the universal human essence, which is probably better represented by "love" than "a different realm," be it perverse curiosity, lust, or physical pleasure.

In fact, it is easy to find in the discourse on "love" the identification of this concept with an unquestionably and universally human feature. In the second chapter I traced the evolution of signifiers in modern Japanese representing "love," many of which utilize the Chinese character *ai*. Matsushita Teizō in his *The Chinese Word "Ai" and Its Compounds* explains the reason: "That its [of the signifier *ai*] connection with the signified of 'love' is based on the universally human and natural sentiment, and that it has served as a momentum to reconsider a human relationship in creating a more democratic, less hierarchial one; these are the reasons why the character has been popular as regards its meaning" (261).

It is significant that Matsushita invokes the notions of "universal," "human," "natural," and "democratic" in one breath in speaking of "love." Throughout this book I have tried to discover certain kinds of universalism and humanism innate in the discipline of comparative literature. In chapters 1 and 2, I discussed the relationship between these beliefs and the notion of "love." In chapter 4, I examined some of the problems involved in the concept of "nature." We now see here another facet of the universalist ideology: "democracy."

A connection between the concept of "love" and that of "democracy" can quite frequently be encountered. A respectable Saikaku scholar, Teruoka Yasutaka, attributes the romantic relationships of a suffragette, Hiratsuka Raichō, who, he thinks, typically resisted feudal morality in favor of the democratization of the society during the Taishō period (1912–1926). Elsewhere, he ascribes the passions of a woman poet, Yosano Akiko, to the same. He polemically argues that such liberation in love was possible given only the ideals of Taishō democracy, with which "a long-awaited goal of democratization" since early Meiji was finally achieved (*Love and Sex* 226).

While it is beyond doubt that the idea of democracy which spread widely in the Taishō period played an immense role in improving, or demolishing, the semifeudal, oppressive human relationships of the time, we should examine the ideological content of "democracy" before declaring it a universal good. The term "Taishō democracy" refers to the popular political movement to obtain suffrage, civil rights and freedom, pursued for about two decades after the end of Russo-Japanese War (1905). It arose in direct response to the proposed peace treaty with Russia, which appeared to the majority of the nation to be humiliating and unworthy of the significant victories won in some of the battles. The colonization of Korea and Manchuria was conceived as a natural goal of the Japanese Empire, for the sake of which the war with Russia was manifestly fought. During this period it was largely felt that the reform of the nation to accomplish modernization-Westernization was more or less completed. Japan was now obliged to expand. The masses accused the oligarchical government of being infirm in this policy. "Democratic" government was considered necessary in order to fully pursue the colonialistic scheme.

Democracy not only did not contradict stronger government or colonial expansion, but was, on the contrary, instrumental to them. Hence, a writer of the day, Maruyama Toranosuke, commented that a slavish, submissive people could not serve the expanding nation, and that only the nation that had rational patriotism and a sense of obligation and honor could achieve this goal (*On Suffrage* 34; qtd. in Matsuo 5). Suffrage and, consequently, democracy were sought so that the entire nation might be able to participate in the decision-making, which would promote the colonialistic move toward other Asian countries. Taishō Democracy was, at least initially, imperialistic in its intention. As late as 1917, a politician from the city of Tottori declared in a speech that his political position represented, domestically, democracy (*minpon shugi*) and, diplomatically, "human imperialism" (qtd. in Matsuo 105). He explains the weird expression of "humanitarian imperialism (*jindō teki teikoku shugi*)" as being used in opposition to "aggressive imperialism (*shinryaku teki teikoku shugi*)." Democracy may not necessarily be opposed to imperialism, although it is normally considered to be antithetical to it.[1]

Such an observation about the ideological formulation of democracy in Taishō political movements leads us to question the all-too-easily presumed idea that democracy is *universally* good since it is *essentially* a human (and humane) system. This idea is, however, quite as widespread as the idea that (romantic) love is a universal phenomenon. It is, then, perhaps not a coincidence that many a writer has associated (romantic) love with democratic beliefs. For both are important tenets of humanism and universalism.[2]

It is not, however, my intention to altogether deny the value of democracy, either the Taishō Japanese, the American, or the socialist version of it.[3] I am simply questioning the ostensible eternity, the unquestionable value, and the ubiquity alluringly attributed to the given concept, and the metaphysical gesture implied in such a belief.

If, in terms of politics, the Taishō Democratic Movement featured a campaign calling for suffrage that was championed by Yoshino Sakuzō's theory of *Minpon shugi* (Democracy), its major proponents in terms of culture were the Tolstoyan "Birch Tree School" of literati and the group of philosophers known as the "Humanists" (*kyōyō shugi sha*). A philosopher, Abe Jirō, was a representative figure among the latter. He drew his system of moral philosophy mainly from German idealist philosophers such as Immanuel Kant and, especially, Theodor Lipps, a representative of the doctrine of "personalism," which exercised a considerable influence on Taishō Japanese thinkers in general. Abe deserves attention here for his *The Art and Society of the Tokugawa Period*, a lengthy treatise on Edo popular culture, particularly on its central principle of sexuality, *kōshoku*, in light of its comparison with Western love.

The book starts with the impression Abe received when he happened to see some *ukiyoe* (woodblock prints) by Utamaro and Sharaku at the Louvre. He relates the experience as a shift from an initial joy at finding native art exhibited on a par with the great achievements of European art, to a subsequent sense of shame. He attributes this shame to his suspicion as to whether the Japanese woodblock prints efflorescing with sensual delight contained elements of self-consciousness and will:

> Is it not that a play of petty wits and ironies which was diverted before accomplishing an ultimate goal, and a consciously resistant *kōshoku*, which Edo citizens could not but indulge themselves in even when they expected a censuring voice—is it not that these factors spoiled the purity of talent and sensuality, thus diverting Edo art away from the mainstream of art? (14)

His main dissatisfaction with Edo art consists in his conception of it as being too vulgarly "sensual." In this Abe shares an opinion with such Meiji writers as Kitamura Tōkoku. Extending the dichotomous notion of spiritual love versus carnal lust that Meiji romantics opened up, the Taishō philosopher theorizes that the sexual life must be given a moral ground by sublimating (*erheben*) the biological instinct into the idea (*Idee*) of love (*ren'ai*), which foregrounds moral affection, sacrifice, and spiritual perfection (126). In another essay, he equates carnal union with sheer prostitution, which, incidentally, was a major mode of (masculine) sexual life in Edo city life: "Another point of contact where a man and a woman seek each other is a carnal and sensual desire. . . . However, if they make a bond in this point, it is only a prostitutional relationship. I do not think they are at the stage of association as two personalities" (*Personalism* 412–13). The carnal, that is, prostitutional, element of a sexual relationship should be overcome by spiritual and moral features.

Thus, Taishō liberal humanists perfected the importation of the Western paradigm of love in modern Japan. As we have earlier seen, it had started around 1890 with the efforts of early Meiji Christian writers such as Iwamoto Yoshiharu and Kitamura Tōkoku to explore a notion of love that was based on the distinction between spiritual love and carnal desire. They also opened up the field of signification where love was a moral achievement. Somewhat later the sexological discourse added to the new paradigm of romantic love dimensions of perversion, insanity, and delinquency. Subsequently, the Taishō humanists made "love" a imperative in

ethics, an achievement of free "personalities," or moral individuals (jinkaku; an editor of Abe's Personalism [jinkaku
shugi] paraphrases jinkaku as "an absolutely free, sacred being, chastened and elevated from the beastly existence"
[486]). "Love" became an important tenet in their humanistic philosophical system, which combined individualism
and spiritualism.[4]

Now, to add one more twist to the premodern paradigm of sexuality, Abe associated this quest for the spiritual and the moral in the sexual field with the belief in
universalism. That Edo art is amusing but not elevating, and
that Edo sexuality is lascivious but not moralizing, is due, according to Abe, to the parochial character of Edo culture.
There were two major features in the Edo system of sexuality that caused the culture to degenerate. One was licensed
prostitution; the other was a Confucian morality whose foremost imperative was to "produce an heir." Only within the
boundary of this imperative, he insists, was Edo Confucian-
ism ascetic. However, he further reasons that, as the Confucian ideology conceived sexuality as an expression of physical
desire and did not realize its spiritual element, it was easily
wedded to the first feature of prostitutional sexuality: "[Con-
fucian asceticism ultimately leads to] the witty but perverse
debauchery which is mitigated by the teaching of 'producing an heir.' It cannot have enough spirituality even to coop-
erate with an impulse to aestheticize sexual desire" (137).

While I agree with his insight about the complicity of
Confucian asceticism and the system of sanctioned prostitution, I do not share his opinion that it was the absence of
spiritualization that was at stake. My protest is directed not
so much against his preference for spiritual and moral love
over physical desire, as against his dualistic conception of
sexuality itself, which, as I attempted to demonstrate in
chapter 4, is a historical construct. In this sense, Abe is arguing doubly as a humanist-moralist, that is to say, first, in
his value judgment concerning the spirit/body dichotomy
(superiority of the former over the latter), and secondly, in
this Cartesian conceptual division per se.

Nevertheless, Abe seems to be firm about his epistemological and axiological position which he paraphrases as "universal." Hence, his critique of Edo culture and its sexual paradigm on the ground that it "withered universal humanity." Is it, however, so obvious as Abe might have us think that the paradigm of sexuality foregrounding morality and spirituality is more universal? Or, even if it is, is the universal so self-evidently more important than the parochial?

We may remember the anthropologist Linton's comment, which was quoted in chapter 1, that from the scholarly point of view the common elements are more significant than the eye-catching differences. The preference for the universal seems to be the acknowledged choice of value in the modern academic disciplines. This judgment, in turn, is endorsed by the belief that the universal is represented by a higher civilization.

Such a framework is not challenged even by scholars engaged in the study of more marginal cultures. For instance, one of the leading scholars of Eskimo cultures in the world, Miyaoka Osahito, to whom I largely owe insights on their languages, also appears to be trapped in this idea, namely, the idea that a local paradigm (for instance, the Eskimo articulation of "snow") expresses a limited, hence inferior, interest:

> Within a vocabulary of a certain language, there are areas where relatively abundant words are available, rendering it possible to make subtle distinctions (for instance, Eskimo "snow"). There are also areas where only a very rough expression can be made.
>
> The mapping of these areas and the "density" of the vocabulary are different from language to language. An imbalance of the density is considerable in the languages of uncivilized or semicivilized races, which have not arrived at the stage to take a universal interest in the world surrounding them and in the internal world. (*Languages* 2)

The reader is led to believe that the intricate vocabulary for snow of the Eskimo language is an "unnatural" imbalance.

It reflects their "uncivilized or semicivilized" status as races miserably struggling with the physical world. The universal, the civilized, the internal, are unquestionably enshrined as superior. The uncivilized-physical/civilized-internal dichotomy is naturally reread into, and fortified by, the carnality/spirituality dichotomy. However, what is the basis for the judgment that the Eskimo method of articulating "snow" is more parochial, less universal, and therefore, less civilized? What is the ground for judging that the Eskimo system of vocabulary is "unbalanced" (in comparison with English, Russian, or Japanese)? Why can we say that having only one word for "snow" is more balanced and normal than having dozens of them for it? The question becomes all the more serious if the English articulation of "snow," as we examined in chapter 2, is not only different from the Eskimo articulation, but also from the Japanese and the Chinese. Is it not that every language possesses a different way of segmentation that, nonetheless, somewhat overlaps the English "snow"? Yet the Eskimo paradigm is conceived as irregular simply because of its "uncivilized" condition.

Tsvetan Todorov relativizes the civilized/barbarian dichotomy, reducing it to linguistic difference: "[E]ach of us is the other's barbarian, to become such a thing, one need only speak a language of which that other is ignorant" (*Conquest* 190). A paradigm different from one's own is always the more parochial while one's own is more universal.

Universalism as Disguised Eurocentrism

However, Todorov's theorem should in no way render barbarism a totally relative concept. The hierarchization of the two different paradigms into the civilized/uncivilized, and therefore more universal/more parochial, pair is a rereading of a difference of a language into a difference deriving from other orders, some of which may include: imperialist forces that create the discourse of barbarity concerning their colonies, modern humanism that favors the universal over the parochial and the internal over the external, and industrialism that supports ever higher civilization and development. One's own linguistic paradigm can be barbarian according to these political conditions. This is why Abe dismissed his own cultural heritage as less universal. The dismissal testifies to the "colonization" of modern Japanese culture when intellectuals had to speak in the Western paradigm. Or it may also be argued that for Abe, who spoke from the cultural tradition of German idealist and moralist philosophy, Lippsean personalism, and Tolstoyan humanism, Edo popular culture was already a paradigm different from his own. At any rate, too often it is European cultural tenets that are given the honorary title of being universal, tacitly to perpetuate Eurocentric presuppositions. Such Eurocentrism is contingent not so much upon linguistic difference as the politico-economic history of the modern world.

Abe makes the following distinction between the Edo system of sexuality and the Western "culture of love," characterizing the former as "aestheticization of sexual life," the latter as "moralization" of it:

> I strictly distinguish "aestheticization" of the sexual life, which we have examined as a force of cultural production of the pleasure quarters in the Tokugawa period, from the moralization of the sexual life through "love," and the aestheticization which is realized through this moralization. . . . It would not be an exaggeration to say that the aestheticization [through moralization] of the sexual life in this sense emerged in Japan for the first time after the Meiji Reformation. (*Art and Society* 45–46)

I am not particularly concerned with his distinction itself, however schematic it may be. What I object to is his absolute valorization of the Western sexual paradigm. His ideal of moral love did not emerge in Japanese culture for two thousand years, but was achieved when it awoke to Western cultural tenets after the onset of Westernization in the Meiji period. The Japanese moralist thus stigmatizes the entire premodern history of Japan, which finally and happily turned "human" through access to the Western paradigm. Abe makes his dichotomous scheme clearer when he specifies in the passage that follows that "the latter [moralization of the sexual life] is an idea traditionally cherished by Western art." He also writes that virgin worship and the ideal of refusing to violate one's lover are the purest, if not the sole, form of moral love. These are ideas far more rooted in European sexual ideology. This leads to Abe's enthusiasm about the radical asceticism proposed in Tolstoy's *The Kreutzer Sonata*, which, incidentally, as we saw in chapter 3, Futabatei argues to be in complete contradiction with the paradigm of sexuality of Edo Japanese culture. Abe argues: "Tolstoy's teaching of absolute chastity is qualified for this [universality as an ideal]. . . . The eternal ideal can function as a force to purify present sexual life in infinitely various degrees and nuances. Conversely, the teaching to 'produce an heir' [his characterization of the Confucian sexual ideology] does not contain such universality" (*Art and Society* 136–37).

I need to reconfirm here, though, that the aim of my analysis in this section is not to revalorize the Edo system of sexuality, which was, to be sure, irrevocably oppressive and patriarchal. Also, though I seek the roots of Abe's "Eurocentric" ideas in the cultural imperialism that Japan was exposed to after the Meiji Reformation, we should also take note of the imperialistic tone of Abe himself toward other non-Western cultures. He writes about a song of a Korean prostitute which he describes as "a song foreboding national ruin" (21), while he thinks Tokugawa art was full of sensual delights in spite of its problems. He adds that the Korean people need not be pessimistic, though, since they have a *few* splendid paintings in the state museum.

The principle of moralization and purification that, according to Abe, characterizes Western sexuality is universal, and hence human, while that of aestheticization and sensualization peculiar to Edo culture is parochial, and hence distorted. Likewise, to him, it is the couples in Goethe's novels (*Wilhelm Meister's Apprenticeship* and *Elective Affinities*), who in his view demonstrate the sense of purity, morality, and repression of the carnal that represent the universal ideal of love (399–400), but not even those in Chikamatsu with his double suicides, let alone Shunsui, who exclusively depicted the late Edo "libertines."[5] The universal and the superior are Western; the parochial and the inferior are Japanese.

A subtler substitution of the Western for the universal concerning the paradigm of sexuality is observed in a comment by René Etiemble, who speaks for humanism and universalism. First, he cites an example where a common language of sexuality is absent in works from different cultures:

> When exalting a woman's breasts, the [Tamil] author, whoever he was, of those "scandalous" Jeoup'ou-t'ouan compares them to "two eggs freshly out of a hen's belly, which would burst when one pressed down on them," I am afraid he thoroughly discourages the French reader, since the image of "fried eggs, sunny side up," rather than an aphrodisiac would be, to him, an anaphrodisiac. (*Crisis* 51)

However, himself dislodging the example just given, Etiemble then invokes a case where such a common language is available:

> When the Chinese poet evokes love with images of war, siege, strategy, horse and rider, garden and flower stands, shoe and shoe-tree, goat and stake, sea-like movements of mingled lovers, we feel at ease and at home. (51)

From this, he draws the following conclusion:

> Could it be that we are here confronted with what, in the expression of the sentiment of love, corresponds to what must be called human nature? (51)

This conclusion subtly, but inevitably, must imply that the Tamil poet does *not* demonstrate human nature because his vocabulary does not please the French reader (while the Chinese does). Tamil poets do not articulate sexuality as a French reader would. Etiemble sounds as if he were encouraging us to understand and accept the difference. But, then, he turns to the metaphors, comparable to the French ones and comprehensible for the Western readers: war, siege, flower, and other rhetorical expressions. Obviously, he feels at ease here. However, the problem is that he attributes his relief to "human nature." In his conception of love, the Chinese represent human nature precisely because they speak a language of love similar to the French. Then, does the Tamil expression not correspond to "human nature"?

What Etiemble, in this rather careless passage, unwittingly underwrites is the cultural imperialist formulation of "humanity" in which whatever fits the French (and, in large measure, Western) paradigm will be regarded as part of "human nature." Whatever does not will be dismissed silently and hastily as inhuman. Universalism does not necessarily contradict Eurocentrism. In fact, it is often a disguised form of it.

Comparative Literature as a Universalist Discipline

Now, returning to the Japanese philosopher Abe's conception of sexuality, his exhortation of Western sexual ideology as more universal, personal (*jinkaku teki*), moral, and human, is a natural result of his use of the term *ren'ai*, which he defines as "a union based on the admiration for each other's personality" (*Personalism* 414) in accordance to the Western conception. He speaks of the problems of *ren'ai* (love) in the Edo period as an absence of a moralizing, purifying, and sublimating tendency. This is tantamount to a tautology if *ren'ai*, as we saw in chapter 2, is a translation for "love," created in the Meiji period in order to connote the morality and chastity involved in the Western term. What he calls "the culture of love" (*ren'ai bunka*) of Edo sexual life becomes inescapably distorted as it is made to be represented by the Western conception *ren'ai*, or "love," that is to say, by an idea it does not foreground.

The appropriation and stigmatization of the local paradigm is thus closely interrelated with the use of terminology. A programmatic essay by an American comparativist, Henry Remak, is a case in point. He contends, in defense of the American method, that "[t]he sagas of the Vikings and Polynesian sagas of the same period, all dealing with explorations, show remarkable similarities that are bound to shed new light on literature and culture at a certain stage of history" ("Comparative Literature at the Crossroads" 8). What, however, legitimatizes his naming Polynesian narratives "sagas"? Even if those two "sagas" show sufficient similarities, as he claims, to authorize such a comparison, would it bring forth the same result if he decided to use a Polynesian concept as an axis of comparison? What if a comparativist first seeks a counterpart to a Viking version of a Polynesian *ka'ao* ("legend"), and then compares? A transcivilizational comparison is, probably, never reversible. It does not lead to a *tertium comparationis*, in relation to which Polynesian and Viking cultural assets occupy symmetrical positions. A Polynesian's idea about the Viking version of a Maui myth can never be identical to the Western perception of the Polynesian myth using the concept of "saga." By switching an axis of comparison from one civilization to another, and by changing the tool for representation, the results of comparative research will be different. In other words, the conclusion of a comparative project is already somewhat foreseen when an axis has been selected, or more concretely, when a comparativist has chosen to call Polynesian oral stories based on voyages "sagas" of some kind, making a decision to rely on the Western concept. For the resulting analysis will conform to the critical standards developed to understand Viking sagas, but not Polynesian legends.

That Remak does not even give a native term for what he calls a "Polynesian saga" is itself significant. As a matter of fact, there does not appear to exist an independent genre in the Polynesian "literary" tradition that can be termed "saga." Remak is probably referring rather vaguely to the body of orally inherited "myths," "legends," "epics," "songs," and so forth, on the theme of voyages from the Polynesian islands. According to Prof. Nakamoto Nobuyuki of the Tokyo Institute of Foreign Languages, stories or poems about voyages do not constitute a clear-cut, independent genre in Polynesian "literatures."

The concealed presumption of transcivilizational comparisons that explore "sagas" of Northern Europe and Polynesia is that one can speak of both Polynesian and Viking "sagas," since both represent, say, the "universal" experience of a marine adventure. Reversibility of comparison, namely, the legitimacy of starting either from the Polynesian "saga" or the Viking sagas, is, then, expected to be authorized. In fact, however, this is an act of universalizing the parochial (Viking), and of giving it an illusory authority. It is also an act of making the irreversible reversible, that is, of making us believe that a comparison of a saga to a Maui counterpart is identical to that of *ka'ao* to a Viking counterpart. Not only are these two comparisons not identical, but also the latter kind of comparison generally does not take place. Universalism is, then, the substitution of the parochial (the European) for the universal, that is, the imperative to make the European paradigm stand for the whole of humanity.

Such a problem is often silenced by a claim for the neutrality of critical terms. A comparativist, it is held, can transcend the parochiality of the paradigms by making use of more abstract, theoretical terms, which are by nature universal. Remak obviously considers "saga" as a term more or less fulfilling this condition. Similarly, Etiemble demands: "In order to serve our discipline well, it is necessary . . . to endow it, first of all, with a precise vocabulary having a *universalist* meaning" (*Crisis* 41; emphasis mine). Consequently, Etiemble, in order to link Chinese (and other Asian) "novels" with European ones, that is, in order to compare them, resorts to a notion of "the permanent elements of the genre of the 'romance,' those elements without which there can be no novel" (54). He requires that they be distinguished from historical contingencies, namely, "those constituent parts of the genre which result, more or less arbitrarily, from historical circumstances" (54). By shedding the contingent, "the essential" takes shape. By resorting to the notion of "Romance," a comparativist can expect to compare "romances" of the world, one form of which happens to be the European novel. But is there an original, ideal "Romance" purely independent of historical contingencies? Is it not that the moment one chooses to utter "romance," the concept is functioning within the hermeneutic horizons of Western literature and literary criticism?

Such a gesture is, as we discussed in chapter 1, a metaphysical move to seek the origin: "When poetry renounces rhyme, then rhythm, then speech, then the meaning of words, then punctuation, then words, to present itself under the form of isolated letters or groups of consonants which cannot be pronounced and are scattered at random on the page; and when the novel is sold in the form of a sheaf of papers which each reader can shuffle like a deck of cards, the comparative analysis of the structure of poems would permit us, perhaps, to discover the sine qua non qualities of the poem or novel per se" (Etiemble, *Crisis* 55). The original, ideal meaning for Etiemble is something that cannot be "pronounced."

As a matter of fact, "romance" is just another historically specific concept, commonly referring to the medieval tales of adventure and love. René Wellek and Austin Warren even regard a romance and a novel as completely opposing genres: "The novel is realistic; the romance is poetic or epic: we should now call it 'mythic.' . . . The two types, which are polar, indicate the double descent of prose narrative: the novel develops from the lineage of non-fictitious narrative forms. . . . The romance, on the other hand, the continuator of the epic and the medieval romance, may neglect verisimilitude of detail" (*Theory of Literature* 216).

We are not concerned here with the veracity of the statement: whether it is Etiemble or Wellek and Warren who grasp the essence of the "novel" more accurately is not at issue. At stake here are the problematics of the Ur-conceptions examined in chapter 2. The given case also shows that the moment one supposes a certain Ur-concept, it is invariably challenged by its ostensible ramifications and then collapses. Etiemble's expectation to use "romance" as the universal point of reference is immediately challenged by the novel and other forms of narrative, including non-Western ones.

Nonetheless, within the confines of (American) comparative scholarship, there has been a constant effort to find universalist, ultimate meanings. This is not to be wondered at, for one cannot pursue a transcivilizational comparison without such an Ur-concept, so original as to be universally applicable. However, the attempt to locate a central meaning is inevitably accompanied by an act of declaring all other meanings marginal. If "Romance" is a universalist meaning, *monogatari, baihua xiaoshuo, ukiyo zōshi,* and so on,[6] have all to be reduced to the ramified reincarnations of the original "Romance." Likewise, the instant a certain account of the voyage in the Polynesian culture is conceived of as a version of a Viking saga, the former becomes a deviation, the latter an original. The moment *iro-otoko* is conceived as a Japanese Don Juan, *iro-otoko* becomes a "crippled" dwarf in front of the giant, Fatherly figure of Don Juan, who has sired all the other sons.

Ramification envisages pathologization. Abe asks himself: Is Saikaku's *ukiyo zōshi* (a kind of pulp fiction of the Edo period), *The Life of an Amorous Man,* a romance or a novella? Unable to categorize it under either of the rubrics, Abe concludes that it falls somewhere in between these two (authentic, universal) categories. Therefore, it is a failed romance, a "'homunculus' born premature" that ended as a mere collection of short stories, or *Novellenkranz* (*Art and Society* 145).

As soon as one compares, as soon as one conceptualizes "a Japanese Edo romance," *ukiyo zōshi* becomes the more contingent, hence more lame; a romance becomes the more universal, hence, the essential, the normal. Furthermore, as we have seen, the less universal all too easily translates into the less civilized. Often, it can even surreptitiously be reread as "inhuman."

Eugene Eoyang argues in a more comprehensive manner that the application of Western critical terminology to the non-Western is categorically dubious. He ironically argues that a question like "Is there a Chinese tragedy?" should sound absurd if asking why there are no dynastic histories in the West, or why the West has produced no counterpart to the *Shih ching*, is considered pointless (11). If "*Shih ching* of the West" is an absurd frame in which to raise a question, why is "a tragedy of China" usually considered not to be? Why is "an Edo romance" not meaningless, whereas "a German *ukiyo zōshi*" is?

An opinion anticipating Eoyang's was long ago voiced by Posnett. His *Comparative Literature* (1886) expresses a similar doubt about the universality of critical standards, in the period when the discipline of comparative literature did not particularly transcend the boundary of Europe in its application of "cosmopolitanism":

> [U]nless we limit the range to which our criticism shall apply, we may find ourselves applying the standards of the Athenian to the Japanese drama, or those of the Greek lyric to the *Shih King* [sic] of ancient China. Clearly such limitless criticism has done much to obscure all ideas of literary development, and consequently to make the conception of literature the medley we have found it. (12)

Let us take note that Posnett is referring to the application of the standards of Athenian theater to the Japanese drama as something paradigmatically absurd.[7] The force of his arguments, if there is one, derives from the absurdity of the example. Today, however, with (American) comparative literature approving East/West comparisons, the application of the concepts of Athenian tragedy to Japanese drama no longer sounds so unthinkable. The reason for this is probably not that contemporary Westerners have come to know the Japanese drama sufficiently well to negotiate the difference of the standards, but that American comparativism has successfully convinced us that such terms as "tragedy," or the literary standards of the Athenian drama and the Greek lyric, possess universal applicability.

It is not, however, my intention to stigmatize a comparison altogether if it means nothing more than an attempt to find similitudes and differences to and from an unknown or little known signification. A Western reader is free to sense similarities and differences between, say, the genres of *monogatari* (tales or prose narratives of various kinds, often including poems [Miner, *Princeton Companion*]) and "romance," and interpret the Japanese narrative on the basis of that framework. A sign is always open to a possibility of being decoded according to a system different from the one in which it was encoded. Conversely, a sign is destined to be more or less misinterpreted since the above two systems never completely coincide. In this sense, a reading of a work within the same system of coding also involves problems of interpretation. For linguistic and cultural differences are diachronic as well as synchronic. As classical Japanese is a different language from modern Japanese, *monogatari* in both languages function in a different way. Therefore, the contemporary attempt in modern Japanese of interpreting *The Tale of Genji* is already a reading-in, as its translation into English is. In any act of interpretation, an original signified can be almost identical to the newly decoded one, or completely different. The former, that is, a historicist reading (an attempt to construct the original meaning), however, should in no way ostracize a transcivilizational reading (an act of projecting a new meaning [of a target language] onto the original meaning).

A problem, however, lies in the desire to find, through a translinguistic interpretation, not the common (and differing) fields of signifieds, but a "universalist meaning": for instance, a move not so much of measuring the similitudes and the differences between "romantic love" and *kōshoku* as to locate them on the coordinates of "Love," from which spring all versions of "love" in the cultures of the world. A supposedly universal coordinate, or an original idea of "Love," however, has to be verbalized if it is a "meaning" at all. But can there be "Love" independent of a language and a culture? I would argue that one only chooses a certain sign among others as an ideal entity. The result is the valorization of that sign and the decentering of all the others. Translinguistic readings have led to the affirmation of such deceptive universalist convictions. The quest for a universalist meaning, in turn, has brought about hierarchization.

As we have seen, such an ideal entity is almost always taken from Western critical categories. The reverse formulation, the theorization of the literary and cultural phenomena of the world under the rubric of a non-Western critical category, has seldom, if ever, taken place. If Etiemble could propose a comparative study of "romances," a comparable study of various world versions of *ukiyo zōshi* has never been conceived. Or, if we are encouraged to compare *The Tale of Genji* and European novels from the framework of "romance," an opposite move of comparing the narratives of the world from the framework of *monogatari* has never been made.[8] What is the force that encourages the former and prohibits the latter, that is, that assumes "romance" to be more universal and *ukiyo zōshi* more parochial, other than the force of cultural imperialism?

This irreversibility is a sign of the colonized status of non-Western culture. It is also a case of Orientalism where Eastern conceptual frameworks have to be represented by the Western. The latter is considered more human, general, and superior, making the former more marginal, parochial, and inferior. However, within the confines of universalist comparativism, the "universality" claim of Western categories has never been attributed to historically contingent factors, that is to say, to the overall political, economic, and military superiority of the West in the last two or three hundred years. For these categories to be universal, they have to be innately so. Modern (Western) humanism has turned a human being into a raw monad, possessing a limited number of human essentials that are later to be forged into a culturally parochial form. Conversely, if the universalist claim is to be sustained, the fact must be suppressed that so-called human essences such as "love," "Don Juanism," and "sexuality," and cultural essences such as "romance," "tragedy," and "literature," are the ideological formations of the West. They have to be absolute categories, independent of political factors.

At this point, the parochial is converted to the universal. For instance, Guillén proposes a "supranational" comparison of Don Juans of the world on the comparative axis of "Seduction." As I argued in chapter 1, however, "Seduction" is a concept specific to a particular paradigm of culture and a particular social system. If this is the case, his use of upper case to indicate the ostensible universality of the concept is significant. For the upper case also demonstrates that it is a proper noun. "Seduction" and the other concepts Guillén proposes are at once an origin and a local (European) paradigm. The capital S that sanctions comparison is an apparatus that transforms locality into universality.

As an opposite expression of the interplay of parochialism and universalism, a case can be observed where parochiality is appreciated, too. In a queer reverse move to valorize the provincial, *nihonjin ron* (discourses on the Japanese) have recently flourished in Japan. If the applicability of Western concepts to the rest of the world is a proof of the superiority of the former, their inapplicability can be another. In this case, it is the claim to uniqueness of Japanese culture that makes the Japanese paradigm inapplicable to other cultural tenets, and inaccessible to foreigners, that testifies to its superiority.

In fact, the Japanese seem to have recently launched on a new strategy, too, a strategy of not emphasizing the uniqueness but the universality of their culture. A leading comparativist stated in a lecture delivered at the national convention of the Japanese Comparative Literature Association that the Greek American writer, Lafcadio Hearn, is particularly popular in Japan since he well expressed the sense of dependence (*amae*), which is often considered one of the unique traits of the Japanese culture. He continued, however, that dependence is a universal human characteristic based on the mother-child relationship, but that it has received full articulation almost exclusively in the Japanese cultural system (June 4, 1995). This shift in the strategy is not to be wondered at. As we have seen with the Western version of universalism, uniquism and universalism are two sides of the same coin. Precisely what is unique is what is universal.

Now, the theme of universalism brings us back to the issue of comparativism, this time with regard to its practical relevance. Wellek and Warren emphasize the connection between universalist humanism and comparativism: "[Comparative literature] asks for a widening of perspectives, a suppression of local and provincial sentiments, not easy to achieve. Yet literature is one, as art and humanity are one; and in this conception lies the future of historical literary studies" (*Theory* 50). Note that the expansion of one's horizons translates into a suppression of the supposedly parochial.

Furthermore, it is remarkable that Wellek and Warren's claim to universalism is underscored by the urge to downplay linguistic differences: "Possibly, it would be best to speak simply of 'literature' [instead of 'comparative' and 'general' literature]. Whatever the difficulties into which a conception of universal literary history may run, it is important to think of literature as a totality and to trace the growth and development of literature without regard to linguistic distinctions" (49). In a queer twist of conceptions, literature and literary criticism transcend language. Wellek and Warren's comment is all the more illuminating read in the light of Todorov, who largely relates the issue of the Other to the difference in languages. Universalism calls for downplaying of language, or rather, languages.

We have to explore more closely the practical politics involved in the universalist-humanist ideas, the principles of comparison, and latent Eurocentrism. Remak, in the epigraph to this chapter, speaks of the "irresistible human urge to reduce the diverse to one." But the question is: Which one?

"Suppression" of the local in the name of the "One" may not be just a metaphor in the domain of epistemology and axiology. In a hierarchical system that entails the dichotomies of civilized/barbarian, normal/abnormal, central/marginal, and so forth, the parochial is often expected effectively to perish. Abe Jirō declares in *The Art and Society of the Tokugawa Period* that he wrote the book in order to "address the last words to the Tokugawa art" (404). In it, writing about the later Edo erotic narrative genre of *ninjō bon*, he insists on the removal of a "libertine," *iro-otoko*, whom *ninjō bon* fictions feature, represented by the hero of *The Plum Calendar*, Tanjirō, not as a literary type, but as a "race" that exists in real life:

> The genre of *ninjō bon* cannot contribute to the development of "the culture of love"; it merely defiles the soul of love. At its best, it represents nothing more than a type of love for Tanjirō's kind who are good-natured in an intrepid and irresponsible way. In this sense, not only does it express a symptom of a past time, but it still affects the society powerfully, and is producing among part of the Edoites (probably, among also the young men native to the large cities like Osaka and Kyoto) a race to be called *iro-otoko*. They are harbingers of corruption. They have to be eliminated by the new age. (349)

In the previous chapters, we have observed how the concept of the *iro-otoko* has been appropriated by that of Don Juan, reduced to a mere shadow of the latter. He is now compelled to become extinct. Abe's judgment is hard to justify all the more because it contradicts his almost diametrically opposite opinion about (Western) Don Juans: "A man like Don Juan still has a potential of having preserved a sense of chaste emotions" (111).

Interestingly enough, the humanist philosopher, Abe, had a keen interest in the discipline of comparative literature, publishing a monograph on it. He explicitly states what he sees as the first principle of comparativism, that is, a quest for the universally human: "Cultural differences, provided they allow comparison, necessarily require the idea of universal humanity. A comparative study cannot be realized where a basis of universality in some sense is not presumed" (*Introduction* 226–27).

One does not, however, speak of "parochial humanity." The universal is the human. At this point, comparison becomes a political issue. For it is a surreptitious move to subsume other paradigms to the Western framework by virtue of "universality" and "humanity." Todorov puts it this way: "The comparativist puts certain *objects*, all of which are external to him, on the same level, and he himself remains the sole *subject*. . . . [One] does not put the Other on the same level as oneself, and does not call into question one's own categories" (*Conquest* 240; emphasis in original). Gadamer makes a similar point: "The essence of comparison presupposes the freedom of the knowing subjectivity, which is in control of both members of the comparison" (206). Comparison, then, is a will to control another paradigm with one's own.

Comparative Literature as a Marshall Plan

In such a manner, at the heart of transcivilizational comparativism is a will to subsume and assimilate other cultural systems. In the history of comparative literature, it has taken the form of a belief in the integrity of the Euro-American paradigm, a tacit assumption that it is universally valid, and, therefore, an effort to dominate all the other cultural paradigms. Non-Western texts have thus been colonized by Western cultural imperialism.

It is significant, then, that American comparativism was launched at the Chapel Hill Congress in 1948, only one year before George Marshall's monumental speech at Harvard, which ushered in a change in American diplomacy. For if the Marshall Plan was a policy predicated on the restoration and domination of Western civilization, American comparativism, as we saw above, was also an effort to solidify the hegemony of European culture. A move to find the universal principle of (comparative) literature was thus instigated precisely when the diplomatic policy of the United States itself was experiencing an immense shift: from the Monroe doctrine to the Truman doctrine, that is, from isolationism to the determination to reign over global politics.

If, however, a comparison of comparative scholarship to the Marshall Plan sounds too eccentric, I am not alone in such an idea. It was actually voiced by one of the founders of American comparativism, Werner Friederich, in an address to the French comparativists:

> [W]e [Americans] feel, with joy and with pride, that what we are doing is part of the deeper meaning of the Marshall Plan, that our vigorous activity somehow goes beyond the realm of mere book-learning, that we are here to help each other, to understand each other, and to save together with you [French scholars], the great cultural heritage that belongs to us, the Western World. (*Challenge of Comparative Literature* 10)

As is well known, the Marshall Plan had two main agenda: the rehabilitation of (Western) Europe and the containment of the communist world. Not in contradiction with these agenda, comparative literature at this point was an ideology of the "Free World," that is, the antisocialist world, which in turn was paraphrased as the "democratic" world. Anticommunist sentiment was quite explicit in the writings of comparativists during this period. Friederich himself declares in the above address: "[After reading Sholokhov] you will thank God for living in America" (55). This connection between comparativism and the capitalist system was neatly underscored by the relatively meager status of comparative literature in the former Soviet Union (especially during the Stalin regime).

Later in the same address Friederich reveals his politics more systematically. Friederich's political agenda, which had a direct bearing on the discipline of comparative literature, can be encapsulated as follows.

1. A belief that American civilization is essentially Western: "We, in America . . . are facing Europe as a whole, as a cradle of our civilization, as the former homeland of all our people" (28).

2. A belief that, consequently, comparativism should contribute to the preservation and the unity of Western Civilization (comparative literature as a Marshall Plan): "Every Humanities Division should have on hand a few specialists devoted to the task of showing what the various literatures taught at a college or university have in common, what they gave to, and borrowed from, one another and how, each in its own way, they are spiritual heirs to, and important representatives of, our Western tradition" (16); "[O]ur own age, with the old tragedies and the new hopes of its post-war adjustments, is in dire need of constant reassurance of the political and cultural unity of our Western World" (22).

3. A politics of incorporation, that is, a call for the non-Western world to imbibe Western culture under the guidance of the United States (a Marshall Plan directed toward the non-Western world): "With regard to a Japan opened up to Western influences only a hundred years ago, it is again the United States that has become the land of the middle, passing on its own and general European literature at an

accelerating speed since the victory and the occupation of 1945" (47).

The United States attains the position of (cultural) protector of the world, Western and non-Western, in the name of the integrity and supremacy of Western civilization. "[The United States is] the leader and the hope of the entire Free World" (57).

Admittedly, the politically fervent language of Werner, perhaps, simply reflects the ambience of the postwar world, and may not be shared by contemporary comparativists. The end of the Cold War structure, reconfirmed by the Bush administration (September 1989, presidential address in Texas) has put an end to the anticommunist fervor of early American comparativists. Oddly, however, as we have explored in the previous chapters, the basic ideology of American comparativism, that it is a theory of universal humanity, democracy, and hence the (Free) World (where the United States is still the "leader") does not appear to be considerably shaken even when the Cold War politics typically represented by the Reagan administration is outdated.

For Friederich, too, politics, culture, and military affairs are closely intermingled. Hence, his comment about "India, with rich cultural possibilities and pitifully inadequate military means" (47). Definitely, he thinks that power and culture are complementary. Thus, the postwar American policies of expansion and assimilation are faithfully reproduced in the field of comparative literature. A shift from the French school of comparativism to the American, that of European literary history to transcivilizational comparisons, displays a clear parallel to the development of geopolitics: a move of the global center from Europe to America, and the subsequent change of American diplomacy from isolationism to expansionism.

The goal of the assimilation of non-Western civilizations to the Western is justified by the American championship of the (Free) World against communism. For instance, Friederich incorporates Blacks into the cultural politics of the United States on the ostensible ground of "deep seated loyalty of the American Negro, and his innate strength in refusing to be ensnared by Communist propaganda" (56):

> Be proud, if you can, that the voice of the Negro, for the first time in human history appeared right here in America, and that, since the end of the eighteenth century, he has added, timidly at first, submissively, unsure of himself, but ever more boldly later, his voice to the voices of Anglo-Saxons, Spaniards, Irishmen, Scandinavians, Frenchmen, Germans, that have contributed to the greatness not only of American literature, but to the greatness of the political dream that is America. (55)

If Black culture is a non-Western tradition within the United States, the same logic can be easily applied to the non-Western world beyond the frontier: Japan, China, India, and all the non-Western nations should join the voice of "Anglo-Saxons, Spaniards, Irishmen, Scandinavians, Frenchmen, Germans" to achieve the great political dream that is America, of its becoming or remaining "the leader of the world."

It is true, however, that American comparativism has been a discipline of internationalism while French comparative literature has been that of nationalism. René Wellek insisted in his polemical paper "The Crisis of Comparative Literature" that comparative literature of the French school was an ideological apparatus of nationalism in spite of its initial intent:

> Comparative literature arose as a reaction against the narrow nationalism of much nineteenth-century scholarship, as a protest against the isolationism of many historians of French, German, Italian, English, etc., literature. . . . But this genuine desire to serve as a mediator and conciliator between nations was often overlaid and distorted by the fervent nationalism of the

time and situation. . . . A cultural power politics is rec-
ommended: everything serves only the strength of
one's nation. (287–88)

In contrast, American comparativism, authorizing transcivilizational comparison, has been expected to represent
internationalism and cosmopolitanism. Nevertheless,
Friederich's above-cited triumphant declaration calls its program into question as a naive expectation. The internationalism of comparative literature is an ideal where all kinds
of voices are united under the flag of Western civilization,
and ultimately, of America, the leader of the (Free) World.
The ideal of cosmopolitanism becomes, then, suspect. Imperialism is by nature internationalism; incorporation of the
Other is no doubt an expansion of the horizons.

A similar note is observed in an essay by Henri Peyre,
who makes a connection between the American methods of
comparativism, which "have one advantage over European
ones" (7), and America's political position. For Peyre attributes the transcivilizational comparative method of the
American school to the fact that "it fell to the lot of America
to be, not only the greatest power on this planet, but the obvious link between Europe and Asia, and between the past
and the future of mankind" (1).

Because internationalism as advocated by comparativism may be nothing other than an expression of imperialism and Pan Americanism at its highest stage of
development, I cannot entirely agree with Jonathan Culler's
hopes for comparative literature: "Disciplines such as comparative literature can be particularly important, for, noto-
riously, comparative literature is defined as literary study
that does not take a national literature as the natural and
inevitable unit of study and thus is not linked to the pieties
of nationalisms and their secular religions. Every comparativist will have favorite examples of how knowledge of
other literature deflates the partisan pretensions of nationalistic critics" (*Framing the Sign* 51). The conventional French
school of comparativism merely complemented, and thus

endorsed, the concept of national literatures. But even in Friederich's Pan-American system, a broader horizon only serves to endorse the centrality of America as a state-ideology. It does not contradict American nationalism. On the contrary, it reinforces it both by reconfirming its cultural unity and identity, and by subsuming other cultural heritages.

Admittedly, Werner Friederich is not a "true" American comparativist (if there is one), and, therefore, he may not represent the "American school." He received his training in comparative literature in France, studied with such authoritative European comparativists as Baldensperger and van Tieghem, and then moved to America. His support for American civilization may have something to do with his being a German-speaking immigrant in the United States in the 1940s. Yet, after all, he *was* one of the most influential founders of American comparativism. In fact, David Malone, in the preface to Friederich's collection of addresses, ascribes his fervor in the advocacy of (American) comparative literature to "Mr. Friederich's Americanization" (ix).

What may be, however, more significant is the attribution by Malone of the reason for Friederich's endorsement of American comparativism not only to his "Americanization" but also to "his profound, innate commitment to the universality of human values" (ix). To be a national of America, where Western civilization finds its most politico-economically powerful posterity, and where all the non-Western traditions get assimilated, is tantamount to being "universal" and "human."

Such have been the political implications of American comparativism, licensing a comparativist to make trans-civilizational comparisons and to appropriate the non-Western paradigms by conceiving them as Oriental versions of Western forms. If the term "appropriation" sounds disproportionate and improper (since at issue here is a matter of culture, but not economics), we may recall Henry James's panegyric to American civilization, cited by a British comparativist in an attempt to demonstrate the promises of American literature and comparativism. James wrote to a friend about the advantage of being born an American: "[W]e [Americans] can deal freely with forms of civilization not our own, can pick and choose and assimilate and in short (aesthetically &c.) claim our property wherever we find it" (Gifford 86). One does not fail to understand what James means by "aesthetically *&c.*"

If, however, American comparative literature has been an attempt to subsume the cultures of the world under the pretext of humanistic values into the Western civilization, a similar politics is found in the disciplines of comparative literature of Eastern countries, too. For instance, the Japanese school of comparative literature, by trying to revitalize the cultural connection with Asian cultures, a move itself welcome, displays a political intention of subsuming Asian powers as opponents to the Western influence, with Japan as a center. If the humanist values and the cultural unity of European countries form a "ground for comparison" for Western comparative literature, the alleged cultural affinity of Asian countries works similarly for the Japanese. A professor of the department of comparative literature at Tokyo University, which has served a function similar to that of the Sorbonne in France, speaks of "the Greater East Asia *Cultural* Co-Prosperity Sphere," unabashedly echoing the prewar military slogan of the Greater East Asia Co-Prosperity Sphere. The revival of the colonialism of the Japanese Empire is explicit. The idea of "community," where *cultural* heritage is common, conceals a colonial ambition which Japan failed to achieve half a century ago.

We may propose through these examples a hypothesis that the scope of the universal in theory is in proportion to the political scheme for colonial annexation. If the universalism of American comparativism reflects the range of influence American imperialistic ideology craves to assert, the theory of "the Greater East Asian Cultural Co-Prosperity Sphere" represents Japan's effort at countering American geopolitics by gaining control over a somewhat smaller "universe" than the political dream of America.

Obviously, today the scope of the Japanese "universe," namely, an area under the politico-economic influence of Japan, is expanding at a tremendous rate. If Japan is to continue to grow as an imperialistic force, the claim of the uniqueness and the parochiality of Japanese culture represented by *nihonjin ron* (discourse on the Japanese) may soon be replaced by the ideal of Greater East Asian cultural integrity represented by Japanese culture, and eventually by a call for a "humanity" whose concealed identity is Japanese. I have taken issue with the appropriation of the Japanese (and non-Western) paradigms through such conceptualizations as a "Japanese Don Juan." However, this should in no way mean that the current appropriation be replaced by another kind of appropriation, that is, to conceptualize Don Juan as a "European *iro-otoko*," who has unfortunately failed to ideally represent the essential quality of masculine sexuality, *kōshoku*.

Conclusion: The Violence of Comparison

Comparative perception, which discovers similitude, inevitably involves exclusion. Exclusion is marginalization. The universal/identical is maintained only through constantly relegating differences to the field of deviation, barbarism, perversion, illegitimacy, abnormality, and inhumanity. By defining as an abnormality a cultural phenomenon which dismantles initial comparative axes, a comparativist conveniently shuns the necessity of problematizing that coordinate, and of finding alternatives.

Translinguistic/civilizational comprehension, then, is invariably an act of violence of some sort. For it cannot be achieved except by a distortion of the object in accordance to the viewer's paradigm. Perception of cultural alterity is already an exercise of power, a political act, that calls for the assimilation, if not the extinction, of the other paradigms.

The procedure of such relegation and distortion is supposedly remedied by a humanist belief, though, that is, the
belief that there exists an essential human nature to be universally found among those who are acknowledged as "humans." In truth, however, we find in the Other what we
already know in our own system of signification. Humanism happily tells us that it is the human essential. For, if
finding and knowing a difference is painful, universalizing
one's own paradigm is a pleasure.

Comparison, then, is realized through the imposition
of the observer's paradigm upon the other. "Reality" to be
perceived (and compared) is a result of an episteme, not vice
versa. A comparativist's consciousness that evokes a comparison of Don Juan and *iro-otoko* arises as a result of the
(modern) Western paradigm of "love," "lust," and "sexuality." A comparative analysis does not commence from the
universally human phenomenon of Don Juanism. Schemes
of comparison have not been stored in the indices of research topics all along, awaiting exploration, interpretation,
and grants; they are, on the contrary, a consequence of the
perception according to a certain paradigm and the linguistic system that endorses it. After the installation of the paradigm, however, the "reality" apparently becomes natural as
if it had been permanently out there.

My book has been an attempt to trace the emergence
of a "modern" sexual paradigm in Japan, in accordance to
which a comparison of Don Juan and *iro-otoko* was for the
first time made meaningful, obvious, and transparent, but
not historical. Romantic love, spiritual love, Don Juanism,
love as a human sentiment, perversion, sexuality—these are
all concepts that were produced exactly when Japanese society accepted, largely under the threat of the cultural imperialism of the West, the episteme of modernity that
invoked the belief that "Love is universal; love is human."
Instead, the difference of paradigms came to be seen as
the embodiment of parochialism. "General" features of
humanity that were ostensibly shared transculturally and

ahistorically were, then, retrospectively constructed: human essences such as "love" had always been there—at times in action, at times dormant—to be found even in premodern Japanese culture. Such was, and is, an epistemological trap which we moderns are entangled in. We do not observe in, or induce from, the examples taken from cultural texts, categories of "love" and "sexuality" (or "desire," "morality," "democracy," "humanity," and so on). Conversely, it is the Western cultural ideology and the paradigm of humanism that compel us to see these qualities.

Such violence of comparativism may only be mitigated by an infinite act of relativization of the universalist, humanist ontology. When a "different" paradigm is perceived, compared, and articulated as (partially) "different" but essentially the "same," initial assimilation and marginalization have already taken place. If so, it is not tolerance in the face of a "different" paradigm that is called for. Instead of the "more accurate" understanding of the other, radical problematization of the comparative hermeneutics per se is required.

The most systematic and most pervasive form of such violence of perception was, and to a considerable degree still is, a Western episteme. Todorov writes: "Since the period of the conquest, for almost three hundred and fifty years, Western Europe has tried to assimilate the other, to do away with an exterior alterity, and has in great part succeeded" (*Conquest* 246). This continues, both culturally and politically, to be a manifest duty of America and Western civilization, that which Michel Foucault aptly called "the great historico-transcendental destiny of the Occident." Trans-civilizational comparativism has been a will to defend and pursue such a destiny.

notes

Chapter 1. Problematizing Comparative Literature

1. This is suggested by the etymology of the word "compare" in most Indo-European languages: com*pare*, ver*gleich*en, s*ravn*it', and so on).

2. It appears quite certain to me, though, that the author, Goncharov, was sufficiently familiar with *Hamlet*.

3. I agree with Claudio Guillén that the distinction of the so-called two schools of comparative literature was far more ambiguous than this simplified dichotomous framework leads us to believe. Consequently, he uses, in his *The Challenge of Comparative Literature*, the terms "the French *hour*" and "the American *hour*." I myself will stick to the conventional terms of "the French school" and "the American school" with the presumption that these be understood as an insufficient formula.

4. Of course, according to Raymond Williams, the use of "civilization" in the plural form, and, hence, its acquired meaning of a conglomerate of several national (cultural) traditions itself is quite recent, appearing only in 1860s (*Keywords*).

5. Given this, it was an irony of history that Asian comparativists, who, naturally, paid major attention to East-West issues, mostly began by following the French model.

6. All Japanese and Chinese names throughout this study appear with the family name first, followed by the first name without a comma, in accordance with the traditional order. Occasionally, the first name is used to refer to a writer when it is more common, especially in the case of a pseudonym (for instance, Tōkoku for Kitamura Tōkoku). Readers are advised to consult the Index to obtain full reference.

7. Etiemble's original text uses a term less intense than "force": "*s'imposer.*"

8. I hasten to add, though, that it is not my intention to establish the American method, or the French, as the gist of comparativism, opposing the two camps as flatly conflicting

academic ideals. In the end, the French method, as we shall see, is also directed toward the discovery of "analogy" and "affinity."

9. There are a wide range of arguments as to the real nature of the Edo period: whether it was "feudal/agricultural," "mercantile," "bureaucratic/centralized," "semibourgeois/semi-industrialized," and so on. It has become more and more clear that the schematic understanding of the era as "feudal" or "premodern" as opposed to the "modernized," "civilian," post-Meiji Reformation Japan is insufficient. Consistent efforts have been made to locate the modernization process well before the onset of Westernization. Although I approve of such a new tendency in historical comprehension, the present book attempts to demonstrate the function of different discursive practices that helped shape the forms of "modern" Japanese culture, thus emphasizing the effects of newly introduced Western discourses.

10. Armando M. Janeira in his *Japanese and Western Literature: A Comparative Study* attempts a similar comparison of Don Juan types. He is, however, engaged not so much in comparative analysis of Don Juan and *iro-otoko*, or a Japanese "amorous man" as in the parallel description of both traditions.

11. The Japanese translator somehow omits the homosexual aspect of Yonosuke's orientation, rendering the given passage thus:

> Overwhelmed at last by all this bleakness but hopeful of the joys to be found in romantic old Kyoto, he set out for the imperial capital. Ah, he mused expectantly, there he would pursue the charms of beautiful women and the pleasures of wine!
>
> Yumesuke, "the Man of Dreams," they called him in Kyoto. (*The Life of an Amorous Man* 11)

12. The hero of a Chinese story, *Jingpingmei* by Xiaoxiao Sheng (Hsiaohsiao Sheng); one abridged edition of an English translation of the story is subtitled: *Don Juan of China*.

13. Transcivilizational comparison can, then, also be considered a kind of structuralist project. A researcher is required to reduce multifarious phenomena until the undividable element of humanity is arrived at: ideal "prima signata" such as a "character-eme," or a "theme-eme," as it were, of Don Juan.

14. For Kant, a third point is "time."

15. But does it have to be *he*? This is not an extravagant question when one thinks of a pair of works that Ihara Saikaku composed as *The Life of an Amorous Man* (*Kōshoku ichidai otoko*), whose hero, Yonosuke, is a candidate for a Japanese Don Juan, and *The Life of an Amorous Woman* (*Kōshoku ichidai onna*).

16. The example just cited is a celebrated one, taken up in Derrida's *Of Grammatology*. Derrida speaks of it with a slightly different focus from mine, though. That is, whereas, through this example, he calls in question the primacy of sound (or, more precisely, speech) over writing in the Western tradition, I am simply pointing to the privileging of a signified over a signifier.

17. This reminds us of the wonderful scene in Chekhov's *Three Sisters* where Masha, in disgust over the love of her husband, a teacher in Latin, utters the table: *amo, amas, amat* . . . (Act III).

Chapter 2. The Introduction of "Love" into Modern Japan

1. Just as there are so many conflicting views concerning the nature of the Edo period (1603-1868), historians disagree (as in the famous debate on the nature of Japanese capitalism among the Marxists in 1920s and 30s) upon the characterization of the Meiji period, whether it was "modern," "semifeudal," "absolute monarchical," "parliamentarian," "semibourgeois," and so on. As I suggested in note 9 to chapter 1, the purpose of my book is not simply to contrast "feudal," "premodern" Edo society with the "modern" Meiji system, but to display the formation of a number of new discursive practices that emerged in the late nineteenth- and early twentieth-century Japan.

2. His aim was, however, to suppress their once sexual bond. Also, their relationship was a hierarchical one in spite of such "friendly" forms of address.

3. For more details, see my "Lovers in Disguise." Incidentally, I say "heterosexual" because a term "dear friend," *nen'yū*, had been used in the context of male homosexuality.

4. Ivan Morris translates the passage thus: "Outside the company of courtesans there can be few girls so versed in the ways of the world that at a time like this they should conceive the desire of bringing to prompt consummation a tender bond" (66).

5. Before we move on, though, it has to be remembered that my arguments in this book will be strictly limited to the classes that produced and consumed "literature." The above-cited episode about the argument on translation between Futabatei and Tsubouchi whether an egalitarian speech is a feature of "proletarian" couple or not, clearly demonstrates that it was a class issue. To a certain degree, "equality" of speech had been already achieved in the lower class of urban Japanese society. The task was to create it for an upper class that could still differentiate itself from the proletarian style. While the absence of attention to the

lower classes puts a limitation upon my study, which I hope to remedy in the future, I suggest at this point that if the representation of love in literature was a class issue, it was so exactly because literary discourse was one, too. Western discourse including literature was monopolized and controlled by the newly formed upper and middle classes, which evolved mainly from the middle-class samurai and the wealthier citizens of the Edo Shogunate. Consequently, a male-female relationship according to the Western model, which at first could be attributed to "proletarian sentiments" by the doctor-professor Tsubouchi, slowly demarcated itself from them, and developed into a part of culture to be appreciated by the higher classes. The debate between Futabatei and Tsubouchi attests to the moment when the discourses of high (literary) culture, new bourgeois ideology, traditional samurai philosophy, proletarian subculture, modern Western thought, and so forth, were struggling with one another, striving to be articulated in their proper places.

Conversely, since the new discourse was largely unavailable to the masses, for all the "modernization" process that the society on the whole was experiencing, their ideology of sexuality remained basically the same for some time even after the Meiji Reformation (in spite of the changes in practice described by Yanagita in his *Social History of Meiji and Taishō*). And since it was the upper class that began to absorb and monopolize romantic love ideology as represented in European literature, Western "love" had to be excluded from lower-class discourse. General dissemination of the European notion of love was not fully achieved until the end of World War II. Any discussion on the conflict between the Japanese and the Western notions of "love" in Meiji Japan has to be restricted to upper- and middle-class discourse.

6. Cited by Teruoka Yasutaka in *Kōshoku* (115). Despite Teruoka's quote, the original passage in Russian reads "Vasha..." (Turgenev 187), literally meaning "I am yours." It is an almost obsolete expression in the sense of "I am devoted to you."

7. Incidentally, as in this example, the usage of *rabu(-suru)* was usually associated with students, a class that was to form an upper- and middle-class governing body with knowledge of Western civilization. For instance, in the above-cited *The Characters of Modern Students*, any romantic involvement of the students is automatically termed *rabu* independent of its nature; the English *rabu* is used even when the implied concept is obviously traditional, as in the example just quoted. This is another instance where "love" was a class issue in exact proportion to the fact that "literature" was one. "Love" was part of the knowledge that the

dominating class (or, the class that was to become hegemonical in future) monopolized.

8. Hereafter, I follow Umberto Eco's usage in *Semiotics and the Philosophy of Language* of single slashes to indicate expression, and guillemets to indicate corresponding content, when the distinction is particularly necessary. For example, «love» is a concept of love, a signified, or the content for the signifier /love/.

9. It has to be remembered, though, that, if we are to regard such an idea as Orientalist, it is one also held by a great number of modern Japanese literati themselves such as Tōkoku.

10. For the linguistic theory of a core meaning (core sense), see George Miller (101-103).

11. Or, we should call it "same-sex love," for the concept of homosexuality, different from sodomy, as a form of "perversion" and a sexual orientation that determines one's identity, is a product of modernity (see Weeks chap. 4).

12. For details, see my "The Purity Campaign as a Literary Context."

13. Whorf does not give the original Eskimo words or their definitions, but only illustrations. According to Miyaoka Osahito, southwest Alaskan Eskimo has four different words for snow: *qanuk* (falling snow), *pirtuk* (snow storm), *aniuq* or *apun* (fallen snow), and *utvak* (a cut-out lump of snow) (*Eskimo: Ethnographical History of the Far North* 157).

There have been many counterarguments to Whorf's idea, pointing to the linguistic inaccuracy of his account. Laura Martin criticizes his failure to scientifically document sources, his oversimplification of "Eskimo" dialects, and his insufficient understanding of them. According to her, if we disregard cognate forms, there are only two distinct roots: *qanik* (snow in the air; snowflake) and *aput* (snow [on the ground]). Therefore, she contends, "Eskimo has about as much differentiation as English does for 'snow' at the monolexemic level: snow and flake" (422). I take issue with her argument. "At the monolexemic level," flake (in English) is *not* snow while *qanik* is.

Moreover, she displays the universalist/essentialist belief which we have been criticizing when she gives an ontotheological status to "(English) snow" by referring to it as "snow *itself* (and not, for example, to [Eskimo] drifts, ice, storms, or moisture)" (422).

Also, as I follow the framework of arguments outlined by Whorf, I will simply use the term "Eskimo" to denote Northern Canadian natives, though its origin may be sought in a discriminatory address, and though such a generalization is rather questionable.

14. The linguist, George Lakoff, makes a similar criticism in *Woman, Fire, and Dangerous Things* (323).

15. The grammatical distinction of SAE between a verb and a noun as applied to Chinese is contestable, however.

16. The subject *"mizu* and [*o-*]*yu"* is already questionable, though, establishing a mathematic equation: "[English] water" = "[Japanese] *mizu* + *yu"* = "[general] Water."

17. Critics (Jonathan Culler, Maruyama Keizaburō, et al.) have attempted to show that such a nomenclaturative notion of a sign, which *Course* may appear to suggest, is not necessarily Saussure's original idea, but may have stemmed from the ideas of the disciples-editors. While I have no reason to contest such an opinion, it is not in my interest to reconstruct the "real" Saussure behind the text of *Course*, either. Besides, my argument is that any theory which foregrounds the distinction of referent/signified is nomenclaturative in the final instance.

18. These four terms are taken from the Osaka dialect. The Tokyo dialect gives a slightly different set.

19. Such a textualist formula is also in contradiction with an essentialist theory of sexuality which legitimizes heterosexual passion on account of biology and instinct. If desire is constructed as a text, one's sexuality can take any form according to its discursive formulation. We will return to this issue in chapter 4.

20. We are here dealing only with translation of words. But even with an expansion of the definition of a "sign" to include a sign as a sentence (as Eco suggests in *Semiotics and the Philosophy of Language* ch. I), we arrive at the same conclusion.

Chapter 3. The Emergence of Don Juanism

1. Kitamura Tōkoku uses *kōshoku* and *iki* almost synonymously in his writings. More precisely, *kōshoku* 好色 is associated with the ancient concept of *iro-gonomi* 色好み, while *iki* is a later invention, mostly applicable to the fashionable culture of the capital Edo in the latter half of the Tokugawa era. A more or less similar concept associated with Osaka, a center of culture before Tokyo (Edo) obtained that status, is represented by such terms as *sui* and *tsū*.

2. Admittedly, Futabatei is aware of the power of his rival Noboru's pragmatism which brings him success both in business and in love. The author is also aware of the infeasibility of the new ideals that make the hero a tragicomical caricature of the time. The ideals, however, appear to remain intact, at least at this stage of

the writer's career. In later life, Futabatei would completely lose faith in the idea of romantic love.

3. See, for instance, Satō et al., *References to Foreign Literatures in Modern Japan*.

4. Of course, the concept of bestiality (*jūyoku*) was used in a Buddhist context and formed a counterculture to the hegemonical prostitutional discourses and practices. However, the term *jūyoku* refers to sexuality in general. In contrast, "lust" or "bestiality" is something defined only in opposition to spiritual, chaste love, which can lead one to celestial heights. Bestiality and *jūyoku* are not to be identified since they represent two different ways of segmenting the continuum. They can be considered comparable only when one presupposes the higher category of "sexuality" that the Buddhist notion comprehensively covers, but that the European notion divides into two. (This allegedly higher category of "sexuality" will be put to question in the next chapter.)

5. Relevant here may be the fact that, while the authors of the Edo pulp fictions were exclusively male, their readership was largely female.

6. Not to mention, though, that the total identification of "chivalry" with spiritual love is merely a myth that Tōkoku introduced.

7. The editor mistranslates "out of love" as meaning "without love." We are, however, more concerned about his mistranslation of "love" into "a patron's affection toward a courtesan" as a significant cultural phenomenon.

8. Whether reproduction is of a "sexual" order or not is an ideological decision. It may simply belong to the constellation of conceptions called "sexuality," which, in turn, can be historicized. We will return to this issue in chapter 4. Such terms as "sexual" and "sexuality," therefore, should be read with quotation marks hereafter.

9. One also finds a similar, total rejection of (sexual) love and an indulgence of extreme misogyny in Christian theology, however. In modern times, it has been more or less co-opted by romantic love ideology, which sees a possibility of spiritual love with an ideal woman. Tolstoy's writings on sexual love are a protest against this later development and an attempt at restoration of what he viewed as the original Christian idea which he sought in the Pauline epistles. See my "Man Seen as a Beast, Male Seen as an Animal."

10. Thus, *kōshoku* in the Edo period was mainly a masculine ideal of hedonism. It takes a much more gloomier form in *Kōshoku ichidai onna* (*The Life of an Amorous Woman*).

11. Except, perhaps, one episode in which Yonosuke is harassed by the ghosts of the spiteful women with whom he has had an affair (ch. 4, episode 3).

12. The project was resumed five years later. The piece, this time entitled *Dan Jūza*, was published in the journal *Kokoro no hana*.

13. The French original does not have an expression corresponding to "passion": "forcer pied à pied toutes les petites résistances qu'elle nous oppose" (*Dom Juan ou le Festin de pierre* 719). This omission possibly indicates that the Japanese translator used the English translation. Charles H. Wall's English translation, the edition often used by the translators of Molière in the Meiji period, renders the given passage as: "It is a most captivating delight . . . to force, inch by inch, all the little obstacles she opposes to our passion; to overcome the scruples upon which she prides herself, and to lead her, step by step, where we would bring her" (*Don Juan; or the Feast of the Statue* 73).

14. In the case of parasitic playboys in the late Edo fictions such as Tanjirō it is the financial means, not chastity, that he deprives.

15. There are, however, cases when courtesans are compared to bodhisattva figures. See, for instance, *Ukiyo monogatari*, vol. 5, episode 5: "There once was a princess-courtesan in Eguchi, who was a reincarnation of bodhisattva Samantabhadra. She slept with travelers, offering them a chance to understand the Buddha's way. This reminds me of Vasumitrā, one of the fifty-five Good Friends in Flower-Wreath Sūtra, who is reported to have been a courtesan. These were magnificent women" (Asai 252).

16. I say "modern" since, in contrast with sodomy, the concept of homosexuality as a form of "perversion" and a sexual orientation that determines one's identity is a product of modernity (See note 11, chap. 2).

Chapter 4. Sexuality as a Historical Construct

1. For instance, the critic Uchida Roan in his criticism of the novel writes: "I do not hesitate to praise the bold attempts by Japanese naturalist writers to investigate human sexual desire. They have touched upon the [latest] European thoughts even before academics. My only problem is that most of them appear to possess minimum knowledge of the ways in which sexual desire is explained and interpreted by Western authorities. . . . Any author who has an intention of making sexually explicit descriptions should acquaint himself with the basic writings of Forel and

Krafft-Ebing. I regret that Dr. Ōgai's *Vita Sexualis*, which is the most daring and most scientific description of sexual desire, was banned by the police" ("*Vita Sexualis*" 255).

2. A passage from Krafft-Ebing's *Psychopathia Sexualis*, concerning "the gradual development of civilisation and the influence exerted by sexual life upon habits and morality" (2), may be relevant, although the author does not mention Japanese society. The German doctor continues: "The gratification of the sexual instinct seems to be the primary motive in man as well as in beast. Sexual intercourse [in uncivilized societies] is done openly, and man and woman are not ashamed of their nakedness. The savage races, e.g., Australasians, Polynesians, Malays of the Philippines are still in this stage" (2).

3. One might oppose this view, citing an episode from *The Life of an Amorous Man* in which Yonosuke peeps on a maid taking a bath in a tub, and, afterwards, pressures her to have a sexual relationship with him if she wishes that he keep his mouth shut (vol. 1, "Through a Spyglass"). The major force of his threat, however, seems to me to consist not in her act of taking a bath (and of being naked) but in her having been (shamefully) engaged in masturbation. Otherwise, Yonosuke's threat would not have had force.

4. This also shows that the construction of sexuality was a class issue. Houses like Ōgai's of the upper samurai class were normally equipped with small private baths, thus offering no chance of visiting a public bath even if there was one in his native town.

5. A peculiarly Japanese genre of a narrative having an autobiographical nature whose main concern was, and is, to make a radical confession, and to faithfully reproduce the most minute details of everyday life. It has, as a form of a novel, become canonical in the naturalist movement.

6. That it does not create *male* nudity as a private and erotic entity is an interesting topic for feminist criticism which I would like to explore in future. On the whole, the discussion in this chapter is restricted to "sexuality" in the masculine system.

7. Portions of *Psychopathia Sexualis* appeared in Japanese for the first time in *The Journal of Forensic Medicine* (*Hōigaku zasshi*). They were later published in book form as *Shikijōkyō hen* (*On Sexual Perversions*) in 1894. It was banned and never reached a wide audience. Meiji literati read the German sexological classic mostly via English translation.

8. Incidentally, it appears that it was also through sexological writings in Japanese translations that China came to use *sei* (or *xing*) in the sense of sexuality. The new usage was introduced by

Chinese students (Guo More, Zhang Tuzhao, et al.) who studied in Japan.

9. I offer my own rather literal translation since the rendering by Ninomiya-Goldstein does not adequately convey the meaning of the original passage. The pagination refers to vol. 5 of *The Complete Works of Mori Ōgai*.

10. Cf. the same qualifier (*seiyoku teki*) that Hasegawa Tenkei uses in "The Miseries of Revealing the Reality" which we read earlier. *Seiyoku teki* (concerning sexual desire) in the sense of "sexual" is obsolete today, and has been replaced by *sei teki* (concerning sex or sexuality, that is, sexual).

11. Weeks writes about the interplay of biological knowledge and the concepts of nature and humanity that shaped the sexological notion of sexuality: "[Darwin's idea of sexual selection] allowed a legitimate revival of interest in the sexual aetiologies ('origins') of individual behaviour and a sustained effort to delineate the dynamics of sexual selection, the sexual impulse, and the differences between the sexes. Biology became the avenue into the mysteries of Nature, and its findings were legitimised by the evidence of natural history. What existed 'in Nature' provided evidence for what was human" (67).

12. Relevant here may be the etymological connection between English "root" and German "Würzel," which is sometimes used as slang for the male organ.

13. Or what André Béjin defines as "protosexology." Béjin calls for its differentiation from later sexology represented by Masters, Johnson, et al., who stressed the achievements of "normal" orgasmic sexuality. I agree with his distinction although my view on sexology in general, which, in my opinion, rests on the normal/abnormal dichotomy, remains essentially the same.

14. The adjective "promiscuous" in English apparently followed a similar trajectory of meaning, shifting from "indiscriminate" (early seventeenth century) to "sexually mischievous" (early nineteenth century). Incidentally, the specific reference in the definition of "promiscuity" given by the OED to "low civilization" ("Promiscuous sexual union, as among some races of low civilization") is remarkable as this shows that the shift was probably created in parallel with colonialist ideology. Undoubtedly, it was the background for the moral change in Japan, too.

15. In truth, as mentioned in note 7, most writers of the Meiji period read Krafft-Ebing and other sexologists in English translation. I suspect, although I have not been able to substantiate the hypothesis, that the well-known last scene of the naturalistic novel *The Quilt*, where the hero-author smells the futon on which slept

his beloved disciple, is a representation of fetishism, an image taken from sexological writings.

16. Pozdnyshev, the hero of Lev Tolstoy's *The Kreutzer Sonata*, which was the initial model for Futabatei's novel, does not use the sexological term "satyriasis," but accuses himself of having been a Don Juan in his youthful search for carnal pleasure, mainly with prostitutes (sect. V).

17. We should remember here that in sexological discourse an excess of sexuality, hyperaesthesia, is much more problematic, and is paid far greater attention, than a lack of it, frigidity. *Psychopathia Sexualis* dismisses the issue of frigidity with a bare minimum of examples.

18. A term *iro-kichigai* (one with a crazily acute interest in sexual matters), which lacks the medical/psychological association, has been used since the early nineteenth century.

19. Except that, of course, it is not a naked, but a dressed body that *kaimami* allows the onlooker to see. The very concept of *kaimami*, then, demonstrates the constructedness of a "sexual" act of peeping. It is a difference, not the ontological status of the object to be peeped, that establishes it as sexually appealing. If nakedness is a difference from "dressedness," Japanese aristocrats found erotic glimpsing ladies wearing "twelve layers" of dress because they were concealed behind the curtains, but not in the open air.

20. Since this is the case, that is, as Debakame's buckteeth symbolize his perverted condition but do not necessarily have to be a fact, we need not be bothered by the alternate theory as to the etymology of the pseudonym, Debakame. Some correspondents reported that the murderer was nicknamed Debakame as he, being violent in nature, was wont to abuse his family and terrify them, brandishing a large kitchen knife (*deba*).

21. Also, a shift in the concepts of madness and perversion from something contingent to something essential is documented in detail by Foucault in his *Madness and Civilization* and *Discipline and Punish*.

22. In Japan, the emergence of lust and perversion took place almost simultaneously. This explains why the term *hentai* (perversion) is very often used in combination with the qualifier *kōshoku* in the sense of mere lust.

23. Not that I advocate the Japanese Edo system of male sexuality. My point is that the immoral "sexual" system of Edo Japan was not necessarily replaced by a more truly "human" system of the "modern" era. I simply object to the concept of a "human essence" that is to be sought after and revealed as "Truth." A change

from the Edo to Meiji sexual ideologies, as I see it, was one system of sexual regime being substituted for another, as repressive as the previous one. For more detail on this issue, see my "The Purity Campaign as a Literary Context."

24. As a matter of fact, the term *"die Schürzenjäger,"* or "a hunter of *aprons"* already precludes the very possibility of love with prostitutes that *kōshoku* foregrounds, but Don Juanism generally does not.

Chapter 5. Politics of Comparative Literature

1. In fact, such a usage of "imperialism" is in line with the original usage of the word in nineteenth-century England (See Williams, *Keywords* 159–60).

2. In this regard, I must thank a member of the audience to a lecture I gave at York University (March 1992) on the incompatibility of the concepts of "love" in various cultures for making me realize this connection. She pointed out that it was wrong of me to question the universality and hence the value of romantic love. There were, along with "love," she claimed, several unquestionably valuable human essentials, such as democracy.

3. For the difference in the meanings of "democracy" between the English and the socialist usages, see Williams, *Keywords* 93–99.

In the issue of the difference between capitalist and socialist versions of "human" values, the concept of romantic love dearly cherished by bourgeois liberalism has been quite nonchalantly inherited by socialist cultures after the initial attempt at "revolutionizing" the sexual relationship represented by "the glass of water theory" (a defence of promiscuity on the grounds that one should satisfy the sex drive as one satisfies thirst [Clements 231]) was demolished. Hence, an opinion by a Soviet education scholar, Anton Makarenko, endorsing the Western moral sense of love: "A sexual relationship is justified through love. . . . [An egoistic man] often shows strong sexual feelings, but tends always not to respect a woman that attracts him, not to cherish her spiritual life, or not even to interest himself in it" (412–13). What we observe in this passage is the stigmatization of lust, which is egoistic, the dichotomy of spiritual love/(vulgar) sexual feelings, and the sense of "respect" that should accompany "love," three of the typical features of Western romantic love which we examined in chapter 2.

4. Incidentally, this leads Abe, as a natural matter of course, to take an explicitly antisocialist position. In another essay, "An

Alternative View on the Labor Problem," he contends that the labor movement will not solve current social problems since it comes down to a demand for an equal distribution of wealth, and therefore, is a "desire for luxury." The reform of the society, he claims, can be achieved only through the establishment of a moral relationship between capitalists and workers.

5. Although one may wonder about the virtues of the heroes and the heroines of *Elective Affinities*. At least, Abe regards them as far more sincere than Edo lovers.

6. Etiemble invokes: "the *Genji monogatari* of the Japanese, the *Shilappadikaram* of the Tamils, the *Kim Van Kieu* of the Vietnamese" (54).

7. Given this opinion of Posnett, I should moderate the criticism against him that I voiced in chapter 1, that he, after radically questioning the concept of "literature" as a point of reference of comparative literature, ended by giving it a commonsensical definition of "imaginative writing." For he may be supposing the applicability of this definition solely to Western "literature."

8. Earl Miner's *Comparative Poetics* may be, as far as I know, the only attempt to subvert this irreversibility of critical terms. When he speaks of *monogatari* as a certain mode of unallegorical narrative, he uses it as an independent critical unit.

bibliography

Abe Jirō. "An Alternative View on the Labor Problem (Rōdō mondai ichimen kan)." *Abe Jirō zenshū*. Vol. 6. Tokyo: Kadokawa shoten, 1961.

———. *The Art and Society of the Tokugawa Period (Tokugawa jidai no geijutsu to shakai)*. Tokyo: Kaizō sha, 1948.

———. *An Introduction to Comparative Literature (Hikaku bungaku josetsu)*. *Abe Jirō zenshū*. Vol. 9. Tokyo: Kadokawa shoten, 1961.

———. *Personalism (Jinkaku shugi)*. *Abe Jirō zenshū*. Vol. 6. Tokyo: Kadokawa shoten, 1961.

Aldridge, A[lfred] Owen. General Introduction. "The Purpose and Perspectives of Comparative Literature." *Comparative Literature: Matter and Method*. Ed. Aldridge. Urbana: U of Illinois P, 1969.

Althusser, Louis. "Ideology and Ideological State Apparatus." *Lenin and Philosophy*. Trans. Ben Brewster. New York: Monthly Review P, 1971.

———. "Marxism and Humanism." *For Marx*. Trans. Ben Brewster. London: Verso, 1990.

Asai Ryōi. *Ukiyo monogatari*. *Nihon koten bungaku taikei*. Vol. 90. Tokyo: Iwanami shoten, 1965.

Badinter, Elizabeth. *The Myth of Motherhood: An Historical View of the Maternal Instinct*. Trans. Francine du Plessix Gray. London: Souvenir P, 1981.

Bassnett, Susan. *Comparative Literature: A Critical Introduction*. Oxford: Blackwell, 1983.

Bataille, Georges. *Eroticism: Death and Sexuality.* Trans. Mary Dalwood. San Francisco: City Lights, 1986.

Béjin, André. "The Decline of the Psycho-analyst and the Rise of the Sexologist." *Western Sexuality: Practice and Precept in Past and Present Times.* Trans. Anthony Forster. Ed. Philippe Ariès and André Béjin. Oxford: Blackwell, 1986.

Berger, Peter L. and Thomas Luckmann. *The Social Construction of Reality.* New York: Doubleday, 1966.

Brunetière, Ferdinand. "European Literature." *Comparative Literature: Early Days.* Ed. Hans-Joachim Schulz and Phillip H. Rhein. Chapel Hill, NC: U of North Carolina P, 1973.

Byron, George Gordon. *Don Juan.* London: Penguin Books, 1982.

Chamberlain, Basil Hall. *Things Japanese.* 5th ed. London: Murray, 1905.

Clements, Barbara Evans. *Bolshevik Feminist: The Life of Aleksandra Kollontai.* Bloomington, IN: Indiana UP, 1979.

Cohen, Walter. "The Concept of World Literature." *Comparative Literature East West: Traditions and Trends.* Ed. Cornelia N. Moore and Raymond A. Moody. Honolulu: The College of Languages, Linguistics and Literature, U of Hawaii, and the East-West Center, 1989.

Culler, Jonathan. *Ferdinand de Saussure.* Ithaca, NY: Cornell UP, 1986.

———. *Framing the Sign.* Norman, OK: U of Oklahoma P, 1988.

Da Ponte, Lorenzo. *Don Giovanni.* Milan: Ricordi, 1986.

Deleuze, Gilles. *Masochism.* Trans. Aude Willm. New York: Zone Books, 1989.

Derrida, Jacques. *Of Grammatology.* Trans. Gayatri Chakravorty Spivak. Baltimore: Johns Hopkins UP, 1976.

———. *Margins of Philosophy.* Trans. Alan Bass. Chicago: U of Chicago P, 1982.

———. *Speech and Phenomenon.* Trans. David B. Allison. Chicago: Northwestern UP, 1973.

————. *Writing and Difference*. Trans. Alan Bass. Chicago: U of Chicago P, 1978.

Doi Kōka. *Women's Learnings in Recent Times (Kinsei onna daigaku). Onna daigaku shū.* Ed. Ishikawa Matsutarō. Tokyo: Heibon sha, 1977.

Ducrot, Oswald and Tsvetan Todorov. *Encyclopedic Dictionary of the Sciences of Language.* Trans. Catherine Porter. Baltimore: John Hopkins UP, 1979.

Dworkin, Andrea. *Intercourse.* New York: Free P, 1988.

Eco, Umberto. *Semiotics and the Philosophy of Language.* Bloomington, IN: Indiana UP, 1984.

Ellis, Havelock. *Studies in the Psychology of Sex.* New York: Random House, [1942].

Engels, Friedrich. *The Origin of Family, Private Property, and the State, in the Light of the Researches of Lewis H. Morgan.* Trans. Eleanor Burke Leacock. New York: International Publishers, 1972.

Eoyang, Eugene. "Polar Paradigms in Poetics: Chinese and Western Literary Premises." *Comparative Literature East West: Tradition and Trends.* Ed. Cornelia N. Moore and Raymond A. Moody. Honolulu: The College of Languages, Linguistics and Literature, U of Hawaii, and the East-West Center, 1989.

Etiemble, René. *The Crisis in Comparative Literature.* Trans. Herbert Weisinger and Georges Joyaux. East Lansing, MI: Michigan State UP, 1966. Trans. of *Comparison n'est pas raison: La Crise de la littérature comparée.* Paris: Gallimard, 1963.

————. *Essais de littérature (vraiment) générale.* Paris: Gallimard, 1975.

Feyerabend, Paul. *Farewell to Reason.* London: Verso, 1987.

Fish, Stanley. *Is There a Text in This Class?: The Authority of Interpretive Communities.* Cambridge, MA: Harvard UP, 1980.

Forel, August Henri. *Sexual Ethics.* London: New Age P, 1909.

————. *The Sexual Question*. Brooklyn, New York: Physicians and Surgeons Book Company, 1931.

Foucault, Michel. *The Archaeology of Knowledge*. Trans. Alan M. Sheridan Smith. New York: Pantheon Books, 1972.

————. *The Birth of the Clinic*. New York: Vintage Books, 1975.

————. *The History of Sexuality: An Introduction*. Trans. Robert Hurley. New York: Vintage Books, 1990.

————. *The History of Sexuality: Use of Pleasure*. Trans. Robert Hurley. New York: Pantheon Books, 1985.

————. *The History of Sexuality: The Care of the Self*. Trans. Robert Hurley. New York: Vintage Books, 1988.

————. *Madness and Civilization: History of Insanity in the Age of Reason*. Trans. Richard Howard. New York: Vintage Books, 1988.

Freud, Sigmund. *Beyond the Pleasure Principles*. Trans. James Strachey. New York: Norton, 1975.

————. *Three Essays on Sexuality and Other Works*. Ed. Angela Richards. London: Penguin Books, 1977.

Friederich, Werner P. *The Challenge of Comparative Literature and Other Addresses*. Chapel Hill, NC: U of North Carolina P, 1970.

Fujimoto (Hatakeyama) Kizan. *The Great Mirror of the Art of Love (Shikidō ōkagami)*. *Zoku enseki jusshu*. Vol. 2. Tokyo: Kokusho kankō kai, [1927].

Futabatei Shimei. "About *Mediocrity* (*Heibon* monogatari)." *Futabatei Shimei zenshū*. Vol. 5. Tokyo: Iwanami shoten, 1965.

————. *An Adopted Husband*. Trans. Mitsui Buhachiro and Gregg M. Sinclair. New York: Knopf, 1919. Trans. of *Sono omokage*. *Futabatei Shimei zenshū*. Vol. 3. Tokyo: Iwanami shoten, 1964.

————. "Confession of My Life (Yo ga hansei no zange)." *Futabatei Shimei zenshū*. Vol. 5. Tokyo: Iwanami shoten, 1965.

————. *Japan's First Modern Novel: "Ukigumo" of Futabatei Shimei*. Trans. Marleigh G. Ryan. Ann Arbor, MI: The Center for

Japanese Studies, 1990. Trans. of *Ukigumo* (*Drifting Clouds*). *Futabatei Shimei zenshū*. Vol. 1. Tokyo: Iwanami shoten, 1964.

——. *Mediocrity*. Trans. Glenn W. Shaw. Tokyo: Hokusei dō, 1927. Trans. of *Heibon*. *Futabatei Shimei zenshū*. Vol. 4. Tokyo: Iwanami shoten, 1964.

——. "Turmoil of a Writer (Sakka kushin dan)." *Futabatei Shimei zenshū*. Vol. 5. Tokyo: Iwanami shoten, 1965.

Gadamer, Hans-Georg. *Truth and Method*. Trans. G. Barden and J. Cumming. New York: Crossroad, 1984.

Geertz, Clifford. *The Interpretation of Cultures*. New York: Basic Books, 1973.

Gendarme de Bévotte, Georges. *La Légende de Don Juan: Son Évolution dans la littérature des origines au romantisme*. Paris: Hachétte, 1906.

Gifford, Henry. *Comparative Literature: Concepts of Literature*. London: Routledge and Kegan Paul, 1969.

Goncharov, Ivan A. *The Precipice* (*Obryv*). *Sobranie sochinenii*. Vols. 5 and 6. Moscow: Khudozhestvennaia literatura, 1979–1980.

Guillén, Claudio. *The Challenge of Comparative Literature*. Trans. Cola Franzen. Cambridge, MA: Harvard UP, 1993.

Guyard, Marius-François. *La Littérature comparée*. Paris: Presses Universitaires de France, 1951.

Handey, Jack. *Deeper Thoughts*. New York: Hyperion, 1993.

Hasegawa Izumi. *A Study of Ōgai's "Vita Sexualis"* (*Ōgai "Vita Sexualis" kō*). Tokyo: Meiji shoin, 1991.

Hasegawa Tenkei. "Miseries of Revealing the Reality (Genjitsu bakuro no hiai)." *Meiji bungaku zenshū*. Vol. 43. Tokyo: Chikuma shobō, 1967.

Hattori Bushō. *A New Guide to Metropolitan Tokyo* (*Shin Tokyo hanjyō ki*). *Meiji bungaku zenshū*. Vol. 4. Tokyo: Chikuma shobō, 1969.

Hawks, Francis L., ed. *Narrative of the Expedition of an American Squadron to China Seas and Japan, Performed in the Years 1852, 1853, and 1854, under the Command of Commodore M.*

C. Perry, United States Navy, by Order of the Government of the United States. New York: Appleton, 1856.

Heine, Wilhelm. Reise um die Erde nach Japan an Bord der Expeditions-Escadre unter Commodore M. C. Perry in den Jahren 1853, 1854, und 1855, unternommen im Auftrage der Regierung der Vereinigten Staaten. Leipzig: Costenoble, 1856.

Hibbett, Howard. The Floating World in Japanese Fiction. London: Oxford UP, 1959.

Hjelmslev, Louis. Prolegomena to a Theory of Language. Trans. Francis J. Whitfield. Madison, WI: U of Wisconsin P, 1961.

Hoffmann, E. T. A. Don Juan or A Fabulous Adventure that Befell a Musician. Tales from Hoffmann. Ed. Christopher Lazare. New York: Wyn, 1946.

Hsiaohsiao Sheng (Xiaoxiao Sheng). Ching P'ing Mei: Don Juan of China. Rutland, VT: Tuttle, 1960.

Ihara Saikaku. Five Women Who Loved Love. Trans. Ivan Morris. The Life of an Amorous Woman and Other Writings. New York: New Directions, 1963. Kōshoku gonin onna. Nihon koten bungaku taikei. Vol. 47. Tokyo: Iwanami Shoten, 1957.

———. The Great Mirror of Male Love (Nanshoku taikan). Trans. Paul Gordon Schalow. Stanford, CA: Stanford UP, 1990.

———. The Life of an Amorous Man. Trans. Hamada Kengi. Rutland, VT: Tuttle, 1984. Trans. of Kōshoku ichidai otoko. Nihon koten bungaku taikei. Vol. 47. Tokyo: Iwanami shoten, 1957.

———. The Life of an Amorous Woman. Trans. Ivan Morris. New York: New Directions, 1963. Trans. of Kōshoku ichidai onna. Nihon koten bungaku taikei. Vol. 47. Tokyo: Iwanami shoten, 1957.

Inoue Tetsujirō. The Dictionary of Philosophy (Tetsugaku jii). Tokyo: Tokyo University, 1881. 2nd ed. Tokyo: Maruzen, 1912.

Ishii Kendō. The Origins of Things and Customs That Began in Meiji (Meiji jibutsu kigen). Tokyo: Meiji bunka kenkyū kai, 1969.

Janeira, Armando Martins. Japanese and Western Literature: A Comparative Study. Tokyo: Tuttle, 1970.

Kaibara Ekiken. "How to Educate Women (Joshi o oshi-yu-ru hō)." *Onna daigaku shū*. Ed. Ishikawa Matsutarō. Tokyo: Heibon sha, 1977.

Kamei Katsuichirō. *A Search for Truth and "Iro-gonomi" of the Heian Court (Ōchō no gudō to iro-gonomi)*. Tokyo: Bungei shunjū sha, 1963.

Kanekawa Mitsuo. "Molière in Japan (Nihon ni okeru Moriēru)." *Moriēru zenshū*. Vol. 4. Tokyo: Chūō kōron sha, 1973.

Kant, Immanuel. *Critique of Pure Reason*. Trans. J. M. D. Meiklejohn. London: Dent, 1934.

Karatani Kōjin. *Origins of Modern Japanese Literature*. Trans. Brett de Bary. Durham, NC: Duke UP, 1993.

Katō Bunnō et al., trans. *The Threefold Lotus Sutra*. New York: Weatherhill/Kosei, 1975.

Kawamura Keikichi, ed. *Mori Ōgai's Miscellaneous Writings on Sexual Desire (Mori Ōgai: Seiyoku zassetsu)*. Tokyo: Nihon iji shinpō shuppan bu, 1949.

———. "Mori Ōgai's View on Sexual Desire (Mori Ōgai no seiyoku kan)." *Mori Ōgai zenshū geppō* 29 (1953): 7–9; 30 (1953): 3–5.

———. *The Sorrows of Young Mori Ōgai (Wakaki Mori Ōgai no nayami)*. Tokyo: Gendai sha, 1957.

Kitamura Tōkoku. *The Works of Kitamura Tōkoku (Kitamura Tōkoku shū)*. *Meiji bungaku zenshū*. Vol. 29. Tokyo: Chikuma shobō, 1976.

———. "The Democratic ideals in the Tokugawa period (Tokugawa-shi jidai no heimin-teki no risō)." *The Works*.

———. "*Kyaramakura* and *Shinhazueshū* (*Kyaramakura to Shinhazueshū*)." *The Works*.

———. "*Manfred* and *Faust* (*Manfureddo to Fōsuto*)." *The Works*.

———. "On *Iki* with Criticism of *Kyaramakura* (Iki o ronjite *Kyaramakura* ni oyobu)." *The Works*.

———. "On the Inner Life (Naibu seimei ron)." *The Works*.

———. "The Pessimist-Poet and the Woman (Ensei shika to josei)." *The Works*.

———. *The Song of Fairyland (Hōrai kyoku)*. *The Works*.

———. "Upon Reading *Utanenbutsu* (*Utanenbutsu* o yomite)." *The Works*.

Koch, Max. Introduction to *Zeitschrift für vergleichende Literaturgeschichte*. *Comparative Literature: Early Days*. Ed. Hans-Joachim Schulz and Phillip H. Rhein. Chapel Hill, NC: U of North Carolina P, 1973.

Kokuritsu kokkai toshokan, ed. *The Catalogue of Translations in Meiji, Taishō and Shōwa (Meiji Taishō Shōwa hon'yaku bungaku mokuroku)*. Tokyo: Kazama shobō, 1959.

Krafft-Ebing, Richard von. *Psychopathia Sexualis: A Forensic Study*. Chicago: Keener, 1901. Trans. of *Psychopathia Sexualis mit besonderer Berücksichtigung der Konträren Sexualempfindung: Eine Klinisch-Forensische Studie*. Stuttgart: Verlag von Ferdinand Enke, 1892. *Shikijōkyō hen*. Tokyo: Nihon hōigakkai, 1894. *Hentai seiyoku shinri*. Trans. Kurosawa Yoshiomi. Tokyo: Dainihon bunmei kyōkai, 1913.

Kuhn, Thomas S. *The Structure of Scientific Revolutions*. Chicago: U of Chicago P, 1970.

Kuki Shūzō. *The Structure of "Iki" (Iki no kōzō)*. Tokyo: Iwanami shoten, 1930.

Lacan, Jacques. *Écrits*. Trans. Alan Sheridan. New York: Norton, 1977.

Lakoff, George. *Woman, Fire, and Dangerous Things*. Chicago: U of Chicago P, 1990.

Lenin, Ivan. *Imperialism as the Highest Stage of Capitalism (Imperializm kak vyshaia stadiia kapitalizma)*. *Polnoe sobranie sochnenii*. Vol. 27. Moscow: Izdatel'stvo politicheskoi literatury, 1969.

Levin, Harry. *Grounds for Comparison*. Cambridge, MA: Harvard UP, 1972.

Linton, Ralph. *The Cultural Background of Personality*. London: Routledge and Kegan Paul, 1947.

Lipking, Lawrence. "Donna Abbandonata." *Don Giovanni: Myths of Seduction and Betrayal.* Ed. Jonathan Miller. New York, Schocken Books, 1990.

Makarenko, Anton S. *Lectures on the Education of the Children (Lektsii o vospitanii detei). Sochneniia v sem' tomakh.* Vol. 4. Moscow: Izdatel'stvo Akademii pedagogicheskikh nauk, 1957.

Marino, Adrian. *Etiemble ou le comparatism militant.* Paris: Gallimard, 1982.

Martin, Laura. " 'Eskimo Words for Snow': A Case Study in the Genesis and Decay of an Anthropological Example." *American Anthropologist* 88.2 (June 1984): 418–22.

Maruyama Keizaburō. *Philosophy of Saussure (Soshūru no shisō).* Tokyo: Iwanami shoten, 1981.

Marx, Karl and Friedrich Engels. *German Ideology.* Ed. C. C. Arthur. New York: International Publishers, 1989.

Masaoka Shiki. "An Idle Essay by an Idle Man (Kanjin kanwa)." *Meiji bungaku zenshū.* Vol. 53. Tokyo: Chikuma shobō, 1975.

Matsushita Teizō. *The Chinese Character "Ai" and Its Compounds (Kango "ai" to sono fukugō go: Shisō kara mita kokugo shi).* Kyoto: Aporon sha, 1982.

Miller, George. "Semantic Relations among Words." *Linguistic Theory and Psychological Reality.* Ed. Morris Halle et al. Cambridge, MA: Harvard UP, 1978.

Miller, Jonathan. Introduction. *Don Giovanni: Myths of Seduction and Betrayal.* Ed. Jonathan Miller. New York: Schocken Books, 1990.

Miner, Earl. *Comparative Poetics.* Princeton, NJ: Princeton UP, 1990.

Miner, Earl, Odagiri Hiroko, and Robert E. Morrell. *Princeton Companion to Classical Japanese Literature.* Princeton, NJ: Princeton UP, 1985.

Miyaoka Osahito. *Eskimo: Ethnographical History of the Far North (Esukimō: Kyokuhoku no bunka shi).* Tokyo: Iwanami shoten, 1987.

———. *The Languages and Cultures of Eskimos (Esukimō no gengo to bunka).* Tokyo: Kōbun dō, 1977.

Molière. *Dom Juan ou le Festin de pierre. Oeuvres complètes.* Vol. 1.
Ed. Robert Jouanny. Paris: Garnier, 1962. *Onna tarashi.*
Trans. Kusano Shibaji. *Kabuki* 93.1 (1908), 94.5 (1908). *Dan
Jūza.* Trans. Kusano Shibaji. *Kokoro no hana* 17.1–12 (1913).
*Don Juan; or the Feast of the Statue. The Dramatic Works of
Molière.* Vol. 2. Trans. Charles Heron Wall. London: Bell,
1919. *Don Juan.* Trans. Tsubouchi Shikō. *Moriēru zenshū.*
Tokyo: Ten'yū sha, 1920. *Don Juan.* Trans. Suzuki Rikie.
Tokyo: Iwanami shoten, 1952.

Mori Ōgai. *Vita Sexualis. Mori Ōgai zenshū.* Vol. 5. Tokyo: Iwanami
shoten, 1972. Trans. Kazuji Ninomiya and Sanford
Goldstein. Rutland, VT: Tuttle, 1972.

———. *The New Theory of Hygiene (Eisei shinpen). Mori Ōgai zenshū.*
Vols. 31 and 32. Tokyo: Iwanami shoten, 1974.

Morse, Edward. *Japan Day by Day.* Boston and New York:
Houghton Mifflin, 1917.

Nakamura Masanao. "An Opinion for Creating a Good Mother"
(Zenryōnaru haha o tsukuru setsu)." *Meiji bungaku zenshū.*
Vol. 3. Tokyo: Chikuma shobō, 1967.

Nakamura Shin'ichirō. *Sex and Love Observed in Classical Japanese
Literature (Nihon koten ni miru sei to ai).* Tokyo: Shinchō
sha, 1975.

———. *The Structure of "Iro-gonomi": The Depths of the Courtly
Culture (Iro-gonomi no kōzō: Ōchō bunka no shinsō).* Tokyo:
Iwanami shoten, 1985.

Niwa Jun'ichirō, trans. *Karyū shunwa. Meiji bungaku zenshū.* Vol.
7. Tokyo: Chikuma shobō, 1972.

Ochiai Shigeru. *Ethnography of Washing (Arau fūzoku shi).* Tokyo:
Mirai sha, 1984.

Ōshima Tadashi. *Invitation to Spanish Literature (Supein bungaku
eno izanai).* Tokyo: Sōseiki, 1978.

———. *A Study of Don Juan Types (Don Howan no genkei no kenkyu).*
Tokyo: Hakusui sha, 1966.

Peyre, Henri. "A Glance at Comparative Literature in America."
Yearbook of Comparative and General Literature 1 (1952): 1–8.

Posnett, Hutcheson Macaulay. *Comparative Literature*. London: Trench, 1886.

Pullum, Geoffrey K. *The Great Eskimo Vocabulary Hoax and Other Irrelevant Essays on the Study of Language*. Chicago: U of Chicago P, 1991.

Pushkin, Aleksandr S. *The Stone Guest*. Trans. A. F. B. Clark. *The Works of Alexander Pushkin*. Ed. Avrahm Yarmolinsky. New York: Random House, 1936.

Rank, Otto. *Don Juan*. Trans. David G. Winter. Princeton, NJ: Princeton UP, 1975.

Remak, Henry H. H. "Comparative Literature at the Crossroads: Diagnosis, Therapy, and Prognosis." *Yearbook of Comparative and General Literature* 9 (1960): 1–28.

―――. "Comparative Literature, Its Definition and Function." *Comparative Literature: Method and Perspective*. Ed. Newton P. Stallknecht and Horst Frenz. Carbondale, IL: Southern Illinois UP, 1961.

Romaine, Suzanne. *Bilingualism*. Oxford: Blackwell, 1989.

Rorty, Richard. *Contingency, irony, and solidarity*. Cambridge: Cambridge UP, 1989.

―――. *Philosophy and the Mirror of Nature*. Princeton, NJ: Princeton UP, 1979.

Rousseau, Jean-Jacques. *Julie, ou La Nouvelle Héloïse*. Paris: Garnier-Flammarion, 1967.

Said, Edward. *Orientalism*. New York: Vintage, 1979.

Santō Kyōden. *Grilled Playboy Edo Style* (*Edo umare uwaki no kabayaki*). *Nihon koten bungaku zenshū*. Vol. 47. Tokyo: Shōgakkan, 1971.

Satō Haruo. Postscript. *Ōgai zenshū chosaku hen*. Vol. 3. Tokyo: Iwanami shoten, 1951.

Satō Teruo. *"La Chanson de Roland" and "The Tale of Heike"* (*"Rōran no uta" to "Heike monogatari"*). Tokyo: Chūō kōron sha, 1973.

Satō Teruo, Tomita Hitoshi, et al., eds. *References to Foreign Litera-tures in Modern Japan: Periodicals (Kindai nihon ni okeru seiyō bungaku shōkai bunken: zasshi hen)*. Tokyo: Yūkyū shuppan, 1970.

Saussure, Ferdinand de. *Course in General Linguistics*. Trans. Roy Harris. La Salle, IL: Open Court, 1983.

Schneider, Lucien. *Dictionnaire français-esquimau du parler de l'Ungava et contrées limitrophes*. Québec: Les Presses de l'Université Laval, 1970.

Searle, John R. *Speech Acts*. Cambridge: Cambridge UP, 1969.

Sedgwick, Eve Kosofsky. *Between Men: English Literature and Male Homosocial Desire*. New York: Columbia UP, 1985.

Seeber, Edward. "On Defining Terms." *Comparative Literature: Method and Perspective*. Ed. Newton P. Stallknecht and Horst Frenz. Carbondale, IL: Southern Illinois UP, 1961.

Sōgō Masaaki et al., eds. *The Dictionary of Meiji Terms (Meiji no kotoba jiten)*. Tokyo: Tokyo dō, 1986.

Suehiro Tecchō. *Plum Blossoms in the Snow (Secchū bai)*. Meiji bungaku zenshū. Vol. 6. Tokyo: Chikuma shobō, 1967.

Takizawa Bakin. *The Crescent Moon (Chinsetsu yumihari zuki)*. Nihon koten bungaku taikei. Vol. 60. Tokyo: Iwanami shoten, 1958.

Tamenaga Shunsui. *The Pleasure Quarters in the Northeast (Shunshoku tatsumi no sono)*. Nihon koten bungaku taikei. Vol. 64. Tokyo: Iwanami shoten, 1962.

———. *The Plum Calendar (Shunshoku umegoyomi)*. Nihon koten bungaku taikei. Vol. 64. Tokyo: Iwanami shoten, 1962.

Tayama Katai. *The Quilt (Futon)*. Meiji bungaku zenshū. Vol. 67. Tokyo: Chikuma shobō, 1968.

Teruoka Yasutaka. *Kōshoku*. Tokyo: Yūki shobō, 1958.

———. *Love and Sex of the Japanese (Nihon jin no ai to sei)*. Tokyo: Iwanami shoten, 1989.

Todorov, Tzvetan. *The Conquest of America: The Question of the Other*. Trans. Richard Howard. New York: Harper-Perennial, 1984.

————. *On Human Diversity: Nationalism, Racism, and Exoticism in French Thought.* Trans. Catherine Porter. Cambridge: Harvard UP, 1993.

Tolstoy, Lev N. *The Kreutzer Sonata.* Trans. David McDuff. London: Penguin Books, 1985.

Tsubouchi Shōyō. *A Calynx of a Parsimon (Kaki no heta).* Tokyo: Chūō kōron sha, 1933.

————. *The Characters of Modern Students (Tōsei shosei katagi).* 17 vols. Tokyo: Bansei dō, 1885–86.

————. Introduction. *Shōyō senshū.* Supplement. Vol. 2. Tokyo: Shun'yō dō, 1927.

————. *Recollections in Leisure (Kaisō mandan). Shōyō senshū.* Vol. 12. Tokyo: Daiichi shobō, 1977.

Turgenev, Ivan S. *Asia. Polnoe sobranie sochnenii.* Vol. 5. Moscow: Izdatel'stvo Nauka, 1980.

Uchida Roan, trans. *Crime and Punishment (Tsumi to batsu). Meiji bungaku zenshū.* Vol. 7. Tokyo: Chikuma shobō, 1972.

————. "Vita Sexualis." *Meiji bungaku zenshū.* Vol. 24. Tokyo: Chikuma shobō, 1978.

van Thieghem, Paul. *La Littérature comparée.* 4th ed. Paris: Libraire Armand Colin, 1951.

Walker, Janet A. *The Japanese Novel of the Meiji Period and the Ideal of Individualism.* Princeton, NJ: Princeton UP, 1979.

Weeks, Jeffrey. *Sexuality and Its Discontents: Meanings, Myths, and Modern Sexualities.* London: Routledge and Kegan Paul, 1985.

Weinstein, Leo. *Metamorphoses of Don Juan.* Stanford, CA: Stanford UP, 1959.

Weisstein, Ulrich. *Comparative Literature and Literary Theory.* Bloomington, IN: Indiana UP, 1974.

Wellek, René. "Comparative Literature Today." *Comparative Literature* 17.4 (1965): 325–37.

————. "The Crisis of Comparative Literature." *Concepts of Criticism.* New Haven, CT: Yale UP, 1963.

————. "Name and Nature of Comparative Literature." *Discriminations: Further Concepts of Criticism.* New Haven, CT: Yale UP, 1970

Wellek, René and Austin Warren. *Theory of Literature.* Harmondsworth, UK: Penguin Books, 1985.

Williams, Raymond. *Keywords.* New York: Oxford UP, 1985.

Wittgenstein, Ludwig. *Tractatus Logico-Philosophicus.* Trans. D. F. Pear and B. F. McGuiness. London: Routledge, 1974.

Whorf, Benjamin Lee. *Language, Thought, and Reality: Selected Writings of Benjamin Lee Whorf.* Ed. John B. Carroll. Cambridge, MA: MIT P, 1956.

Wrenn, C[harles] L[eslie]. *The Idea of Comparative Literature.* Cambridge: Humanities Research Association, 1968.

Yanabu Akira. *How Translations Were Created* (*Hon'yaku go seiritsu jijō*). Tokyo: Iwanami shoten, 1982.

Yanagida Izumi. *A Study of the Translations of Foreign Literature in Early Meiji* (*Meiji shoki hon'yaku bungaku no kenkyū*). Tokyo: Shunjū sha, 1961.

Yanagita Kunio. *Social History of Meiji and Taishō* (*Meiji Taishō shi: sesō hen*). Tokyo: Chikuma shobō, 1984.

Yokota-Murakami (Murakami) Takayuki. "The Birth of Sexual Life: Rethinking *Vita Sexualis* and Naturalism (Sei seikatsu no tanjō: *Vita Sexualis* to shizen shugi saikō)." *Comparative Literature Studies* (Jap.) 65 (1994): 118–29.

————. "Futabatei Shimei and Russian Literature: A Problem of Modernity in Comparative Scholarship (Futabatei Shimei to rosia bungaku: hikaku bungaku teki kenkyū ni okeru kindai)." Ed. Matsumura Masaie. *For Beginners in Comparative Literature* (*Hikaku bungaku o manabu hito no tameni*). Kyoto: Sekai shisō sha, 1995.

————. "Lovers in Disguise: A Feature of Romantic Love in Meiji Literature." *Comparative Literature Studies* (USA) 38.3 (1991): 213–33.

————. "Man Seen as a Beast, Male Seen as an Animal: On the Concept of 'Bestiality' Examined through *The Kreutzer So-*

nata." Vision of History. Vol. 2 of *Proceedings of the XIIIth Congress of the International Comparative Literature Association.* Ed. Margaret R. Higonnet and Sumie Jones. Tokyo: Tokyo UP, 1994.

———. "The Purity Campaign as a Literary Context." *A Journal of Japanese Studies* 2 (1994): 25–30.

———. "Translating Literature, Love, and Sexuality: Negotiation of the Ideologies in Early Modern Japan." *Translation and Modernization.* Vol. 4 of *Proceedings of the XIIIth Congress of the International Comparative Literature Association.* Ed. Teresa Hyun and José Lambert. Tokyo: Tokyo UP, 1994.

Yoshida Kenkō. *Essays in Idleness: The Tsurezuregusa of Kenkō.* Trans. Donald Keene. Tokyo: Tuttle, 1981.

index

221

ST. JOHN FISHER COLLEGE LIBRARY

0 1220 0059432 7

PN 57 .D7 Y65 1998
Yokota-Murakami, Takayuki.
Don Juan East/West